Issues in the Taxation of Individuals

This is a volume in the series of studies commissioned as part of the research program of the Fair Tax Commission of the Government of Ontario. The Fair Tax Commission's research publication series is intended to inform public discussion of tax policy issues. In making this report available the commission does not necessarily endorse the results or recommendations of the authors.

Issues in the Taxation of Individuals

KATHLEEN M. DAY and STANLEY L. WINER

JONATHAN R. KESSELMAN

JAMES B. DAVIES

MAUREEN A. MALONEY

PETER DUNGAN

JAMES B. DAVIES and DAVID G. DUFF

Edited by

ALLAN M. MASLOVE

Published by the University of Toronto Press in cooperation with the Fair Tax Commission of Ontario

UNIVERSITY OF TORONTO PRESS
Toronto Buffalo London

© Queen's Printer for Ontario 1994

All rights reserved. No part of this publication may be reproduced, stored in a retrieval system, or transmitted in any form or by any means, electronic, mechanical, photocopying, recording, or otherwise, without the prior written permission of University of Toronto Press Incorporated.

Printed in Canada

ISBN 0-8020-7603-3 (paper)

Printed on acid-free paper

Canadian Cataloguing in Publication Data

Main entry under title:

Issues in the taxation of individuals

(Research studies of the Fair Tax Commission of Ontario)
ISBN 0-8020-7603-3

1. Taxation – Ontario.   I. Day, Kathleen Mary,
1958–   .   II. Maslove, Allan M., 1946–   .
III. Ontario.   Fair Tax Commission.   IV. Series.

HJ2460.06177 1994   336.2'009713   C94-931706-3

Contents

Foreword

The Ontario Fair Tax Commission was established to examine the province's tax system as an integrated whole and, in conjunction with its working groups, to analyse individual components of the system in detail.

It has been many years since the Ontario tax system was subjected to a comprehensive examination. However, a great deal of research on taxation has been undertaken over the past two decades. This work, based in several disciplines, has been both theoretical and applied, and in this context the research program of the Fair Tax Commission was formulated.

The research program has two broad purposes. The first is, of course, to support the deliberations of the commissioners. The second, more novel objective is to inform public discussions of tax matters so that the commission's formal and informal public consultations can be of maximum value. For this reason we have opted to publish volumes in the series of studies as they are ready, rather than holding them all until the commission has completed its work. While our approach is more difficult from a technical and administrative perspective, we believe that the benefits will justify our decision.

The research program seeks to synthesize the existing published work on taxation; to investigate the implications for Ontario of the general research work; and, where required, to conduct original research on the context and principles for tax reform and on specific tax questions. We thus hope to add to the existing body of knowledge without duplicating it. The studies included in these publications are those that we believe make a contribution to the literature on taxation.

I would like to extend my thanks to my fellow commissioners and to the members of the FTC secretariat. I also thank the many members of the working groups and the advisory groups who have contributed to the research program and to the overall work of the commission.

Monica Townson, Chair

Introduction

This volume contains several papers requested by the Fair Tax Commission to assist its consideration of the direct taxation of individuals. These studies cover a range of policy issues relevant to the reform of existing taxes and the possible (re)introduction of a new tax on personal wealth. The first three papers deal with more general issues relating to individuals' responses to taxation, compliance, and tax mix. The remaining three papers address policy issues specifically related to income, sales, and wealth taxation respectively.

One type of potential response to tax measures (or government actions more generally) is for individuals to migrate to jurisdictions offering them the promise of larger "fiscal surpluses." If such migration occurs, it could have significant negative impacts on economic efficiency and on the ability of governments to redistribute income in the affected jurisdictions. The survey article by Kathleen Day and Stanley Winer examines these questions based on a review of empirical studies that asked whether policy-induced migration in fact exists. They find that there is some evidence that benefits such as unemployment insurance, education, and health care do influence interprovincial migration flows, but that evidence of similar flows in response to tax differences is weaker. An important ancillary question is whether policy-induced migration results in capitalization of net benefit differentials in housing and land prices. Day and Winer note that the results found by various credible studies range from zero to complete capitalization. They conclude that, because of this uncertainty, capitalization cannot be assumed to compensate for inequities in property taxation.

Jonathan Kesselman examines emerging issues in tax compliance, enforcement, and administration, primarily from an economic perspective. He reviews evidence on the extent, nature, and motivation for compliance behaviours and their relevance for achieving tax fairness. He distinguishes three types of non-compliance "unintentional" non-compliance, which results from tax complexity, ambiguity, or administrative procedures; tax evasion, which is intentional violation of tax laws; and tax avoidance, which satisfies the letter of the tax laws while violating its intent. Both vertical and horizontal equity may be undermined by non-compliance although the appropriate compensating policy responses will differ. Kesselman discusses how one might consider non-compliance problems as they relate to existing taxes and to new forms of taxation. Among other things, his paper discusses several approaches to addressing the non-compliance problem, including the merging of provincial sales taxes with the federal GST.

Governments typically rely on a mix of taxes to raise their revenues. In contrast, academic studies often identify a single "ideal" tax base. James Davies addresses the issue of tax mix in achieving tax equity by comparing the three main competitors for the title of ideal tax base: the annual income tax, a consumption (expenditure) tax, and a lifetime income tax. Davies reviews the essential characteristics of each tax and demonstrates, theoretically, the circumstances under which they would be equivalent. The essential distinguishing feature among these taxes is the treatment of time, and the "borderline" issues that arise when moving from one tax period to another. Davies argues that while our tax system may appear messy from the vantage point of one of the "ideal" tax bases, this "messiness" reflects a popular ambivalence among these ideal types. Moreover, a tax mix composed of a variety of bases offers a measure of flexibility to adjust the tax system as perceptions about these ideal types change.

The designation of the appropriate tax unit (mainly) for income tax purposes has generated renewed interest in recent years. Participation of women in the paid workforce and changing ideas about what constitutes a "family" raise the question: Should tax be determined based on the income of the individual, the "marital" unit, or the "family" unit? Maureen Maloney's paper explores the issues involved in the determination of the tax unit. She argues that individual notions of taxpaying ability enhance autonomy and self-sufficiency, especially for women and poorer partners. Yet, individual taxation may be unfair between differently situated, economically dependent individuals. However, the evidence on how couples and families share income and wealth is quite unsatisfactory. Maloney discusses five categories of tax provisions that take into account, in some fashion, couple or family income: affirmative action, dependency, economic mutuality, anti–tax avoidance, and welfare provisions. Each category is analysed ideologically and practically to ascertain the underlying rationale for utilizing joint incomes in each circumstance. Maloney suggests that the tax system be changed to recognize specific groups disadvantaged for reasons of disability, race, or gender.

The option of merging the provincial retail sales tax with the federal Goods and Services Tax was an obvious option for the Commission in its consideration of sales tax reform. A major issue in that consideration was the likely macroeconomic impact of a harmonized system. (The other major issue, the distributional consequences of harmonization, was addressed in the incidence study conducted for the Commission entitled "Incidence of Taxes in Ontario in 1991." See Block and Shillington 1994.) The paper by Peter Dungan addresses this issue and reports on the results of an analysis of harmonization using the macroeconomic model of the Institute for Policy Analysis at the University of Toronto. The major potential impacts arise from the removal of sales tax on business inputs and the extension of the base for the provincial tax to include services currently taxed by the GST but not by the existing provincial sales tax. Dungan reports on the nature of the simulation exercises conducted and concludes that harmonization is likely to increase Ontario's GDP, at least in the longer term. Initial increases in consumer prices are unlikely to lead to ongoing inflation. Because the removal of the sales tax from business inputs and the extension of the base to include services roughly offset each other, the revenue-neutral rate for a GST-type provincial tax is approximately the same for the existing retail sales tax.

Investigating the desirability and feasibility of introducing a wealth tax in Ontario constituted another important component of the commission's mandate. In the final study, James Davies and David Duff analyse the impacts of two alternative forms of wealth tax on the distribution of wealth and estimate potential government revenues that they might yield. Most OECD countries assess either a wealth transfer tax on gifts and bequests or an annual net wealth tax, and a few levy both. Davies and Duff discuss the design of both forms of tax, the major compliance and other behavioural response issues associated with each, and present simulations of potential revenue and distributional impacts of each type of wealth tax.

Allan M. Maslove

Issues in the Taxation of Individuals

1 Internal Migration and Public Policy

An Introduction to the Issues and a Review of Empirical Research on Canada

KATHLEEN M. DAY and STANLEY L. WINER

Introduction

Migration continues to play an important role in the demographic history of Canada. As table 1 records, between 1976 and 1986 emigration from other parts of the world added over half a million people to a total population in 1986 of about 25 million, with approximately 45 per cent of the immigrants going to the province of Ontario.

Internal migration as well as international migration has been, and continues to be, influential in establishing population patterns across the country. The figures in table 1 show that in the decade after 1976, out-migration from poorer provinces to the rest of Canada, particularly from Newfoundland, New Brunswick, Manitoba, and Saskatchewan, was more important than immigration from abroad in determining overall population changes in these provinces. In-migration from other parts of Canada to Alberta and British Columbia and out-migration from Quebec to the rest of Canada have also been substantial. Over the ten-year period illustrated in the table, net internal migration to Alberta and from Quebec was, in each case, over twice as large as the corresponding international inflow.[1]

In this paper we are concerned with the nature and strength of relationships between internal migration, public policy, and the economic well-being of Canadians. We review empirical research that considers how public policies influence internal migration in Canada as well as empirical work on how policy-induced migration can, in turn, influence other economic variables.

TABLE 1
International and Internal Migration, Canada and the Provinces, 1976–1986

	Population 1986 (1)	Population distribution (2)	National increase (3)	Net international migration (4)	Distribution of (4) by province, percent (5)	Net interprovincial migration (6)	Net interprovincial migration rates, 1986, percent (7)	Interprovincial vs. international migration (6)/(4) (8)
				(Thousands)				
Newfoundland	568.3	2.2	63.9	-0.6	-0.1	-34.0	-1.01	56.7
P.E.I.	126.6	0.5	9.1	0.4	0.1	-0.1	-0.06	-0.3
Nova Scotia	873.2	3.4	54.0	1.8	0.3	-0.2	-0.15	-0.1
New Brunswick	710.4	2.8	54.6	-1.8	-0.3	-10.4	-0.27	5.8
Quebec	6,540.2	25.8	486.7	106.8	18.6	-237.8	-0.08	-2.2
Ontario	9,113.0	35.9	620.5	262.4	45.7	63.9	0.37	0.2
Manitoba	1,071.2	4.2	80.3	28.9	5.03	-44.9	-0.21	-1.6
Saskatchewan	1,010.2	4.0	95.4	11.8	2.06	-12.7	-0.69	-1.1
Alberta	2,375.1	9.4	280.6	67.3	11.7	154.7	-0.16	2.3
B.C.	2,889.0	11.4	206.2	97.0	16.9	130.0	-0.16	1.3
Yukon	23.5	0.1	3.8	0.0	0.0	-3.7	-2.32	n.a.
N.W.T.	52.2	0.2	11.2	0.1	0.01	-4.9	-2.10	-49.0
Canada	25,353.0	100.0*	1,966.1	574.1	100.0*	0.0*		

Notes: An asterisk (*) indicates that numbers do not sum to total because of rounding. A minus sign in column 7 indicates a net outflow. A minus sign in column 8 indicates interprovincial and international net flows are opposite in direction. The migration rates in column 7 are net interprovincial migration flows in 1986 divided by provincial population in 1986 times 100.

Source: Statistics Canada Catalogue No. 91–210, June 1991 and Beaujot (1991, Table 3, 165).

Sometimes the effect of government policies on internal migration is readily apparent. It is reasonable to suspect that the large outflow of people from Quebec to the rest of Canada in the 1976 to 1986 period (shown in column 6 of table 1) is closely connected to the actual or anticipated nature of public policy in Quebec following the election of a separatist government in 1976. However, the election of the Parti Québécois was a dramatic development in the history of the country of the sort that does not often occur. In the absence of such events, the relationship between migration and the public sector is hard to study. In "normal times," people move to take a better job, to get married, for adventure, to retire, or for other life-cycle–related reasons that have little to do with the public sector. Migration decisions may also be influenced in normal times by public policies that affect the quality of schools, the generosity of social welfare programs like unemployment insurance and public housing, and the size of tax burdens. Common sense tells us that all of these factors together, to a greater or lesser extent, weigh in the decision to migrate. The social scientist who wishes to study the connection between public policy and migration faces the delicate task of untangling the multiple causes of migration decisions in an environment where there is a substantial risk of confusing the influence of small policy changes with the influence of many private factors, including changes in the nature of employment opportunities over the course of business cycles. The problem is inherent in the empirical studies we review, all of which are based on data from what we have referred to as "normal times," a fact to which we shall return when assessing the implications of empirical results for the making of public policy in the future.

We preface our survey of empirical work with an introduction to the theoretical literature on policy-induced migration, emphasizing issues that are of particular concern in Canada. The discussion explains why the study of policy-induced migration is of interest to policy-makers concerned with the aggregate level and distribution of economic well-being and provides a useful background against which the empirical research may be viewed. In the survey of empirical work that follows we emphasize what the Canadian data have revealed and attempt to be comprehensive in doing so. We also briefly consider selected findings based on data from other countries. In a final section we assess the implications of the empirical results for the making of public policy and offer some suggestions for further research.

Why Is Policy-Induced Migration of Interest?

Suppose that the provision of public services in all fiscal systems at all levels of government, both here and abroad, is based on the benefit principle. In other words, assume that the nature of public services received by any individual depends completely on his or her own payment for them. Suppose also that all redistribution consists of voluntary payments by individual donors who care only about those to whom they directly give. In such a situation, migration decisions may be affected by fiscal systems. High demanders of public services may move to jurisdictions where they can purchase quality public services, or poor people may move to be near rich donors. But this migration, if it occurs, carries with it no implications for either efficiency or distribution in society as a whole that are not fully taken into account by migrants and stayers.

The benefit principle is not feasible as a basis for organizing the public sector, however, because of the problem of determining individual preferences for public goods that can be consumed even if individual taxpayers cheat on their tax contributions.[2] We therefore require other reasonable principles upon which to levy taxation, such as ability to pay, that do not rely on knowledge of individual preferences. Moreover, almost all political jurisdictions pursue redistributional objectives with ability-to-pay taxes being an essential part. In this more realistic situation, as the ensuing discussion demonstrates, migration is of substantial interest to policy-makers concerned with the allocation and distribution of scarce resources. The basic reason for concern is that in the absence of benefit taxation and purely voluntary, person-to-person redistribution, individuals who find it advantageous to move in order to receive a higher fiscal surplus – the difference between the benefits of public services and the taxes levied to pay for them – will not generally internalize all the social consequences of their migration decision.

Of course mobility of labour is not perfect and is much less than that of capital because of the need for migrants to change their place of residence as well as their place of work. A personal decision to move carries with it substantial transactions and psychological costs that do not burden investors in capital markets. The high personal cost of migration means that migration decisions made in the absence of benefit taxation and voluntary redistribution are of greater interest when viewed from the perspective of medium- or longer-term horizons, or when migration is between closely adjacent jurisdictions such as between municipalities within a large metropolitan area.

Policy-Induced Migration and the Regional Allocation of Labour

Consider figure 1 (taken from Watson 1986) in which the line AEC shows the gain in private real income, $Y_w - Y_m$, experienced by successive migrants from province or region M to province W, assuming those with the biggest gains leave first. To fix ideas, we might think of migration from the Maritime provinces in Canada to the Western province of Alberta during the oil boom of the mid-1970s. The optimal level of migration (to which will correspond an optimal regional allocation of labour) is OA, where the real income of the last or marginal migrant is the same in both origin and destination. Only with this amount of migration will aggregate real income and output in the economy as a whole be maximized. However, as Boadway and Flatters (1982a, b) and many others have noted, in the presence of fiscal surpluses that are not identical across provinces, this efficient reallocation of labour will not occur.[3]

The line through point B in figure 1 records the difference in comprehensive or post-fisc incomes between jurisdictions W and M, $F_w - F_m$, including fiscal surpluses, and is drawn to reflect a situation in which the fiscal surplus is higher in W than it is in M for every individual. Given the nature of the fiscal surplus, rational decision-makers will migrate until comprehensive incomes are equalized at point B, and so too much labour will move into region W where the public sector offers more than it does in M. At B, excess migration has depressed the marginal productivity of labour in W and thus real incomes by an amount (equal to BC) that just offsets the fiscal advantage from consuming public services in W rather than in M.

The attractiveness of the public sector in W relative to that in the destination and the corresponding degree of inefficiency in the allocation of labour will, in principle, depend on three basic factors (Winer and Gauthier 1982a, 28–9): the overall level or scale of public services in each location; their mix in terms of education, health, and so on; and the incidence of public services and taxes collected to pay for them. Presumably, people will take into account both the current structure of the public sector and its anticipated future structure.

If the fiscal advantage in favour of W remains, so will regional

FIGURE 1
Policy-Induced Migration and the Regional Allocation of Labour

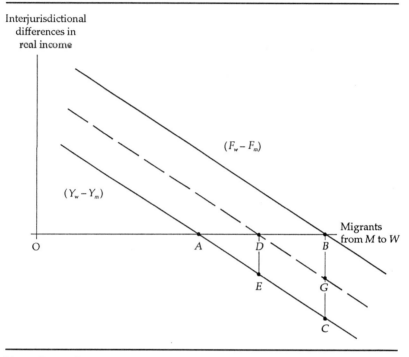

Notes: Y_i = real income in region i
F_i = comprehensive income in region i, equal to Y_i plus the net fiscal surplus associated with region i.

disparities in earned incomes. What is sometimes referred to as the "transfer dependency thesis" (see, for example, Courchene 1978) focuses on this important point. In this view, disparities in earned incomes between richer and poorer regions persist primarily because the fiscal system subsidizes the location decision of individuals who choose to live in relatively underdeveloped parts of the country.

Mobility and Redistribution

In addition to its consequences for the allocation of resources and for regional disparities in earned incomes, policy-induced migration has important implications for the design and effects of redistributive taxation. It has long been recognized that the ability of a government to redistribute is severely restricted if those being taxed to finance this redistribution are mobile.[4] Attempts to redistribute may ultimately affect primarily the income of immobile factors, especially lower-income workers, since more mobile people who enjoy higher incomes and capital tend to leave a jurisdiction whenever coercive redistribution becomes too onerous. In the limit, only fiscal systems based on the benefit principle may survive.

The likelihood that taxes will be shifted to relatively immobile factors raises the question of whether the target group for purposes of redistributive policy should consist only of residents who can be easily reached by the policy, or rather should be extended to citizens wherever they may live and whatever the cost of enforcing the redistributive policy. The standard view of the appropriate policy response to the consequences of migration for redistributive policy is stated by Oates (1972) in his treatise on fiscal federalism and has been recently summarized in the following way by Wildasin (1991b, 757): redistributive activity should be centralized because lower-level jurisdictions that engage in redistribution will experience "a kind of adverse selection: redistribution creates locational incentives that attract those who benefit from these policies (the poor) and repel contributors (taxpayers)." Acceptance of this view clearly has important implications for the definition of the target group and for the locus of democratic decision-making on redistributive issues.

The standard view has been challenged by Pauly (1973) on the normative grounds that tastes for redistribution vary substantially across lower-level jurisdictions in a federation. Oakland (1983) argues, in addition, that the costs of migration are substantial enough to make regionally differentiated redistribution viable as a matter of fact, a hypothesis that accords with his observations that cities and states in the United States are conducting programs with substantial redistributive effects, including the subsidization of housing, and that these programs vary widely in generosity from place to place.

Intergovernmental Grants and Fiscal Externalities

There is another policy recommendation, besides centralization of fiscal responsibilities, that is often offered to governments in a federation trying to cope with the consequences of factor mobility. This alternative involves the use of a system of intergovernmental grants to eliminate the interjurisdictional differences in fiscal structure that cause migration. Again, we may use figure 1 to illustrate. If a central authority were to transfer funds from jurisdiction or province W to province M, or were to tax the country as a whole to pay for a grant to M, the fiscal system in M could be made just as attractive as that in W. The solid line representing differences in comprehensive incomes, $F_w - F_m$, would then correspond with the line through point A, provided that the grant were properly computed, and inefficient migration would be eliminated. Canada has a sophisticated system of intergovernmental grants that may, at least in part, be justified in this way (Graham 1964; (Boadway and Flatters 1982a).

Interjurisdictional grants in Canada are not just about efficiency, however. A concern for equity is also evident. Equity in this context, following Buchanan (1950), is usually thought to require that an individual of given economic circumstances receive the same level of public services and pay the same taxes regardless of where in the country the individual might live.[5] This view of equity is made operational in Canada through a system of equalization grants (described in detail by Courchene 1984).[6] Under various names, such grants have been a federal responsibility since Confederation and were formally entrenched in the Constitution in 1982. Equity in the same sense is also regarded as an appropriate rationale for provincial grants that equalize funds available to local school boards and municipalities (Bird and Slack 1983, ch. 7).

One of the most interesting aspects of interregional grants is that the equity and efficiency rationales for them lead to very similar policy recommendations. Grants intended to equalize or improve access to public services in poorer regions will also retard inefficient out-migration induced by the relatively larger fiscal surpluses in more prosperous jurisdictions. As Graham (1964) and Boadway and Flatters (1982a, b) have shown, the theory of grants in the context of interregional migration provides one of the few instances where equity and efficiency concerns do not necessarily conflict with each other. Whether equity and efficiency concerns actually conflict in the real world depends on whether the level of grants is properly computed. If grants are overly generous to less developed regions and do more than is required to equalize fiscal surpluses, then they may indeed retard efficient out-migration from relatively depressed regions (Winer and Gauthier 1982a, 3).

Calculating the size of grants required to avoid a trade off between equity and efficiency is not an easy job. The task is complicated by the presence of congestion and fiscal externalities, as a reading of the analyses by Flatters, Henderson, and Mieszkowski (1974) or by Wildasin (1986, 2–22) demonstrates. When people move into a jurisdiction they may cause a rise in congestion or pollution. If we define real income in figure 1 to be net of the cost of congestion and pollution, the position of the real income line including congestion effects will depend on the extent of migration.

Fiscal externalities refer to the consequences for the fiscal surpluses enjoyed by non-migrants that are not taken into account by migrants. If publicly supplied services are subject to economies of scale, for example, a migrant will raise the per capita tax price of services in the place they leave and reduce it in the jurisdiction to which they are moving. In the presence of fiscal externalities, the position of the line representing comprehensive income differentials in figure 1 will depend on the extent of migration.

With both real and comprehensive income lines in figure 1 responding to migration in complicated ways, it is clear that computing the correct grant to M to forestall inefficient over-migration to W will not be a straightforward task. A further complication in the design of grants is that in a federation like Canada, as in almost every federation, grants are paid to governments rather than to individuals. To do otherwise would seriously weaken the autonomy of the provincial or municipal governments and thereby attenuate federalism. On the other hand, the connection between grants and individual fiscal surpluses is weakened when grants are paid to governments, and the design of the "proper" grant system becomes even more difficult.

Capitalization, the Tiebout Model, and the Operation of Local Fiscal Systems

The last issue we introduce before turning to the empirical research concerns the capitalization of fiscal surpluses into the price of immobile assets. If interjurisdictional differences in fiscal surpluses are expected to persist, then they may, to some extent, be capitalized into the value of immobile assets such as land or housing as new migrants bid up the price of assets that are associated closely with favourable fiscal treatment. The degree of capitalization that actually occurs will depend on such factors as the cost of moving, the cost of information about fiscal systems, uncertainty about future fiscal policy, the nature of zoning regulations in urban areas, and the elasticity of supply of new housing (Yinger et al. 1988).[7]

Much of the theoretical work on capitalization has been stimulated by the Tiebout model. Over 35 years ago, Tiebout (1956) suggested that when individuals are mobile between jurisdictions, migration between jurisdictions in a federal system might lead to the efficient provision of local public services. He sought to rebut Samuelson's (1954) conclusion that no market-like mechanism exists to determine the correct level of public goods. The gist of the argument is described by Musgrave (1991a, 283):

> With benefits of public goods limited to a particular local region, efficient provision calls for individuals with homogeneous public good preferences to congregate in particular regions, a result brought on by the tendency of individuals to move so as to seek a congenial preference environment. In a Tiebout equilibrium, the size of these equal preference communities ... will expand until marginal cost saving (as the cost of the social good is spread to one additional resident) equals the marginal congestion cost introduced by that marginal resident. The size of each jurisdiction is thus determined at the point of lowest average tax cost of providing public services.

In other words, as migrants "vote with their feet" they reveal their preferences for public goods by sorting themselves into equal-preference communities. Such sorting into homogeneous communities permits local governments, who are assumed to be interested in maximizing the welfare of their citizens, to provide the right type and amount of public services at least total cost.

Tiebout's insight about the potential virtues of migration in a system of local governments led to a debate over his unproven claim for the efficiency of the resulting migration equilibrium. Some authors have argued that the existence of congestion, fiscal externalities, or attempts by a jurisdiction to export its tax burdens would invalidate Tiebout's claim. Musgrave (1991b) emphasizes that, in the presence of interjurisdictional mobility, the overall level of taxation may be bid down by competition for factors below the level required to finance desired public services. This theoretical debate is not yet resolved.[8]

The Tiebout model also stimulated a search for evidence that the process he described is, in fact, operative. Following Oates (1969), many authors have used measures of the extent of capitalization of property taxes as evidence that a Tiebout-like process occurs in the real world. The underlying assumption is that capitalization serves as visible evidence of the economic decisions made by migrants during the working out of the Tiebout process. Whether capitalization indicates the Tiebout process is working is a contentious issue, however. Some authors argue that in a long-run Tiebout equilibrium, the fiscal surpluses that motivate Tiebout migrants would be reduced to such a low level by supply-side responses that capitalization would cease to exist. Thus, they claim that the existence of capitalization indicates that the Tiebout process does not work as it is supposed to.[9]

Regardless of whether or not capitalization can be regarded as evidence for the Tiebout process, the existence of capitalization may alter the conclusion that regional policies create or prolong regional disparities in earned incomes (Boadway and Flatters 1982a). Figure 1 can be used to illustrate this point. Partial capitalization into property values of the fiscal advantage to living and consuming public services in jurisdiction W rather than in M can be represented in the figure by shifting the solid line through point B (which shows the difference in comprehensive incomes before capitalization) inwards to the dotted line through D. The extent of inefficient migration to W is thus reduced by an amount DB, with corresponding welfare gain $DECB$. If capitalization is complete – that is, if the price of a house in W increases by an amount equal to the difference in the present values of fiscal surpluses in W and M – the dotted line must be shifted back all the way to point A, and we can see that inefficient migration is then completely eliminated.

Capitalization also has substantial implications for the allocative and distributive consequences of municipal fiscal systems. Property tax systems, even in those cities where systematic assessment errors have been made, become benefit tax systems when capitalization is complete.[10] When capitalization is complete, the value of a house or business receiving systematic preferential treatment from municipal authorities, in the form of better-than-average municipal services or a lower-than-average tax rate, will be bid up by an amount equal to the capitalized value of the fiscal surplus enjoyed by the existing owners.[11] Moreover, to the extent that fiscal surpluses are correctly anticipated by buyers and sellers of property, attempts at vertical redistribution across income classes using the property tax may be unsuccessful even though nominal property tax rates are progressive. This is because the price of homes in the districts inhabited mainly by lower-income people will tend to adjust upwards by the capitalized value of the preferential tax treatment they receive. The horizontal equity of property taxation is also affected by capitalization. If property taxes are correctly anticipated, the tax system will tend to be horizontally equitable in the sense that those property owners who enjoy a given level of services will, after capitalization, pay the same, present value amount of taxes (Hamilton 1979).[12]

When changes in municipal fiscal systems are not anticipated, the implications of capitalization for equity are quite different. Unanticipated changes in taxes or public services will cause current owners of property to suffer a capital loss, or will confer on them a capital gain equal to the present value of the unanticipated stream of fiscal surpluses associated with their property (Feldstein 1976). These capital losses and gains may lead to undesirable vertical or horizontal inequities.

The Empirical Literature on Policy-Induced Internal Migration

While economic theory demonstrates that policy-induced migration, if it exists, may have substantial consequences for the level and distribution of economic welfare as well as for the type of policies actually adopted, such a conclusion is of little practical importance if migration is not, in fact, responsive to policy changes. It is clearly important to know what the data tell us about the nature of the relationship between migration and public policies in the real world.

In this section, we review the studies using Canadian data that have attempted to reveal whether or not policy-induced internal migration in fact occurs, and if it does, which elements of public policy are involved and what the degree of sensitivity to policy changes is. Unfortunately, despite the potential importance of policy-induced migration for economic well-being, there is less work that deals directly with the empirical estimation of its consequences. The few studies that have been done are reviewed in the following section.

Virtually all economic studies of migration behaviour are based on the same underlying hypothesis: that individuals will move to a new location if they believe that their welfare will be increased by such a move. This basic hypothesis is broad enough to allow a very wide range of factors to influence individual migration decisions: income and employment opportunities, environmental quality, climate, culture, both monetary and non-monetary costs of moving, and elements of fiscal structure such as the availability of public services and the levels of taxes and transfer payments. Holding the non-policy determinants of migration equal, one would expect individuals to be attracted to locations with lower taxes, higher transfer payments, and greater availability of publicly provided services. Since we cannot directly observe the impact of each of these factors on the welfare of individuals, the problem facing empirical researchers is to find some means of measuring their approximate impact on migration decisions using data on the observed choices of individuals.

In addition to a common underlying hypothesis, empirical studies of migration tend to share a common structure. All such studies hypothesize that a functional relationship exists between a measure of the migration between locations i and j, M_{ij}, and various determinants of migration:

$$M_{ij} = f(X_{11}, ..., X_{1J}, ..., X_{n1}, ..., X_{nJ}, \epsilon_{ij}) \tag{1}$$

where X_{kj} represents the value of explanatory variable k in location j, J is the total number of locations that individuals can choose between, and ϵ_{ij} is a random error term that accounts for such factors as measurement error and the effects of unobservable variables. As the equation indicates, the characteristics of all possible alternative destinations will be taken into account by individuals and therefore should, in principle, be incorporated in the empirical model of migration.

However, beyond this point, studies of migration behaviour can vary in a number of important ways. First of all, they may differ in their choice of migration flow to examine: intermunicipal, interregional, interprovincial, or international. All but two of the studies to be reviewed here examine interprovincial or interregional migration in Canada; in the interregional case, the regions are aggregates of provinces. The remaining two studies focus on intermunicipal migration flows.

Second, studies may differ in the definition of the migration variable M they examine: for example, net in- or out-migration gross flows between locations, gross migration rates between locations, or individual migration choices. The gross flow of migrants from *i* to *j* is the total number of people who moved from *i* to *j*, while the corresponding gross migration rate is the gross flow divided by the population of the origin, location *i*. A net flow is simply the difference between gross flows in opposite directions; for example, net in-migration to Ontario is the difference between total inflows to and total outflows from Ontario. Net migration rates can also be defined by dividing the net flow by the population of the location under consideration. Only two of the studies examined here use a micro data set that contains information on individual migration choices; the others use data on net or gross migration rates or flows that have been obtained by aggregating over groups in the population.

Third, studies vary in their definitions of the variables chosen to represent the determinants of migration choices, in particular in the variables that represent fiscal structure. Among the explanatory variables that are typically included in studies of migration are wage rates, unemployment rates, indicators of climate, and the distance between the origin and potential destination. In this review, we will restrict our attention to the variables used to represent fiscal structure, which will be discussed more fully below.

Finally, studies vary in terms of their econometric specification and choice of estimating technique, ranging from simple linear models of migration to more complicated logit and probit models. Linear models typically have the form

$$M_{ij} = \alpha_0 + \alpha_{1i}X_{1i} + \alpha_{1j}X_{1j} + \ldots + \alpha_{ni}X_{ni} + \alpha_{nj}X_{nj} + \epsilon_{ij} \qquad (2)$$

where M_{ij} and $_{-ij}$ are defined as above, X_{ki} and X_{kj} are the origin and destination values of the explanatory variable X_k, and the αs are the parameters to be estimated. In a log-linear model, natural logs of both the dependent and the explanatory variables are taken, implying the following relationship between M_{ij} and the explanatory variables:

$$M_{ij} = e^{\alpha_0} \cdot X_{1i}^{\alpha_{1i}} \cdot X_{1j}^{\alpha_{1j}} \cdot \ldots \cdot X_{ni}^{\alpha_{ni}} \cdot X_{nj}^{\alpha_{nj}} \cdot \epsilon_{ij} \qquad (3)$$

where *e* represents the exponential function. In some linear and log-linear models, the origin and destination coefficients of a given explanatory variable are constrained to be the same.

Although the log-linear estimating equation allows for interactions between the explanatory variables while the linear equation does not, both suffer from the same deficiencies. First of all, as indicated in equations 2 and 3 above, linear and log-linear estimating equations contain, at most, the origin and actual destination values of the explanatory variables; if the values for other (potential) locations were included as well there would simply be too many parameters to estimate. Second, the adding-up restrictions that are satisfied by the migration data (for example, the sum over all destinations of rates of out-migration from province i must be one) will not be satisfied by the estimated migration equations unless numerous cross-equation restrictions are imposed on the parameters. Finally, predictions of migration rates derived from equations such as 2 or 3 can be either negative or greater than one, values that are not possible in the real world.

For these reasons, many recent studies of migration have discarded the linear formulations in favour of the discrete choice approach, which recognizes that, from the point of view of the individual, the migration decision is a discrete choice: in other words, the individual has only a limited set of alternatives from which to choose. The multinomial logit (MNL) model, which leads to the following equation describing the probability (or rate) of migration from i to j,

$$M_{ij} = \frac{e^{V_{ij}}}{\sum\limits_{k=1}^{J} e^{V_{ik}}} \qquad (4)$$

$$V_{ij} = \beta_0 + \beta_1 X_{1ij} + \beta_2 X_{2ij} + \dots + \beta_n X_{nij} \qquad (5)$$

has become particularly popular. Some MNL models also allow the parameters β_{-k} to differ between the province of origin and the destinations.

As the definition of V_{ij} indicates, in the MNL model, the characteristics of all the relevant alternatives can enter into the equation for M_{ij} without increasing the number of parameters to be estimated. Furthermore, if equation 4 is summed over all the possible alternatives, the resulting sum will equal one regardless of the parameter values. Last but not least, predictions of migration rates derived from discrete choice models will always lie between zero and one.

Table 2 contains a concise summary of the most important features and results of 15 studies of migration in Canada that investigate the effect of fiscal structure on internal migration. As column two of the table indicates, seven of these studies use a multinomial logit or discrete choice approach, while the others utilize linear or log-linear equations. Column two of the table also describes the migration data used and the sample period covered, while the third and fourth columns of the table describe the variables used to represent fiscal structure and the results of each study regarding the fiscal variables.

Collectively, the studies encompass the period 1951 to 1983. With the exception of Islam (1989), they have restricted their attention to interprovincial differences in fiscal structure, and differ greatly in their choice of fiscal variables to be included in the model. In total, eight different aspects of fiscal structure have been examined by the various studies: intergovernmental transfer payments, transfer payments to individuals, unemployment insurance (UI) benefits, taxes (both direct and indirect), federal purchases, natural resource revenues, government expenditures, and fiscal surpluses.

Of course, measures of fiscal structure are not the only explanatory variables included in the studies summarized in table 2. But because the non-fiscal determinants of migration are not the primary focus of the paper, we pay very little attention to them here. Briefly, the general results with respect to the most commonly included non-fiscal explanatory variables can be summarized as follows: (1) income or wage differentials have a significant impact on migration, with individuals tending to move from low-wage to high-wage locations; (2) distance, which is typically included as a proxy for moving costs, is a strong deterrent to migration; and (3) empirical results with respect to the unemployment rate are mixed, with some studies finding that unemployment rates have the anticipated effect and others finding that they do not.[13] Finally, there is also some evidence that younger and better-educated individuals are the most likely to move (Courchene 1970; Islam 1989).

An Overview of the Canadian Studies

Courchene (1970) was the first to examine empirically the possible effects of fiscal structure on migration. This work, as well as much of the work that followed, was clearly motivated by a suspicion that transfer payments are partly responsible for the persistence of regional disparities in Canada.

Courchene identified two types of policies that he felt would be likely to have a detrimental effect on the efficiency of interprovincial migration: federal transfers to persons, in particular unemployment

TABLE 2
A Summary of Studies of Fiscally-Induced Migration in Canada

Study	Migration data used; model type	Fiscal variables	Results
Courchene (1970)	Gross interprovincial migration rates, 1961 Census; linear model	Intergovernmental transfers per worker in the sending province	Transfers have significant negative effect on out-migration.
	Gross interprovincial migration rates of family allowance recipients, 1952–67; log-linear model	Ratio of total federal transfers to earned income in the sending province, ratio of total UI benefits to earned income in the sending province	Both federal transfers and UI benefits have significant negative effect on out-migration.
Boadway and Green (1981)	Net migration to Newfoundland, 1951–78 (net migration estimated to be annual change in population less natural increase); linear model	Average weekly UI benefits per claim divided by average weekly earnings, per capita federal transfers to Newfoundland	Increases in ratio of average weekly UI benefits to average weekly earnings significantly increase net migration to Newfoundland. However, per capita federal transfers do not seem to have significant effect.
Schweitzer (1982)	Gross in- and out-migration to Alberta, 1961–79; linear model	Per capita provincial government natural resource revenues in Canada relative to those in the rest of Canada	Increase in per capita natural resource revenues in Alberta relative to rest of Canada will significantly increase in-migration to Alberta, but does not have significant effect upon out-migration.

continued

TABLE 2 (*continued*)

Study	Migration data used; model type	Fiscal variables	Results
Dean (1982)	Gross interprovincial migration rates of family allowance recipients, 1972–9; linear model	Personal income tax rate (origin and destination), direct taxes paid as a percentage of personal income (origin and destination)	Origin and destination values of both variables have negative and usually significant impact on out-migration when provinces are pooled.
Winer and Gauthier (1982)	Gross interprovincial migration rates of family allowance recipients, 1951–78; log-linear model	Ratio of average weekly UI payments to average weekly wages, ratio of total federal transfers to persons (excluding UI) to labour income in sending province, ratio of unconditional intergovernmental grants divided by labour force in sending province	Federal transfers and unconditional grants have significant negative impact on out-migration.
Winer and Gauthier (1982)	Gross interprovincial migration rates of individuals in a sample drawn from income tax records, 1967–77; MNL model	Index of UI generosity in both origin and destination; difference between origin and destination in per capita federal purchases; difference between origin and destination in per capita unconditional intergovernmental grants; per capita transfer payments to persons excluding UI benefits; difference between origin and destination in per capita natural resource revenues	Results somewhat mixed. In general, fiscal structure seems to have larger impact on poor and middle income classes than on rich income class. Also, out-migration from Atlantic provinces is negatively related to increases in generosity of UI in the Atlantic region, and positively related to increases in generosity of UI benefits elsewhere.

continued

Mills, Percy, and Wilson (1983)	Gross interprovincial migration rates of family allowance recipients, 1961–78; linear models	Difference in fiscal surplus between destination and origin provinces, where fiscal surplus is defined as per capita provincial government expenditures less per capita revenues from direct and indirect taxes	Positive fiscal difference seems to increase out-migration from Alantic and Western provinces, but not Ontario and Quebec.
Foot and Milne (1984)	Net interprovincial flows, 1961–81; linear model	Real per capita fiscal surplus in region under consideration, defined as difference between federal transfers to persons plus provincial government expenditures less provincial and local direct and indirect taxes and and other transfers to provincial government from persons; weighted average of fiscal surpluses in other regions	Increase in fiscal surplus in province i will increase net in-migration to six provinces; but has no effect or negative effect in Ontario, Manitoba, Saskatchewan, and BC. Increases in fiscal benefits in other provinces have expected significantly negative effect only in case of Ontario.
MacNevin (1984)	Gross interprovincial migration rates, 1962–78; MNL model	Real per capita provincial government expenditures; total provincial and local taxes as a percentage of provincial personal income; provincial and local taxes disaggregated by type (personal taxes deducted from income, and commodity taxes expressed as a percentage of gross provincial expenditures)	Results with respect to government expenditures not robust. Both tax specifications perform well. Higher taxes in origin province will increase out-migration, while higher taxes elsewhere will reduce out-migration.

continued

TABLE 2 (*continued*)

Study	Migration data used; model type	Fiscal variables	Results
Shaw (1985, 1986)	Gross migration rates between 17 census metropolitan areas, 1961, 1971, 1976, and 1981 censuses; MNL model	Average weekly payment of UI benefits in the province divided by the average weekly wage in the CMA (generosity of UI); ratio of total weeks of UI benefits paid to total number of weeks of unemployment in province (probability of receiving UI); real per capita unconditional federal grants to province; real provincial government natural resource revenues	Increased generosity of UI benefits in origin CMA will significantly reduce out-migration. Increased grants to government of destination province will increase out-migration. When sample is restricted to post-1971, generosity of UI benefits in destination CMA and grants to province of origin will also have significant effect on out-migration – positive in first case, negative in second. Changes in natural resource revenues do not have significant effect on migration.
Liaw and Ledent (1987)	Gross interprovincial migration rates, 1961–83; MNL model	Relative unemployment benefit per unemployed person; level of per capita government transfers in province of origin	Unemployment benefits per employed person have no significant effect on out-migration from region, and increases in per capita government transfers provide no more than a weak disincentive to out-migration. Higher relative unemployment benefits in destination province seem to provide significant deterrent to in-migration.

continued

Study	Data and model	Variables	Findings
Rosenbluth (1987)	Rate of net in-migration, estimates based on migration of family allowance recipients, pooled across provinces for the period 1966–83; linear model	Real per capita transfer payments to persons; real per capita government expenditures; real per capita taxes on persons	Increases in real per capita transfer payments to persons significantly increase rate of net in-migration to province. Results with respect to other two variables are not robust.
Liaw and Ledent (1988)	Micro data from the 1981 census, interprovincial moves of elderly only; nested logit model	Per capita government transfers per person, net of UI benefits	Per capita government transfers do not have significant impact on migration of the elderly.
Vanderkamp (1988)	Rate of net out-migration between census years, pooled across provinces for the period 1931–40 to 1971–80; linear model	Fiscal surplus (defined as provincial government expenditures less residence-based taxes) as proportion of earned income	Fiscal surplus appears to act as deterrent to net out-migration.
Islam (1989)	Micro data from the 1981 census; discrete choice model of move/stay choice	Estimated difference between origin and destination in transfers to persons; estimated difference between origin and destination in property taxes	Property tax differentials do not have a significant effect on intermunicipal migration, but differences in transfer payments do. Individuals will tend to move to municipalities where transfer payments are higher.

continued

TABLE 2 (continued)

Study	Migration data used; model type	Fiscal variables	Results
Day (1992)	Gross interprovincial migration rates, 1962–81; MNL model	Real per capita expenditures on health, social services, education, and all other goods by provincial and local governments and hospitals; income and wage variables corrected for income taxes, provincial transfers, and UI benefits	In general, increases in government spending on health and education in a province increase in-migration to that province. But increased spending on social services has significantly negative impact on in-migration. Tax, transfer, and UI variables have a significant impact through income and wage variables.

insurance; and intergovernmental grants from the federal to the provincial governments. With respect to unemployment insurance, his concern was that since eligibility requirements and benefit periods varied with regional unemployment rates, individuals in high-unemployment regions might be discouraged from leaving those regions to seek work elsewhere. Similarly, he argued that intergovernmental transfer payments, by allowing governments in low-income provinces to offer more services at a given level of taxation, would reduce migration from low-income to high-income provinces. Using the ratio of total UI benefits to earned income and intergovernmental transfers per worker in the origin province i (or, in an alternative equation, the ratio of total federal transfers to earned income in the origin) to measure the effects of UI and intergovernmental transfer payments respectively, he estimated a simple equation explaining the rate of migration from province i to province j and found that both his hypotheses were verified.

The studies that built on Courchene's seminal paper can be divided into two groups. The first group consists of studies that continued to use linear specifications for their migration equations, while a second group of studies consists of those that relied on discrete choice models instead of linear ones. Studies that used a linear specification include Boadway and Green (1981), Dean (1982), Schweitzer (1982), Mills, Percy, and Wilson (1983), Foot and Milne (1984), Rosenbluth (1987), and Vanderkamp (1988). Three of these studies – Dean (1982), Mills, Percy, and Wilson (1983), and Foot and Milne (1984) – are concerned primarily with the existence of fiscally induced migration and will be discussed first.

Dean (1982) chose to focus on the effect of taxes on migration. He included both origin and destination values of two tax variables in an equation describing the rate of migration from province i to province j: the personal income tax rate (which is a percentage of basic federal tax) and direct taxes as a percentage of personal income. When the equation was estimated using pooled data for all ten provinces, all the tax variables proved to have significant coefficients. Surprisingly, the coefficients of the origin as well as the destination variables had negative signs, suggesting that high taxes in the province of origin would tend to reduce out-migration rather than increase it. However, Dean reported that the negative sign of the coefficient on the province of origin tax variable disappeared in most cases when separate equations were estimated for each province of origin.

Mills, Percy, and Wilson (1983) and Foot and Milne (1984) tried to examine the combined impact of taxation and government expenditures on interprovincial migration. Both of these studies relied on a single indicator of fiscal structure, a measure of fiscal surplus essentially equal to the dollar amount of expenditures minus taxes collected. As a representation of fiscal structure, this measure is somewhat problematic, because it does not incorporate the subjective evaluation of the benefits individuals receive from government services. Moreover, use of the fiscal surplus precludes investigation of the effects of such aspects of fiscal structure as the mix of government services supplied.

The results of the two studies are not very conclusive. Both found that their fiscal surplus variables have the anticipated effect only in some provinces. It is particularly noteworthy that Ontario is one of the provinces in which both studies find that fiscal surpluses seem to have either no impact on migration, or an effect opposite to that which was anticipated.

The remaining studies that estimated linear models of migration were concerned primarily with the estimation of multi-equation models of migration, employment, and wage determination, rather than with the problem of policy- or fiscally induced migration. In this section of the paper, we discuss only their migration equation results. All of these studies added at least one fiscal variable to their migration equations. Boadway and Green (1981), for example, included both the ratio of average weekly UI benefits to average weekly earnings in Newfoundland and per capita federal transfers to Newfoundland in their equation explaining net migration to Newfoundland, but found that only the former variable had a significant (positive) impact on migration.

Schweitzer (1982) included per capita provincial government natural resource revenues in equations explaining both in- and out-migration to Alberta, but this fiscal variable proved to have a significant (positive) effect only on in-migration to Alberta.

Unlike Boadway and Green (1981) and Schweitzer (1982), Rosenbluth (1987) and Vanderkamp (1988) estimated simultaneous models for all of Canada. Rosenbluth tested three potential fiscal variables in his migration equation, but obtained consistent results with respect to only one of them – real per capita transfer payments to persons. His results indicate that increases in real per capita transfers to persons in a province will significantly increase the rate of in-migration to that province. Vanderkamp, on the other hand, tested only one fiscal variable, and found that it reduced net out-migration from a province. Like Mills, Percy, and Wilson (1983) and Foot and Milne (1984), he used an estimate of fiscal surplus as his measure of fiscal structure.

As was noted above, one problem with linear models of migration is that it is impossible to include the characteristics of more than just the origin and destination regions in the estimating equations without making some extremely restrictive assumptions. Some studies, like that of Vanderkamp (1988), included variables representative of only one province or region. Foot and Milne (1984) did include the characteristics of all regions as explanatory variables in their model, but only by defining "all other provinces" versions of each explanatory variable that were distance-weighted aggregates of the values for nine provinces. Each of the seven studies in table 2, which have yet to be discussed, overcome this problem by estimating a discrete choice model.

The first study of migration in Canada to use a discrete choice model to test whether or not fiscally induced migration exists was that of Winer and Gauthier (1982).[14] They used a number of different variables to represent the fiscal structure of a province: an index of the generosity of UI benefits; the difference between provinces i and j in per capita federal purchases; the difference between i and j in per capita unconditional grants; the difference in per capita natural resource revenues; and per capita federal transfers excluding UI benefits. In addition, their data set allowed them to estimate separate models of migration for each of seven different income classes. Since the impact of fiscal structure may vary systematically with income class, this sort of disaggregation is obviously useful in a study of policy-induced migration.

Apart from the results with respect to unemployment insurance, their results concerning most of the fiscal variables they utilized were inconclusive. Winer and Gauthier (1982) did find that migration to Alberta and the west is significantly positively correlated with natural resource revenues. The possibility remains, however, that this result is tainted by the general collinearity of public- and private-sector variables in the west following the dramatic rise in the price of oil after 1973, a problem that affects all studies that have attempted to look at the role of such tax revenues. Natural resource revenues may simply be a proxy for job opportunities or other private-sector determinants of migration decisions not included in the estimating equations.

The results with respect to UI benefits are much stronger than those for other fiscal variables. Winer and Gauthier (1982) found that out-migration of poorer people from the Atlantic provinces is significantly and negatively related to increases in an index of the generosity of UI benefits in that region, and positively related to increases in the generosity of UI benefits elsewhere. The fact that unemployment insurance payments are a relatively important source of income for poorer people, and for people in relatively depressed regions of the country, enhances the intuitive plausibility of this result.

Using census data, Shaw (1985, 1986) estimated a multinomial logit model that was somewhat similar to that of Winer and Gauthier (1982). He found that real per capita unconditional intergovernmental grants to the destination province will increase migration to that province, while grants to the province of origin either have no effect or an unexpected positive effect on out-migration. The natural resource revenues of a provincial government had no discernible effect on migration flows. But increases in the generosity of UI benefits in the census metropolitan area (CMA) of origin significantly reduce out-migration. Furthermore, when Shaw restricted his sample to the post-1971 period, he found that an increase in the generosity of UI benefits in the potential destinations will tend to increase out-migration from a CMA. Thus, his results with respect to UI benefits support those of Winer and Gauthier.

Two other studies, both by Liaw and Ledent (1987, 1988), also tested the effect of per capita government transfers and UI benefits on interprovincial migration flows. In their first study, Liaw and Ledent found that per capita transfers have only a weak effect on migration, while in their second study, which focused on the migration of the elderly, they found that it had no effect at all. Their results with respect to unemployment benefits, however, contrast sharply with those of other researchers: they found that higher relative UI benefits in the province of origin will actually reduce in-migration, not increase it. They argued that this result was to be expected because they included this variable as a proxy for the unemployment rate rather than as a measure of the UI system.

Liaw and Ledent's (1987) results with respect to their relative UI benefits variable illustrate the difficulties inherent in interpreting econometric results. Average UI benefits, of which their variable is a measure, do rise with unemployment rates because of variable entrance requirements and differences in the maximum benefit period. Thus, unless the unemployment rate is also included as an explanatory variable in the model, which it is not in this case, one cannot distinguish between the deterrent effect of high unemployment rates in a province, and the attraction of higher UI benefits. Therefore, Liaw and Ledent's result does not necessarily contradict the findings of Winer and Gauthier and Shaw; it may simply indicate that the deterrent effect is the stronger of the two. Since Winer and Gauthier included both unemployment rates and UI benefits in their estimating equations, their results are more likely to reflect the true effect of UI benefits on migration.

The poor performance of fiscal variables other than UI benefits in most of the studies discussed thus far seems to suggest that provincial government fiscal policies have very little effect on interprovincial migration flows. However, MacNevin (1984) and Day (1992) disputed this conclusion, arguing that the explanation for the inconclusive results obtained by other studies lay in their choice of variables representing fiscal structure. Individuals making migration decisions are unlikely to pay attention to the levels of interprovincial grants or natural resource revenues received by different provincial governments. Similarly, few individuals are likely to make a detailed calculation of their fiscal surplus in the manner implied by Mills, Percy, and Wilson (1988), Foot and Milne (1984), or Vanderkamp (1988). Instead, the aspects of fiscal structure that individuals are most likely to be aware of are the public services that they consume, the taxes they pay, and the transfer payments (including UI) that they receive.

MacNevin and Day therefore proposed that some measure of the level of public services, rather than intergovernmental grants or natural resource revenues, should appear directly in equations explaining interprovincial migration. A finding that the level of public services has a significant impact on interprovincial migration would provide indirect evidence that intergovernmental grants and natural resource revenues influence migration, since changes in provincial government revenues will clearly have an impact on the supply of public services.

Both MacNevin (1984) and Day (1982) chose real per capita provincial government expenditures as their measure of the level of public services. Although MacNevin's results with respect to this variable were somewhat inconclusive, in that they were not consistent across different specifications of his estimating equations, Day's results were stronger. She found that higher per capita levels of provincial government spending will indeed attract in-migrants to a province, holding all other determinants of migration constant. In addition, she found that the mix of services provided is important. Migrants are attracted to provinces with higher per capita levels of spending on health and education, but repelled by higher levels of spending on social services. Precisely why spending on social services seems to repel migrants is not clear. It is possible that the effect is related to the income or employment status of migrants, or that per capita expenditures on social services are acting as a proxy for types of unemployment that are not adequately captured by the Labour Force Survey measure of unemployment.[15] Unfortunately, the aggregate data set used by Day did not permit the exploration of such possibilities.

MacNevin and Day also included taxes and transfer payments to individuals in their models of interprovincial migration, although they did so in a somewhat different manner than do other studies. Income taxes and transfer payments affect individuals primarily through their effect on disposable income, and thus MacNevin and Day argued that they should be included in migration equations through measures of disposable income, rather than as separate explanatory variables. Day also included UI benefits in the measure of disposable income in some versions of her model. Since the measures of disposable income included by MacNevin and Day do have a significant impact on in-migration to a region (the higher the disposable income in province i, the greater will be in-migration to that province, holding all else equal), income taxes and provincial government transfer payments also have a significant influence on migration via this channel.

Some authors, such as Winer and Gauthier (1982), argued that empirical models of migration should ideally include the expected present value of the gain in disposable income resulting from a move as the appropriate income variable, rather than current disposable income, which is the income variable utilized by Day and MacNevin. This is because the gains from migration are not realized solely in the period immediately after the individual moves, but over an extended period of time after the move is made. Moreover, they argued that individuals may have different expectations about how the different components of disposable income – before-tax income, income taxes, and transfer payments – are likely to evolve through time. If so, and given that it is only possible to approximate the process through which individuals form expectations of these quantities, it may be more appropriate to treat expected before-tax income, expected income taxes, and expected transfer payments as separate explanatory variables rather than use one comprehensive measure of income.

Winer and Gauthier (1982) followed this latter strategy by including separate measures of expected gross or before-tax income and per capita transfer payments to individuals as separate explanatory variables in their estimating equations. They deliberately excluded income taxes because including income taxes would introduce a serious econometric complication: the high correlation between income taxes and before-tax income would make it difficult to identify the separate results of the two explanatory variables.[16] Unfortunately, as indicated above, their results with respect to variables such as per capita transfer payments were inconclusive. For example, a higher level of transfer payments to the province of origin has the expected negative effect on migration only for some migration flows and income classes.

One other study that adopted a similar approach is Islam's (1989). This study usefully differs from most others in that it examines intermunicipal, rather than interprovincial differences in two aspects of fiscal structure: transfers to persons and property taxes. In addition, his is one of only two that use micro data (the other is Liaw and Ledent, 1988), but rather than examine interprovincial migration choices he restricts his attention to the move/stay decision.[17]

Although Islam used after-tax income as his income variable, he chose to include transfer payments and an estimate of property taxes in his estimating equation independently of income. Islam's results indicated that higher transfer payments elsewhere will encourage people to move to a municipality, and that intermunicipal differences in property taxes do not have a significant effect on migration. One difficulty in interpreting Islam's results concerning property taxation stems from the manner in which he constructed his data. Since Islam's data set did not contain direct observation on property tax payments, he estimated them by regressing monthly rental payments on average household income and various characteristics of the housing unit. Because it assumes that variations in individual rental payments from municipality to municipality are due entirely to property taxes, there are some potential problems with this approach to estimating property taxes. Differences in the frequency with which assessed values are changed, among other things, may result in differences across municipalities in the relationship between rental payments and property taxes. In addition, since Islam included renters as well as owners in his data set, differences in the degree of rent control and in the proportion of rental properties that are subject to rent control will also distort the relationship between rental payments and property taxes. Thus it is likely that Islam's estimates of property taxes are subject to measurement error, which will tend to bias the coefficient estimates.

What general conclusions can be drawn from this survey of empirical studies of the relationship between migration and fiscal structure in Canada? One must point out that the existing empirical evidence does suffer from some limitations. None of the studies used recent data, and therefore they missed the period after the 1982 recession during which there were some important changes in the levels and directions of internal migration flows. In addition, only four of the studies attempted to model the interactions between migration and various other economic variables. Economic theory tells us that the movement of people from one region or municipality to another is likely to have an impact on such variables as the wage rate, the unemployment rate, housing prices, and perhaps even government policies themselves if governments are aware of the impact of their policies on migration. If the simultaneity between migration and other variables is not taken into account, the estimates of the coefficients of migration equations may be biased.

Simultaneous equations bias is not as serious a problem in studies that use micro data, since a single individual is unlikely to have a big impact on a region's economy. However, the dearth of studies using micro data is itself a deficiency of the literature, since individual differences in such factors as age and education levels may play an important role in migration decisions. If migrants tend to be younger and better educated than the average population, then regions experiencing high net out-migration may suffer a deterioration in the quality of their labour force as a result. Only studies using microdata can effectively identify the groups in the population that are the most likely to move.

Last but not least, although a wide range of aspects of fiscal structure were considered by the studies surveyed, one class of government policies seems to have been ignored completely by Canadian researchers: policies related to housing. Rent controls and housing subsidies may well have an impact on migration decisions, since housing costs constitute an important component of a household's budget. Because of the lack of empirical evidence, it is impossible to determine the extent to which such policies may influence migration from one location to another in Canada.

Despite these general limitations of the studies reviewed, we can draw some conclusions from them regarding the existence of fiscally induced migration. First, the evidence that provincial or regional differences in UI benefits influence migration is fairly strong. Second, there is some evidence that the level and mix of provincial government spending, as well as provincial taxes and transfer payments, have an impact on interprovincial migration. Much of the evidence regarding interprovincial differences in taxes and transfer payments is indirect, however, as it relies on the use of comprehensive after-tax income variables. While this approach is not incorrect, it remains to be demonstrated that potential migrants actually base their migration decisions on after-tax rather than before-tax incomes. Finally, there does not appear to be any clear evidence that intergovernmental grants or natural resource revenues influence migration directly. It is of course possible, and perhaps even likely, that these policy instruments exert an indirect influence on migration via their role in the determination of provincial government fiscal policies, but this remains to be shown.

As far as migration within a province in response to differences in municipal government policies is concerned, very little can be said since only one study has examined this issue. Although Islam's (1989) results are interesting and indicate that intermunicipal migration responds to differences in welfare benefits, they pertain to only one type of municipal government policy. More research needs to be done using intermunicipal data before definite conclusions can be drawn.

A Comparison with Selected Studies from Other Countries

Researchers in other countries besides Canada have been interested in the effects of public policies on migration. In this section, we review a very small subset of the studies that have investigated the subject using data from the United States, and one study that uses British data.

In the United States, many of the studies of policy-induced migration have focused on the role of interstate differentials in levels of welfare benefits. A number of these studies have distinguished between flows of white and non-white migrants, arguing that whites – who, on average, are better off financially than non-whites – are likely to be repelled by higher levels of welfare benefits because they associate them with higher tax burdens. Non-whites, on the other hand, will be attracted to states with higher levels of welfare benefits because they are more likely to be welfare recipients.

Indeed, the results of Cebula (1979a) confirm this hypothesis. Using census data on interstate migration between 1960 and 1970, Cebula estimated simple linear equations explaining net in-migration for both whites and non-whites. He also included in his estimating equations per capita non-welfare expenditures of state and local governments and found that this fiscal variable too has different effects on white and non-white migrants: white migrants seem to be unaffected by it, while non-whites are more likely to migrate to states with higher per capita levels of non-welfare ex-penditures, holding all else equal.

Many of the other studies surveyed by Cebula (1980) obtained similar results regarding welfare benefits. More recently, Gramlich and Laren (1984) estimated a two-equation model in which the number of recipients of AFDC (Aid to Families with Dependent Children) benefits and the levels of AFDC benefits are jointly de-termined. Their data set covered the period 1974–81, and was pooled over states, but did not disaggregate recipients by race. They found that the number of AFDC recipients in a state was sensitive to the level of benefits, implying that interstate migration flows do respond to benefit levels.[18] Similarly, Cebula (1991), using a 1987 to 1989 data on AFDC recipients in Wisconsin who had recently moved from another state, found that the level of benefits in Wisconsin relative to the level in the state of origin was one of the factors determining the number of new recipients from other states.

Some U.S. studies have examined the effects of fiscal variables other than welfare. For example, Cebula (1977) examined the impact of both the growth rate of per student public expenditures on ed-ucation and per capital property taxes on inter-metropolitan migra-tion between 1965 and 1970. He found that a higher rate of growth of educational spending encouraged in-migration to a metropolitan area, while higher property taxes discouraged it.[19]

In another paper, Cebula (1990) examined the role of state income taxes in the migration decisions of the elderly. Since some U.S. states (six as of 1986) do not impose a general income tax, Cebula simply included in his linear migration equations a dummy variable that took on the value one for states that did impose income taxes and zero for states that did not. He found that the existence of a state income tax was indeed a significant deterrent to the in-migration of the elderly.

Goss and Paul (1990) examined the impact of unemployment insurance on interstate migration of the unemployed in 1982, estimating a discrete choice model of the binary decision of whether or not to move. In the United States, unemployment insurance programs are administered by state governments and, as in Canada, there may be regional differences in the generosity of benefits.[20] However, Goss and Paul ignored this aspect of UI and focused instead on its role as an income supplement for unemployed workers. A UI recipient will experience an increase in non-wage income that may either increase or decrease mobility: by lowering the cost of remaining unemployed, it may reduce the individual's incentive to move in search of a new job; or it may help the individual finance a move and thus increase mobility. Goss and Paul found that individuals who are "involuntarily unemployed" (for example, they have been laid off) are less likely to move if they receive UI benefits, while individuals who are "voluntarily unemployed" are more likely to move if they receive UI benefits.

Goss and Paul's results suggested that UI benefits would influence migration even if there were no regional differences in benefit levels or eligibility requirements. They interpreted these results as an indication that involuntarily unemployed workers use UI benefits to finance their wait for recall, while voluntarily unemployed workers are more likely to use UI benefits to finance the search for a new job. However, these behaviours on the part of unemployed workers are not necessarily undesirable. Instead, they imply that a system of UI benefits can contribute to economic efficiency by helping workers finance their search for a new job.

In Britain, one aspect of fiscal structure that has received some attention in the literature on interregional migration is housing subsidies. Hughes and McCormick (1981) noted that one family in three lives in what is known as "council" housing, and that the allocation policies for such housing are likely to discourage interregional migration. Using data from the 1973 General Household Survey, they estimated a discrete choice model of the option between moving or not moving. The type of housing tenure was included as a dummy variable in the model. They found that council-house tenants were significantly less mobile than owner-occupiers, who, they argued, would otherwise be the least likely to migrate to another region.

This survey of studies of policy-induced migration in other coun-

tries has been extremely selective, but it does indicate that migration
induced by public policy is not a phenomenon that is unique to
Canada. Various types of government policies, from welfare to housing subsidies, have been shown to influence interregional migration
in other countries. These results can only serve to strengthen the
case that public policies are, in many circumstances, significant determinants of migration decisions.

Importance versus Significance of the Results

The preceding review of the empirical evidence suggests that government policies do have a significant impact on individual migration
decisions. However, "significance" in the statistical sense does not
guarantee "importance" in the normal, everyday sense of the term.
The importance of policy-induced migration will depend on its magnitude, which in turn will depend on the size of the coefficients
multiplying fiscal variables in the migration equation and the mag-
nitudes of the fiscal variables themselves. Simulation exercises involving estimated migration equations and hypothetical changes in
fiscal variables can shed some light on the question of whether or
not fiscally induced migration is really an important phenomenon.

   Only five of the studies surveyed in this paper report any results
regarding the magnitude of fiscally induced migration. The first of
these is Dean (1982), who regards his results as very tentative. Using
estimated migration equations that were not reported in his paper,
he estimated the impact of a reduction of 1 percentage point in
the provincial basic tax (applied to the federal tax rate) in Alberta
and British Columbia on in-migration to the two provinces from
several other provinces. He found, for example, that the reduction
in Alberta's tax rate increases the flow of migrants from Newfoundland to Alberta by 6 per cent, while an equal reduction in British
Columbia's tax rate increases the flow of migrants from Newfoundland to British Columbia by 14.5 per cent. The corresponding increases in outflows from Quebec are only 2.6 per cent and 3 per
cent, respectively.

   Dean's simulation results suggest that interprovincial migration
is extraordinarily sensitive to provincial tax rates. Since provincial
taxes are computed as a percentage of the Basic Federal Tax, an
increase in the provincial tax rate of one percentage point implies
an increase in the combined-federal-provincial marginal tax rate of
less than one percentage point. For example, if the federal marginal

tax rate is 25 per cent, an increase in the provincial basic tax of one percentage point will increase the overall marginal tax rate facing an individual by one-quarter of that amount. It is surprising that such a tiny change in the tax rate would have as large an impact on migration flows in a single year as Dean's results indicate.

Winer and Gauthier (1982a) did a number of different simulations, the most interesting of which involved unemployment insurance benefits. They examined the effects of the 1971 reform of the UI system by estimating the migration rates that would have been observed in 1977 had the post-1971 regional variations in the maximum weeks of benefits not been introduced. The results presented in table 5-1 of their study summarize the effects of this change on poor migrants, based on their parameter estimates for an equation explaining rates of out-migration from the Atlantic provinces to provinces outside the Atlantic region. The results indicate that the UI reform reduced the rates of out-migration of poor people from Newfoundland, Nova Scotia, and New Brunswick to Ontario by between 35 and 42 per cent. The reductions in out-migration to Quebec are more modest, ranging from zero to 16 per cent. Thus the introduction of regional differences in the maximum weeks of benefits had a fairly large impact on interprovincial migration flows of the poor.

The numbers obtained by Winer and Gauthier (1982a) are even bigger than those of Dean. However, direct comparisons between the two sets of simulation results are not possible because the changes in policy being examined are so different. The elimination of regional variations in maximum weeks of UI benefits constitutes a much bigger change in policy than a one percentage point increase in a province's income tax rate, and should have a bigger impact on migration flows. Moreover, the results of Winer and Gauthier described here apply only to one income class – the poor.[21] Since UI benefits did not seem to have a significant impact on the migration decisions of individuals in higher-income classes, the impact of their simulation on migration rates for the population as a whole would have been much smaller than the numbers quoted here.

Mills, Percy, and Wilson (1983) did not present any simulation results using their estimated equations. However, they did point out that their estimates suggest that migrants are more sensitive to an extra dollar of fiscal surplus than they are to an extra dollar of wage income.[22]

Like Winer and Gauthier, MacNevin (1984) also did some rough calculations of the predicted effects of certain changes in government policy on migration. First, he considered the effect of a 20 per cent reduction in federal grants to the Atlantic provinces, under the assumption that the reduction in revenues is evenly distributed between provincial government expenditures and taxes. He found that over the 1976–8 period, this reduction in intergovernmental transfer payments would have increased total out-migration from the Atlantic provinces by 15.6 per cent, with 55 per cent of those migrants (3329 people) ending up in Ontario. Then he estimated the effect of a 10 per cent reduction in both commodity and sales taxes in Alberta. Inflows to Alberta between 1976 and 1978 rose by 8.2 per cent as a result, with 27 per cent (1808) of the new migrants coming from Ontario.

Finally, using his small simultaneous model of migration, wage determination, and employment growth, Vanderkamp (1988) carried out a simulation in which fiscal surpluses are equalized across regions. This change caused net out-migration from Quebec and Saskatchewan to fall over the period 1981 to 1991, while net out-migration from the Atlantic provinces increased. Both British Columbia and Ontario experienced increases in net inflows of migrants, with the rate of net in-migration to Ontario rising by 3 percentage points over the decade.

Thus, changes in fiscal variables can have a substantial impact on interprovincial migration rates. It is important to remember, however, that the annual number of interprovincial migrants is quite small in relation to existing provincial populations (as column 7 of table 1 indicates) and that even big changes in migration flows or rates do not necessarily mean that the number of people moving is large in relation to a province's population. In this respect, one may note that the 3329 new in-migrants to Ontario in MacNevin's simulation of the effects of a 20 per cent cut in grants to the Atlantic provinces constituted less than 0.04 per cent of Ontario's population in 1976.

The Economic Consequences of Policy-Induced Migration

Almost all of the empirical work on the economic consequences of internal migration in Canada is concerned either with investigating the role played by migration in the adjustment of provincial labour markets or with estimating the degree to which interjurisdictional mobility has resulted in capitalization of property taxes into housing values. There is one study of the gain in aggregate economic welfare that can be attributed to the effect of the equalization program on interprovincial migration (Watson 1986). The above contributions are surveyed below.

Some empirical work has been done on the effects on the domestic public sector in Canada of immigration from abroad, and there is a substantial volume of research on the effects of immigration on the domestic economy. This work has been thoroughly surveyed by Simon (1989) and de Silva (1992) and will not be reviewed here.

Migration, Provincial Labour Markets, and Fiscal Structure

It is apparent from our introduction to the issues, as well as from the proceeding discussion of empirical research, that much of the interest in interprovincial migration in Canada has been motivated by the potentially important role of migration as a mechanism for interprovincial economic adjustment. However, only a handful of Canadian studies have investigated empirically the relationship between migration and regional labour markets. Perhaps the lack of empirical work in this area can be attributed to two factors: the difficulty of obtaining all the necessary data on a provincial level, and the difficulty of specifying a model that is both simple enough to estimate using simultaneous equation techniques and yet complex enough to capture the relevant differences between provinces.

Two of the four existing studies deal with the problem of complexity by restricting their attention to only one province. In the first of these studies, Boadway and Green (1981) investigated the relationship between migration, wages (as measured by average weekly wages and salaries), and unemployment in Newfoundland using data for the period 1951 to 1978. Their model consists of four stochastic equations that explain the wage rate, net migration to Newfoundland, the labour force participation rate, and the demand for labour. Three non-stochastic equations define population, the labour force, and unemployment. Population in period *t* is given by the last period's population plus migration and natural increase (the latter is assumed to be exogenous to the model). The labour force is simply the population multiplied by the participation rate, while unemployment is determined residually as the difference between the labour force and the demand for labour. Although net migration does not appear directly in the wage equation as an explanatory variable, it exerts an influence through its impact on the labour force, which enters the wage equation with a one-period lag. Via its impact on the wage rate, which enters the equations explaining the participation rate and labour demand as well as the net migration equation, net migration can potentially influence the other variables in the model as well.

Boadway and Green (1981) found when they estimated their model that the influence on the wage rate of local labour market conditions, as measured by the size of the labour force, is small. Wages in Newfoundland appear to be determined primarily by the wage rate in Ontario and the ratio of the Consumer Price Index in Newfoundland to that in Ontario. When they stimulated the model to determine the effect of a one-time decrease of 1000 persons in net out-migration in 1975 (which amounts to over one-third of annual average net out-migration over their sample period), they found that after ten years the wage rate had decreased by only 14 cents from its 1975 level of approximately $196. They concluded that "migration tends to have its prime influence on unemployment levels rather than on wage rates owing in large part to the rigidity of the latter" (Boadway and Green 1981, IV–44).

Schweitzer's (1982) econometric forecasting model of the Alberta economy is much larger than Boadway and Green's model of Newfoundland. Unfortunately, Schweitzer did not perform simulations that isolate the effect of interprovincial migration on the Alberta economy. However, one can get a rough idea of the impact of migration on the wage rate, as measured by labour income per worker, by tracing the links between the rate of wage growth and net migration in the model. As in Boadway and Green's model, net migration forms part of an identity defining the population 15 years of age and over. An estimate of the labour force is obtained by multiplying population 15 and over by the estimated labour force participation rate. Unemployment is defined as the difference between the labour force and employment, and the unemployment rate, in turn, enters a Phillips curve equation that defines the percentage rate of growth of wages.

Schweitzer estimated two alternative Phillips curve equations, one in which the unemployment rate enters a linear fashion, and one in which it is the inverse unemployment rate that influences the rate of wage growth. The derivative of the rate of wage growth with respect to net interprovincial migration is thus

$$\frac{\partial WDOT}{\partial NM_{-1}} = -1.045 \frac{EMP_{-1}}{LF_{-1}^2} \cdot PARTR_{-1} \qquad (6)$$

in the first case, and

$$\frac{\partial WDOT}{\partial NM_{-1}} = -\frac{0.0014}{UR_{-1}^2} \cdot \frac{EMP_{-1}}{LF_{-1}^2} \cdot PARTR_{-1} \qquad (7)$$

in the second. In both equations $WDOT$ represents the rate of wage growth, NM is net migration to Alberta, UR is the unemployment rate, EMP is employment, LF is the labour force, $PARTR$ is the participation rate, and the subscript -1 indicates a one-period lag of the variable in question. In general these derivatives are likely to be quite small, implying that the effect of net interprovincial migration on wage growth is likely to be small.[23] Like Boadway and Green, Schweitzer concluded that changes in migration will affect primarily the unemployment rate, rather than the wage rate, as a result of rigidities in the labour market.

Both Rosenbluth (1987) and Vanderkamp (1988) used pooled time-series–cross-section data sets to estimate small simultaneous models of regional labour markets in Canada. Rosenbluth's model, which is estimated using two-stage least squares and annual data for the period 1966–83, is similar in structure to that of Boadway and Green. It consists of seven equations, of which four – explaining the rate of net in-migration to a province, the provincial labour force participation rate, provincial employment, and the province's wage rate – are stochastic. The remaining three equations are identities defining population, the labour force, and the unemployment rate.

Vanderkamp's model is also estimated using simultaneous equations estimation techniques, and consists of a net migration equation, an employment change equation, an equation for the ratio of employment to potential labour supply, a wage equation, and an identity defining the change in regional labour supply. Because Vanderkamp used census data for the period 1921 to 1981, the time period in his model is a decade. Vanderkamp's model is thus appropriate for the study of longer-run issues.

Rosenbluth and Vanderkamp carried out simulations to explore the effects of government policies on regional disparities. To approximate the effect of provincial government employment creation policies, Rosenbluth performed a simulation in which British Columbia's gross provincial product is exogenously increased by 5.6 per cent in 1984. He found that the effect on regional disparities is small. British Columbia's unemployment rate falls by only 1.1 percentage points, while the wage rate takes 18 years to fall by about three dollars. These results are attributed partly to increases in net migration and in the participation rate, which increase the labour force, and partly to the sluggish adjustment of wages.

Vanderkamp performed a simulation that is of particular interest from the point of view of this paper: he examined the effect on regional disparities during the 1980s of the complete elimination of regional differences in net fiscal benefits. It is interesting that even a shock of this magnitude has virtually no effect at all on regional disparities in wage rates. As far as the employment-to-population ratio is concerned, the Atlantic provinces move slightly closer to the national average, while the Western provinces and Quebec end up slightly worse off. Vanderkamp concluded that "wage disparities are unlikely to disappear or even change much over a decade or two, even in the face of major changes in exogenous variables or policy measures" (Vanderkamp 1988, 289).

Thus, it appears that all four studies of the impact of interprovincial migration on provincial labour markets leads to basically the same conclusion: that changes in interprovincial migration flows have a greater impact on the distribution of unemployment across the country than on regional disparities in wage rates. This result is largely due to the finding that provincial wage rates are not very sensitive to local labour market imbalances. While three of the four studies can be criticized on the grounds that their models are highly simplified and ignore the relationships between the labour market and goods markets – and there is a need to update the results of all four – the consistency of the results obtained gives each of the studies additional credibility.

The Welfare Consequences of Equalization

In our discussion of the theoretical literature concerning policy-induced migration, we noted the possibility that equalization grants may retard inefficient out-migration from the poorer regions of the country. For example, equalization paid to the Atlantic provinces may retard inefficient migration to Alberta aimed at capturing oil rents flowing into the Alberta treasury. In figure 1 we demonstrated the potentially beneficial welfare consequences of equalization grants in such situations. It is useful to recall that in the figure, an equalization program that shifts the comprehensive income line from the point through *B* to the dotted line through *D* reduces inefficient outmigration by *DB* and raises welfare in the country as a whole by an amount equal to *DECB*

Watson (1986) cleverly used the estimates of the migration responses to equalization grants provided by Winer and Gauthier (1982, ch. 5) to actually compute the size of the welfare gain *DECB* in figure 1. This is the only attempt to estimate the aggregate welfare consequences of policy-induced migration of which we are aware.

On the basis of simulations reported by Winer and Gauthier, Watson (303) estimated that the change in per capita equalization paid by the federal government between 1971 and 1977, the line segment *BG* in figure 1, reduced inefficient out-migration by 9712 persons. This change in out-migration represents the line *DB* in figure 1.[24] The line *GC* is given by the fiscal gap in per capita own-source revenues between rich and poor provinces remaining after the payment of equalization. Putting together the measures of these line segments permits Watson to measure the quadrangle *DECB* as 0.5 × *DB* × (*BC* + *DE*). The amount he arrives at is $1.4 million in 1971 dollars. Since the equalization program cost $719.6 million dollars more in 1977 than in 1971, it appears that the program cannot be justified on efficiency grounds.

Watson extended his calculations to include the closing of the entire fiscal gap between rich and poor provinces (represented by the line *BC* in figure 1), which he estimated would have led to a total reduction in out-migration of 82,913 persons (represented by the line *AB*). The resulting welfare gain, the triangle *ACB*, is only $35.4 million, which is swamped by the billions of dollars required to close the fiscal gap *BC*. Watson concluded that a rationale for equalization grants cannot be based on their consequences for economic efficiency and that future debate should focus on the role of such grants in promoting equity within the Canadian confederation (305).

Such a conclusion may be somewhat hasty, however. The differences in equalization payments between 1971 and 1977 are just one piece of a larger picture involving many equalizing or redistributive grant programs that have been in place for many decades. It may be misleading to apply the results of a migration study based on a short time series to simulate the effects of programs that may have influenced migration decisions over long periods. Watson's calculations may only reflect the marginal effect of the grant system on welfare, because the migration study on which it is based may only accurately reflect the marginal effects of grants on migration flows. The total effect of the system of redistributive grants over decades, on migration, on regional disparities in earned incomes and thus on aggregate welfare, may be quite another matter.

As a final comment on Watson's work, we note that it is a pioneering effort. Our criticism of it can neither diminish its originality nor its importance.

Capitalization

The last body of empirical work we review concerns the relationship between interjurisdictional migration and property values. As we noted in our introduction to the theoretical issues, this relationship has attracted a great deal of attention in view of its potential importance for the allocative and distributive consequences of local fiscal systems.

Estimates of the degree to which taxes are capitalized into property values are based on the idea that the value of a house is equal to the present-value of the after-tax services flowing from it. If V is the market value of a house, R is its annual rental payment, T is the property tax (equal to tV where t is the tax rate), r is the owner's real discount rate, and β is the degree of tax capitalization, then (Yinger et al. 1988, 12):

$$V = \alpha + \beta' \cdot TAX + \sum_j \delta_j \cdot X_j + \epsilon \qquad (8)$$

If capitalization is complete, $\beta = 1$, while if there is no capitalization, $\beta = 0$.

Most studies have attempted to estimate β by fitting a variant of the following estimating equation (Bloom, Ladd, and Yinger 1983, 154):

$$\ln V = \ln R - \ln(r + \beta \cdot t) \qquad (9)$$

where V is a house value or sales price, TAX is a property tax variable (either the tax payment T or the property tax rate $t = T/V$), X_j is the housing characteristic such as the level of public services or the number of rooms, and ϵ is an error term. If capitalization exists, the coefficient on TAX will be negative. The degree of capitalization is given by the coefficient on TAX times the discount rate $\beta'r$

Table 3 summarizes the results of the five existing studies of property tax capitalization in Canada. Except for the study by Islam (1989), which indirectly infers the degree of capitalization from migration responses to tax differentials, all of the studies listed in the table utilize micro data to estimate the direct effect of tax liabilities on the sale prices of houses in large suburban centres. Two of the studies use data from a single jurisdiction, two use data representing large metropolitan areas, and the study by Islam uses data from different urban centres.

A quick look at the results recorded in the table indicates that conclusions range from zero capitalization to 100 per cent capitalization, with one study in the middle of this range. Such wide variation in results is not unusual. A recent comprehensive survey of U.S. studies done since 1980 also reveals a very wide range of results, from 15 per cent to 120 per cent (Yinger et al. 1988, 44). The estimates of the reviewers vary from about 16 to about 33 per cent (119), which is similar to the results produced by what they think are the best of the post-1980 U.S. studies (44).

There are two basic reasons why the variation in results reported in the table is not surprising. First, there are difficult econometric issues involved in actually estimating the degree of capitalization; these issues are dealt with in different ways by the various authors. In addition, each study uses a unique data set that may reflect circumstances in which the degree of capitalization is in fact different. Both of these possible reasons for the differences in the results summarized in table 3 deserve some attention.[25]

One of the econometric problems that must be dealt with in estimating the degree of capitalization stems from the fact that the TAX variable in equation 10 on page 48 is correlated with the error term. If the tax rate T/V is used as the TAX variable, as in Wales and Wiens (1974), Chinloy (1978), and Chaudry (1983), there will be a negative correlation between the TAX variable and the error term; an increase in ϵ will increase V and thus reduce T/V. Unless allowed for, this negative correlation will bias the estimate of β' downwards and hence bias the conclusion toward zero capitalization. Most of the studies listed in table 3 include a careful, but different, treatment of this simultaneity problem.[26]

TABLE 3
Empirical Studies on Property Tax Capitalization Using Canadian Data

Study	Housing data used	Fiscal variables	Results	Comments
		1. Within-Jurisdiction Differentials		
Wales and Wiens (1974)	Sale prices of improved residential property, Surrey, B.C, 1972	Tax rates	No evidence of tax capitalization	Results attributed to house-buyers' lack of information about tax assesments and tax rates.
Chinloy (1978)	House prices from Survey of Housing Units, London, Ontario, 1974	Effective tax rate (net of property tax credit), simulated from survey	No evidence of tax capitalization	Stresses the importance of using effective tax rates rather than nominal ones to incorporate housing tax credits.
		2. Within- and Between-Jurisdiction Differentials		
Hamilton (1979)	Sale price of houses in Metropolitan Toronto, 1961	Tax levels and public services (school expenditures per pupil)	Capitalization of intrajurisdictional fiscal differentials at 50%; inter-jurisdictional differentials at 28% (assuming 3% discount rate)	Estimating equation incorporates effect of zoning on supply response. Both tax payments and tax rates used in estimation.

continued

Chaudry (1983)	Sale price of houses in Metropolitan Edmonton, 1977	Complete capitalization of both inter- and intra-jurisdictional tax differentials. Only partial (<20%) capitalization of public service differentials (assuming 2% discount rate).	Two types of estimation, one using tax rates as dependent variable, and one using tax payments. Low benefit capitalization attributed to nature of evaluations of benefits by households.
		3. Between-Jurisdiction Differentials	
Islam (1989)	Sample of 1981 census data for intermunicipal migrants	Tax differentials have no effect on migration decisions.	Results interpreted as indicating complete capitalization.

If the *TAX* variable is the level of property tax payments, then the bias in the conclusion will be in the opposite direction, toward 100 per cent capitalization; an increase in ϵ will increase V, which in turn leads to an increase in tax assessments, so ϵ and the *TAX* variable will tend to be positively correlated. Chaudry also uses tax payments in addition to tax rates and corrects for simultaneity in both cases. Hamilton (1979) uses tax payments as well, but does not explicitly allow for simultaneity.

Another difficult statistical problem that must be confronted is omitted variable bias. In order to estimate the degree of capitalization, all other influences on housing prices must be controlled for. These other influences include supply responses and zoning, both of which tend to reduce the actual degree of capitalization (considered by Hamilton); the effect of property tax credits on the effective tax rate that, when ignored, tend to bias estimates of capitalization upwards (emphasized by Chinloy); the benefits of public services (investigated by Hamilton and by Chaudry); and a long list of other factors such as the size of a house, its proximity to the centre of the city, and so on.

The allowance for the effects of public services is particularly difficult because there is no way to actually measure the subjective value placed on such services by households. Hamilton assumes one dollar of public services is equal in value to one dollar of taxes, estimates the response of house prices to changes in fiscal surpluses (equal to services less taxes), and then computes the degree of capitalization of these fiscal services into house prices. This procedure, which is essentially the same as the one employed by some of the migration studies we reviewed earlier, does not allow for differences in the subjective valuation of services across municipalities or for variation in the cost of providing services (Yinger et al. 1988, 30). The same assumptions are implicit in Chaudry's treatment of expenditure capitalization (see, for example, Chaudry 1983, 89).

A third econometric problem stems from the non-linearity introduced by the discount rate in equation 8. Substituting tV for T, rearranging and taking logs gives another form of the estimating equation, which is non-linear in the degree of capitalization β:

$$V = \alpha + \beta' \cdot TAX + \sum_{j} \delta_j \cdot X_j + \epsilon \qquad (10)$$

Many authors get around this non-linearity by using the linear equation 9 and then converting an estimate of β' into an estimate of β by choice of an appropriate subjective discount rate r. Chaudry uses both linear and non-linear estimation techniques.

Reliance on a linear estimating equation like 9 instead of the non-linear equation 10 gives rise to a fourth statistical problem, that of choosing an appropriate read discount rate. The estimates in table 3 for Hamilton's study are by Yinger et al. (table 2-3, 25) and are based on their choice of 3 per cent as the correct discount rate. Chaudry uses 2 per cent, a figure that would lower Hamilton's implied estimate of intrajurisdictional capitalization recorded in table 3 from 50 per cent (based on a 3 per cent discount rate) to 33 per cent, and his estimate of interjurisdictional capitalization from 28 per cent (using $r = .03$) to 19 per cent.

While differences in the treatment of the statistical issues outlined above may give rise to quite different results, it is also possible that capitalization in fact varies from jurisdiction to jurisdiction. Perhaps one of the most important reasons why this may be so is that supply responses to initial capitalization may vary, a factor emphasized by Hamilton (178). If the supply of housing is perfectly elastic in the long run, all capitalization will eventually disappear. Another factor that also seems important – one singled out by Yinger et al. (129–30) and noted by Wales and Wiens (332) – is that expectations of house buyers concerning future effective tax rates will not necessarily be uniform across jurisdictions. Obviously, expectations about the behaviour of local governments could differ widely.

To complete this review of the issues associated with the estimates of capitalization summarized in table 3, it should be noted that all of the studies referred to in the table are carefully executed. For some reason the challenge of estimating the degree of tax capitalization is attractive to good econometricians, both in Canada and in the United States. Anyone interested in learning applied econometrics could do much worse than to read how the authors listed in the table have attempted to deal with the statistical problems we have briefly outlined.

Policy Implications and Suggestions for Further Research

We conclude the paper by considering the implications of the empirical work that we have reviewed for public policy-making and by offering some suggestions for further research.

The empirical research we have surveyed suggests that policy-makers are not severely constrained by migration responses to interjurisdictional differences in fiscal structure over short time horizons, provided that government policies do not deviate dramatically from those of neighbouring jurisdictions. In any given year, most moves appear to be determined by employment and income considerations, rather than by attempts to profit from fiscal surpluses. What a "dramatic deviation" in fiscal structure may be in this context must be interpreted in the light of the data utilized by the studies. Obviously, the results do not rule out substantial migration responses to unusually big changes in public policies.

It is clear that the econometric results do not provide the basis for further fine-tuning of fiscal structure to accommodate or take advantage of migration behaviour. The fact that changes in migration flows are statistically associated with changes in the generosity of the unemployment insurance system and with migration decisions of lower- but not higher-income people, along with the other empirical results, is reasonably convincing evidence that policy-induced migration in fact exists. But, in our opinion, there is not enough evidence to permit the accurate computation of what the responsiveness to an arbitrarily chosen program change might be.[27] There is not even any consensus to be found in the studies we have reviewed about the sensitivity of migration decisions to the fiscal policies that have been explicitly included in estimating equations.

Perhaps the robust finding that the primary effect of interprovincial migration and, by implication, of policy-induced migration, is on provincial unemployment rather than on wage rates may be of interest to policy-makers in the future. What action should be taken on the basis of this particular evidence remains an unexplored issue, however.

Concerning research on the degree of tax capitalization, it is important to note that the estimated degree of capitalization varies so widely from study to study that one can only assume that capitalization does occur, but that in any particular instance it will be of unknown degree. A risk-averse strategy would be to assume that capitalization cannot be relied upon to remove horizontal inequities in property tax assessments and to assume that the property tax will not be a useful tax for redistributive purposes. Moreover, should the property tax be reformed, say by the implementation of market value assessment, grandparenting and postponed implementation of such a reform is advisable to avoid the possibility that (an unknown degree of) capitalization in the past may lead to new inequities when the reform is undertaken.

The sole study that has tried to estimate the welfare consequences of policy-induced migration in Canada (Watson 1986) concluded that in the case explored, the gain in aggregate economic welfare resulting from the (small) impact of government policy on the regional allocation of labour was not substantial enough to justify the cost of the government program involved. While this study is important, we think it would be a mistake to infer from it that policy-induced migration does not have serious consequences for regional disparities in earned incomes and thereby for aggregate welfare. The same research that indicates that migration patterns are not greatly affected from year to year by public policies can be interpreted as suggesting that persistently applied inducements to migrate to, or remain in, a particular location may be effective in altering the regional allocation of labour and the nature of regional disparities over long periods. Such long-run effects may be particularly important when the policies involved are social programs like unemployment insurance, welfare, or health and education services, since these are the types of programs that have been shown to be most closely associated with migration decisions.

Finally, we offer the following suggestions for further research. Finding better ways to represent public policy in a study of migration decisions continues to be central to progress in the study of policy-induced migration.[28] The province- or municipality-wide aggregate levels of taxes and expenditures that have often been used in estimating equations are not well suited to investigations of why individuals decide to move. These variables reflect the effects of policy on both movers and stayers and are highly correlated with other variables that are also used in migration equations, such as unemployment rates or incomes. It may be preferable to use direct measures of the values of policy instruments, such as effective tax rates or indexes of the generosity of social welfare systems. One should note that use of micro data sets that record the history of individual migrants does not necessarily make it easier to capture the role of public policy. While such data sets may contain indicators of fiscal benefits received or taxes paid by individual migrants, these measures are likely to be affected in important ways by the individual migration decisions rather than simply reflecting decisions made by governments.

Our review of empirical work indicates that, of all the internal migration flows studied so far, migration at the intraprovincial level has received the least attention. Moreover, those studies that have examined intermunicipal migration flows in Canada (Shaw 1985, 1986; Islam 1989) have included measures of provincial rather than municipal fiscal structure in their estimating equations. While the analysis of intraprovincial migration presents researchers with more challenging problems, including how to appropriately measure fiscal structure in this context as well as the problems that follow from the large number of alternative destinations involved, it might also be more interesting precisely because the volume of migration occurring at this level is larger. In addition, there may be opportunities to investigate the effects of policies not considered before such as housing or local welfare policies.

Among the policy issues we introduced in the second section of the paper, the consequences of a relationship between public policy and the regional allocation of labour for the nature of regional disparities remains, in our view, the most important one in Canada. The longevity of the debate in Canada over this issue makes it all the more puzzling why there has been so little empirical research on the matter. Studies such as those by Vanderkamp (1988), which look at the role of fiscal structure in the determination of regional disparities over long time periods, and that by Watson (1986) investigating the consequences for aggregate welfare that can be attributed to the effects of equalization grants on interprovincial migration, deserve company. Research in both the intraprovincial and interprovincial contexts would be of interest. Does the system of equalization grants within the province of Ontario have the same small consequences for economic welfare that Watson attributes to interprovincial equalization? Does policy-induced interprovincial migration in fact play a role in explaining the persistence of regional disparities of earned incomes in Canada over long periods of time, and if so, to what extent? Empirical work that can help to answer these and related questions should be high on the research agenda.

Notes

1 A useful review of Canadian trends and developments in migration is found in Beaujot (1991).
2 This and the next paragraph follow Musgrave (1991a).
3 See Wildasin (1986, ch. 2) for a general introduction to the literature on

the consequences for efficiency of policy-induced migration. Winer and Gauthier (1982, ch. 1) provide a survey of literature that deals with the issue in a Canadian context.

4 For recent discussions of the issue, see, for example, Wildasin (1991a) and Musgrave (1991b).

5 See also The Royal Commission on Dominion-Provincial Relations (1940, Book II, 83).

6 Bird and Slack (1990) provide an interesting critique of the equalization system in Canada.

7 Additional surveys of the literature on the capitalization of the property tax are contained in Wildasin (1986, ch. 4), Mieszkowski and Zodrow (1989) and, in the Canadian context, Kitchen (1991).

8 See Wildasin (1986, chs 4 and 6) and Musgrave (1991b) for surveys of this literature. Recently, Krelove (1992) and Myers (1990) have challenged the view that the existence of fiscal externalities or tax exporting will prevent the provision of the efficient quantity of public goods. Using different models, they argue that these externalities may be internalized if local governments are aware of the immediate consequences of the interregional migration that could be precipitated by their fiscal decisions. In contrast, Hercowitz and Pines (1991) argue that, in a dynamic setting, inefficiency will persist despite government actions in response to migration. It should be noted that Musgrave's argument outlined in the text was originally raised in the context of a discussion of international migration where the existence of national institutions that might constrain unproductive interjurisdictional competition cannot be assumed. However, in the absence of "perfect" institutional arrangements, her concern may be relevant in the domestic context as well.

9 See Wildasin (1986, ch. 4) for further details.

10 The same result occurs when partial capitalization is accompanied by zoning ordinances (and appropriate tax differentials) that lead to homogeneity of types of housing and businesses within well-defined districts (Hamilton 1976).

11 One should note, as do Yinger et al. (1988, 134), that capitalization will not eliminate the distortion from taxing all housing at a rate different from that of other assets.

12 Zodrow and Mieszkowski (Zodrow 1983) review and extend the so-called "new view" of the incidence of the property tax, an important alternative to the analysis of the redistributive consequences of the property tax described in the text (called the "benefit view"). They argue that when non-residental property is taxed everywhere in the country,

the burden of the capital component of the tax falls to a considerable extent on the owners of the capital, whether capitalization occurs or not. Thus, they argue, the non-residental property tax will be progressive since income from capital tends to be distributed progressively across income classes. See also Mieszkowski and Zodrow (1989) and Fischel (1992), who critically examine the role of zoning in models of the incidence and incentive effects of the property tax.

13 For example, Shaw (1986) and MacNevin (1984) find that a high unemployment rate in the destination region will deter in-migration, but that the unemployment rate in the region of origin generally does not have a significant coefficient. Day (1992), who constrains the coefficients of the origin and destination unemployment rates to be the same, finds that the unemployment rate differential does have a negative and significant coefficient, implying that people will tend to move from regions with high unemployment rates to regions with low unemployment rates.

14 Winer and Gauthier also attempted to reproduce Courchene's results by re-estimating his equations using an updated data set. These results are reported in table 3 but are not discussed in the text.

15 Day includes the provincial unemployment rate as a separate explanatory variable in her estimating equations and finds that a higher unemployment rate in province i, holding all else equal, will significantly reduce in-migration to province i.

16 Transfer payments are less highly correlated with income than are income tax payments, and thus pose less of a problem from an econometric point of view.

17 It should be noted that Islam is one of the few researchers who has corrected for (selectivity) bias in the estimation of the income gains attributable to migration, using the procedure of Heckman (1979). To estimate income gains due to migration, which is an important explanatory variable in any migration equation, one has to compare migrants' observed post-migration income with an estimate of what they would have earned had they not moved. A bias in estimating what their income would have been had they not moved may occur if migrants are systematically different from stayers, and this difference is not explicitly allowed for through the use of an appropriate estimation technique. (Ordinary least squares is not an appropriate technique in these circumstances.)

18 Gramlich and Lauren also found that benefit levels are responsive to the number of recipients, indicating that state legislators are aware of the relationship between the levels of benefits and the size of the recip-

ient population, and do take it into account when setting benefit
levels.

19 See Cebula (1979b) for a survey of some additional work on the effects
of other fiscal variables.

20 One important difference between the Canadian and U.S. UI systems is
that the U.S. system incorporates "experience rating" – i.e., a firm's UI
premiums will depend on the amount of benefits paid to its workers in
the past. However, since the premiums paid by individuals do not depend on their past unemployment experience, experience rating will
have no direct effect on individual migration decisions.

21 The poor constituted about 53 per cent of interprovincial migrants in
Winer and Gauthier's tax data sample.

22 It should be noted in assessing this result that only 7 of the 21 equations estimated by Mills, Percy, and Wilson (1983) contain significant
coefficients for both the wage and net fiscal benefit variables.

23 To get some idea of the likely magnitude of these derivatives, we obtained data for 1981 and substituted it into equations 6 and 7. The 1981
data for employment (1152 thousand), labour force (1198 thousand),
participation rate (72.3 per cent), and the unemployment rate (3.8 per
cent) in Alberta were obtained from Statistics Canada catalogue 71-
201, *Historical Labour Force Statistics*. According to the variable definitions
in Schweitzer's paper, the participation rate and the unemployment rate
should enter the equations in decimal form. The results obtained were
0.00061 for equation 6 and 0.00056 for equation 7. Note that these
numbers are only approximations, because the appropriate units of
measurement for labour force and employment were not clear from
Schweitzer's paper (we used thousands). Note also that the numbers
presented in the text are overestimates, because equations 6 and 7 were
derived under the simplifying assumption that the relevant population
variable in the model was the total population. In fact, Schweitzer restricted his attention to the population aged 15 and over. Thus, to be
fully consistent with Schweitzer's model, equations 6 and 7 should
both be multiplied by the proportion of migrants who are aged 15 and
over.

24 Watson based these figures on equations for out-migration from the
Atlantic region to the west of Canada and migration from the rest of
Canada to Alberta and British Columbia.

25 The problems of estimating the degree of capitalization and the reasons
for variation in capitalization across communities is discussed in length
in Yinger et al. (1988, chs 2 and 7), and in Bloom, Ladd, and Yinger
(1983).

26 Bloom, Ladd, and Yinger (1983, 155–6) and Yinger et al. (1988, 30) have criticized the way in which both Wales and Wiens and Chinloy have tackled the simultaneity problem.
27 Quebec may have a lower corporate tax rate (on mobile capital) than Ontario and a higher payroll tax rate (which tends to be borne by immobile francophone workers). But the government in Quebec City could not have chosen the particular tax rates it actually levied on the basis of the empirical research reviewed here. Trial and error is a more likely possibility.
28 On this point, see also Winer (1986).

Bibliography

Beaujot, Roderic. 1991. *Population Change in Canada*. Toronto: McClelland and Stewart.
– 1991. *Population Change in Canada: The Challenges of Policy Adaptation*. Toronto: McClelland and Stewart
Bhagwati, Jagdish N., and John D. Wilson, eds. 1989. *Income Taxation and International Mobility*. Cambridge, MA: MIT Press
Bird, Richard M., and Enid Slack. 1983. *Urban Public Finance in Canada*. Toronto: Butterworths
– 1990. "Equalization: The Representative Tax System Revisted." *Canadian Tax Journal* 38(4): 913–27
Bloom, Howard S., Helen F. Ladd, and John Yinger. 1983. "Are Property Values Capitalized into House Values?" In *Local Provision of Public Services*, ed. G. Zodrow, 145–63. New York: Academic Press
Boadway, Robin, and Frank Flatters. 1982a. *Equalization in a Federal State: An Economic Analysis*. Ottawa: Supply and Services Canada for the Economic Council of Canada
– 1982b. "Efficiency and Equalization Payments in a Federal System of Government: A Synthesis and Extension of Recent Results." *Canadian Journal of Economics* 15: 613–33
Boadway, Robin, and A.G. Green. 1981. "The Economic Implications of Migration to Newfoundland." Discussion Paper No. 189, March. Ottawa: Economic Council of Canada
Boadway, Robin, Pierre Pestieau, and David Wildasin. 1989. "Tax-Transfer Policies and the Voluntary Provision of Public Goods." *Journal of Public Economics* 39(2): 157–76
Brennan, Geoffrey, and James M. Buchanan. 1980. *The Power to Tax: Analytic Foundations of a Fiscal Constitution*. Cambridge: Cambridge University Press

Breton, Albert. 1985. Supplementary Statement. *Royal Commission on the Economic Union and Development Prospects for Canada*, Vol. 3: 486–526, Ottawa: Supply and Services Canada

Brown, C.G., and Wallace E. Oates. 1987. "Assistance to the Poor in a Federal System." *Journal of Public Economics* 32: 307–30

Buchanan, James M. 1950. "Federalism and Fiscal Equity." *American Economic Review* 40: 583–99

Cebula, Richard J. 1977. "An Analysis of Migration Patterns and Local Government Policy toward Public Education in the United States." *Public Choice* 33: 113–21

– 1979a. *The Determinants of Human Migration*. Toronto: Lexington Books

– 1979b. "A Survey of the Literature on the Migration Impact of State and Local Government Policies." *Public Finance* 24: 69–84

– 1980. "Voting with One's Feet: A Critique of the Evidence." *Regional Science and Urban Economics* 10: 91–107

– 1990. "A Brief Empirical Note on Tiebout Hypothesis and State Income Tax Policies." *Public Choice* 67: 87–9

– 1991. "A Brief Note on Welfare Benefits and Human Migration." *Public Choice* 69: 345–9

Chaudry, Anwar M. 1983. "Capitalization of Local Property Taxes and Public Services with Applications to Efficiency and Equity Issues." Unpublished Ph.D. dissertation, University of Alberta

Chinloy, Peter. 1978. "Effective Property Taxes and Tax Capitalization." *Canadian Journal of Economics* 9(4): 740–9.

Courchene, Thomas J. 1970. "Interprovincial Migration and Economic Adjustment." *Canadian Journal of Economics* 3: 550–76

– 1978. "The Transfer System and Regional Disparities: A Critique of the Status Quo." In *Canadian Federation at the Crossroads: The Search for a Federal-Provincial Balance*, ed. Michael Walker, 145–86. Vancouver: The Fraser Institute

– 1984. *Equalization Payments: Past, Present and Future*. Toronto: Ontario Economic Council

Day, Kathleen M. 1992. "Interprovincial Migration and Local Public Goods." *Canadian Journal of Economics* 25: 123–44

Dean, James. 1982. "Tax-induced Migration in Canada, 1972–79." *Western Economic Review* 1: 17–31

de Silva, Arnold. 1992. *Earnings of Immigrants: A Comparative Analysis*. Ottawa: Supply and Services Canada for the Economic Council of Canada

Eden, Lorraine, ed. 1991. *Retrospectives on Public Finance*. Durham, NC: Duke University Press

Feldstein, Martin S. 1976. "On the Theory of Tax Reform." *Journal of Public Economics* 6: 77–104

Fischel, William A. 1992. "Property Taxation and the Tiebout Model: Evidence for the Benefit View from Zoning and Voting." *Journal of Economic Literature* 30(1): 171–7

Flatters, Frank, Vernon Henderson, and Peter M. Mieszkowski. 1974. "Public Goods, Efficiency and Regional Fiscal Equalization." *Journal of Public Economics* 3: 99–112

Foot, David K., and William A. Milne. 1984. "Public Policies and Interprovincial Migration in Canada: A Multiregional Approach." Mimeo. University of Toronto

Goss, E., and C. Paul. 1990. "The Impact of UI Benefits on the Probability of Migration of the Unemployed." *Journal of Regional Science* 3: 349–58

Graham, John. 1964. "Fiscal Adjustment in a Federal Country." In *Inter-Government Fiscal Relationships*. Canadian Tax Paper No. 40, 3–34. Toronto: Canadian Tax Foundation

Gramlich, Edward M., and Deborah S. Laren. 1984. "Migration and Income Distribution Responsibilities." *Journal of Human Resources* 19: 489–511

Hamilton, Bruce W. 1976. "Capitalization of Intrajurisdictional Differences in Local Tax Prices." *American Economic Review* 66: 743–53

– 1979. "Capitalization and the Regressivity of the Property Tax: Empirical Evidence." *National Tax Journal* 32: 169–80, Supplement to No. 2, June

Heckman, J.J. 1979. "Sample Selection Bias as a Specification Error." *Econometrica* 47: 153–62

Hercowitz, Zvi, and David Pines. 1991. "Migration with Fiscal Externalities." *Journal of Public Economics* 46(2): 163–80

Hughes, Gordon, and Barry McCormick. 1981. "Do Council Housing Policies Reduce Migration between Regions?" *Economic Journal* 91: 919–37

Islam, Muhammed N. 1989. "Tiebout Hypothesis and Migration – Impact of Local Fiscal Policies." *Public Finance* 44(3): 406–18

Kitchen, Harry M. 1991. *Property Taxation in Canada*. Toronto: The Canadian Tax Foundation

Krelove, Russell. 1992. "Efficient Tax Exporting." *Canadian Journal of Economics* 25(1): 145–55

Liaw, Kao-Lee, and Jacques Ledent. 1987. "Nested Logit Model and Maximum Quasi-Likelihood Method." *Regional Science and Urban Economics* 17: 67–88

– 1988. "Joint Effects of Ecological and Personal Factors on Elderly Interprovincial Migration in Canada." *Canadian Journal of Regional Science* 11: 77–100

MacNevin, Alex S. 1984. "Fiscal Integration and Subcentral Public Sector

Inducements to Canadian Interprovincial Migration." Ph.D. dissertation, McMaster University

Mieszkowski, Peter, and George Zodrow. 1989. "Taxation and the Tiebout Model: The Differential Effects of Head Taxes, Taxes on Land, Rents and Property Taxes." *Journal of Economic Literature* 27(3): 1098–1146

Mills, K.E., M.B. Percy, and L.S. Wilson. 1983. "The Influence of Fiscal Incentives on Interregional Migration: Canada 1961–78." *Canadian Journal of Regional Science* 6: 207–29

Musgrave, Peggy. 1991a. "Merits and Demerits of Fiscal Competition." In *Public Finance with Several Levels of Government*, ed. Rémy Prud'homme, 281–97. The Hague: Foundation Journal Public Finance

– 1991b. "Fiscal Coordination and Competition in an International Setting." In *Retrospectives on Public Finance*, ed. L. Eden, 276–305. Durham, NC: Duke University Press

Myers, Gordon. 1990. "Optimality, Free Mobility and Regional Authority in a Federation." *Journal of Public Economics* 43: 107–21

Oakland, William. 1983. "Income Redistribution in a Federal System." In *Local Provision of Public Services*, ed. George Zodrow, 131–44. New York: Academic Press

Oates, Wallce E. 1969. "The Effects of Property Taxes and Local Public Spending on Property Values: An Empirical Study of Tax Capitalization and the Tiebout Hypothesis." *Journal of Political Economy* 77: 957–71

– 1972. *Fiscal Federalism*. New York: Harcourt Brace Jovanovich

Oates, Wallace E., and Robert M. Schwab. 1988. "Economic Competition among Jurisdictions: Efficiency Enhancing or Distortion Inducing." *Journal of Public Economics* 35: 333–54

Pauly, Mark V. 1973. "Income Redistribution as a Local Public Good." *Journal of Public Economics* 2: 35–58

Robinson, C., and N. Tomes. 1982. "Self-Selection and Inter-Provincial Migration in Canada." *Canadian Journal of Economics* 15(3): 474–502

Rosenbluth, Gideon. 1987. "The Causes and Consequences of Interprovincial Migration." Discussion Paper No. 87–29, August. University of British Columbia

Royal Commission on Dominion-Provincial Relations. 1940. *Report*. 3 vols. Ottawa: King's Printer

Samuelson, Paul A. 1954. "The Pure Theory of Public Expenditure." *Review of Economics and Statistics* 36: 387–9

Schweitzer, Thomas T. 1982. "Migration and a Small Long-Term Econometric Model of Alberta." Discussion Paper No. 221, December. Ottawa: Economic Council of Canada

Seligman, Edwin R.A. 1921. *Essays on Taxation*, 9th ed. New York: Macmillan

Shaw, R. Paul. 1985. *Intermetropolitan Migration in Canada.* Toronto: NC Press
- 1986. "Fiscal versus Traditional Market Variables in Canadian Migration." *Journal of Political Economy* 94: 648–66
Simon, Julian L. 1989. *The Economic Consequences of Immigration.* New York: Basil Blackwell
Statistics Canada. 1991. *Postcensal Annual Estimates of Population by Marital Status, Age, Sex and Components of Growth for Canada, Provinces and Territories,* 9, June 1, Cat. No. 91–210, Annual
Tiebout, Charles. 1956. "A Pure Theory of Local Expenditures." *Journal of Political Economy* 64(5): 416–24
Vanderkamp, J. 1988. "Regional Disparities: A Model with Some Econometric Results for Canada." In *Regional Economic Development: Essays in Honour of François Perroux,* ed. B. Higgins and D.J. Savoie, 269–96. Boston: Unwin Hyman
Wales, Terrance J., and E.G. Wiens. 1974. "Capitalization and Residential Property Taxes: An Empirical Study." *Review of Economics and Statistics* 56: 329–33
Watson, William G. 1986. "An Estimate of the Welfare Gain from Fiscal Equalization." *Canadian Journal of Economics* 19(2): 298–308
West, E.G., and Stanley L. Winer. 1980. "The Individual, Political Tension and Canada's Quest for a New Constitution." *Canadian Public Policy* 6: 3–15
Wildasin, David E. 1986. *Urban Public Finance.* New York: Harwood Academic Publishers
- 1991a. "Relaxation of Barriers to Factor Mobility and Income Redistribution." Unpublished paper prepared for the 1991 meeting of the International Institute of Public Finance, Leningrad
- 1991b. "Income Redistribution in a Common Labour Market." *American Economic Review* 81(4): 757–74
Winer, Stanley L. 1983. "Some Evidence on the Effect of the Separation of Spending and Taxing Decisions." *Journal of Political Economy* 91(1): 126–40
- 1986. "Challenging Issues in the Study of Fiscally-Induced Migration." *Canadian Journal of Regional Science* 9(3): 381–7
Winer, Stanley L., and Denis Gauthier. 1982a. *Internal Migration and Fiscal Structure: An Econometric Study of the Determinants of Interprovincial Migration in Canada.* Ottawa: Supply and Services Canada for the Economic Council of Canada
- 1982b. "Internal Migration Data: A Supplement to *Internal Migration and Fiscal Structure.*" Technical Paper. Ottawa: Economic Council of Canada
Yinger, John, Howard S. Bloom, Axel Borsch-Supan, and Helen F. Ladd.

1988. *Property Taxes and House Values: The Theory and Estimation of Intrajurisdictional Property Tax Capitalization*. Boston: Academic Press

Zodrow, George R., ed. 1983. *Local Provision of Public Services: The Tiebout Model after Twenty-Five Years*. New York: Academic Press

2 Compliance, Enforcement, and Administrative Factors in Improving Tax Fairness

JONATHAN R. KESSELMAN

Objectives and Organization

This discussion paper presents a brief review of emerging issues in the areas of tax compliance, enforcement, and administration.[1] Its perspective in addressing these topics will be primarily economic. Hence, it will concentrate on the insights provided by economic analysts – theoretical, empirical, and policy oriented. It will focus on the economic motivation of compliance behaviours and the assessment of related policy structures. As far as possible, the treatment will also attempt to direct these findings toward the mandate of the Ontario Fair Tax Commission. This will be done, in part, by establishing the importance of compliance, enforcement, and administrative aspects of taxation in attaining tax fairness. It will be accomplished further by providing overview applications of the economic analysis to selected issues of concern to the commission.

The topics treated here have also been addressed by tax experts from the disciplines of law, accounting, and public administration. Their insights and expertise may be as important to the work of the commission in formulating its concrete policy recommendations as those provided by the economic perspective. Experts from those disciplines will be even more useful than economists are in crafting particular legislative provisions and administrative structures. However, an economic approach can be of great value in any overall policy assessment and in providing a conceptual framework to guide the formulation of tax policy at an early design stage.

This paper is organized in the following way. The second section reviews the terminology of tax compliance, avoidance, and evasion. The third section presents some rough figures on the estimated extent and characteristics of these behaviours. The fourth section provides a verbal, intuitive version of the economic theory of tax avoidance, evasion, and enforcement. The fifth section discusses the relevance of compliance, enforcement, and administration to attaining tax equity. It also uncovers potential conflicts between improved compliance and some notions of equity. The sixth section examines two alternative ways of dealing with compliance problems – at the initial stage of designing tax policies and at the subsequent stages of devising administrative structures and legislative remedies. The final section applies the preceding analyses and insights to selected tax issues relevant to the mandate of the Ontario Fair Tax Commission. Its discussion suggests areas where the commission might benefit from research to learn more about compliance, enforcement, and administrative matters.

Terminology of Compliance

The operation of a tax system involves three sets of agents: taxpayers, intermediaries, and the government. Taxpayers are the entities upon whom taxes are levied, including individuals and businesses (both corporate and unincorporated). Intermediaries are private-sector entities required to withhold taxes and/or provide information reports to the government; examples are employers and payers of interest, dividends, and pensions. The government includes the tax collection agency as well as its enforcement branch. The terms "compliance" and "compliance costs" are applied to both taxpayers and intermediaries. Administration and administrative costs, conversely, refer solely to activities of the government. Enforcement is one aspect of tax administration, and it includes the detection, apprehension, and prosecution of non-compliant taxpayers and intermediaries. Intermediaries can ease compliance for taxpayers (by withholding and remitting their taxes) and can also simplify the government's tax administration task.

It is useful to distinguish three types of non-compliance to the tax system, although in practice the distinctions are not always clear. First is what might be called "unintentional" non-compliance. This is the failure of a taxpayer or intermediary to remit the proper

amount of tax on account of the complexity, vagaries, or even con-
tradictions in the tax legislation or the tax administrative procedures.
Unintentional non-compliance may arise due to inadequate effort
by the taxpayer or intermediary to discover its obligations, but it
can still be distinguished from the other two types of non-
compliance. Tax evasion, the second type of non-compliance, is any
kind of behaviour that knowingly attempts to underpay a tax liability
in ways that clearly violate the letter of the tax law. Typical methods
include concealment or understatement of income sources or sales
and overstatement of business expenses or personal deductions.

The third type of non-compliance is abusive tax avoidance. This
is behaviour that intentionally attempts to reduce one's tax liability
by actions that satisfy the letter of the tax law while violating its
spirit or intent. Of course, a large part of tax avoidance activity
is not abusive, in that it merely attempts to utilize tax incentive
or relief provisions that were purposefully legislated. An analyst
might question the social benefits of some of these provisions, but
so long as taxpayers are utilizing them in ways that are known to
and accepted by the legislators, these behaviours can hardly be described as non-compliant. When taxpayers push the application of
statutory provisions well beyond what was intended or anticipated,
then the avoidance can be considered abusive. Recent Canadian legislation establishing a General Anti-Avoidance Rule (GAAR) attempts to make such a distinction by inquiring whether the taxpayer's actions were primarily motivated by a tax purpose.

Extent of Non-Compliance

There are no systematic or reliable measures of the extent of non-
compliance to various taxes. However, rough indicators of some
types of non-compliance have been produced on occasion. For unintentional non-compliance, news reports have suggested that personal income taxes are beset by frequent errors of interpretation
as well as arithmetic errors on the tax returns. Multiple telephone
inquiries to Revenue Canada about relatively common problems
have produced divergent advice about the interpretation or application of tax provisions. Even expert tax advisers using the same
raw information on a person's situation will arrive at different com-
putations of the tax liability. Unintentional non-compliance usually
stems from the complexity of tax provisions and the difficulty of
applying them to the even more complex situations of the real world.

Unless the individual's tax return is audited, this type of non-compliance typically goes undetected.

Some types of non-abusive tax avoidance may show up in Revenue Canada's tabulations of claims for particular categories of tax deductions. Rough estimates of the associated revenue costs have been made by the Department of Finance in periodic publications on tax expenditures. In fact, without a detailed audit of the individual taxpayer, it is often not possible to ascertain whether tax avoidance has been abusive. Hence, the figures on the use of various tax expenditure provisions may include some abusive behaviour. Much abusive tax avoidance, however, proceeds through devices other than the provisions that are formally designated as tax expenditures, so that no meaningful estimates of this phenomenon are available.

Tax evasion has been subjected to numerous studies in many countries to determine its extent and characteristics. These studies usually attempt to estimate the size of the irregular or underground economy, the existence of which is motivated primarily by tax evasion (but also by welfare fraud and illegal activities). Because such activities are inherently concealed, indirect methods must be used for estimation, resulting in highly variable figures. Estimates of the irregular economy as a proportion of the total economy have ranged widely from 5 per cent to more than 25 per cent in the United States. Comparable estimates for Canada's irregular economy have ranged from 5 to 20 per cent. The proportion of taxes evaded may not be correspondingly large, however, if evasion is concentrated at below-average income levels. Conversely, if much evasion arises through non-reporting of capital incomes, the incidence of evasion may exceed the size of the irregular economy.

More illuminating for tax policy than estimates of the size of the irregular, tax-evading economy are studies that show where tax evasion is most concentrated. In particular, the absence of source withholding and information reporting is most conducive to evasion with respect to income taxes. This can be seen in the results from the Taxpayer Compliance Measurement Program of the U.S. Internal Revenue Service, tabulated below. A sample of individual taxpayers was subjected to intensive audits to uncover any unreported incomes and overstated expense claims. Voluntary reporting percentages (VRPs) are the proportions of true incomes that were actually reported by taxpayers without any enforcement action. For those types of income sources that allow expense deductions, VRPs are reported on both gross and net income bases. Wages and salaries, which were

TABLE 1

Source of income	VRP for gross income	VRP for net income
Wages and salaries	93.9	–
Dividends	83.7	–
Interest	86.3	–
Capital gains	59.4	–
Nonfarm proprietor income	78.7	50.3
Partnership and small business corporate income	78.7	47.0
Farm proprietor income	88.3	−18.5
Informal supplier income	–	20.7
Pensions and annuities	86.9	–
Rents	95.6	37.2
Royalties	61.2	–
Estate and trust income	76.2	74.2
State income tax refunds, alimony, other income	62.0	–
Total income	89.3	87.2

Source: U.S. Internal Revenue Service (1983, pp. 10, 15).

subject to both source withholding and information reporting, had the highest VRP. Types of incomes allowing deductions displayed some of the lowest compliance rates, as seen in the VRPs for net income. Farm proprietors even had a negative VRP for net income, since they reported negative net incomes whereas they had substantial positive net incomes. Informal supplier income, with a VRP for net income of just 20.7 per cent, is heavily concentrated in a few sectors: home repair and additions, food, child care, domestic services, and auto repairs. Moreover, the tabulated figures, which one would expect to have VRPs close to zero, generally omit all incomes derived from illegal activities.

The sectoral concentration of tax evasion can be seen from an Internal Revenue Service (IRS) study, conducted in 1978 for the U.S. Congress. The study was based on a sample of workers classified as "independent contractors" and therefore not subject to source withholding of tax. (Payers are required to file "1099" information returns to the IRS for payees receiving over $600 but are not required to supply a copy to the worker. Yet the study found that over 40 per cent of payers failed to comply in filing the required returns.) This group constitutes workers in the cash or underground economy with the greatest opportunities for tax evasion. The tabulated figures are striking. Fully half of the industries tabulated had zero compliance rates exceeding 50 per cent; in those industries

TABLE 2

| Industry | Per cent of compensation reported | Per cent of payees with | | |
		Full compliance	Partial compliance	Zero compliance
Taxicabs	43.5	32.4	2.9	64.7
Logging and timber	52.1	22.9	7.6	69.5
Warehousing	54.0	16.0	4.0	80.0
Restaurants and bars	58.5	33.1	8.0	58.9
Real estate construction	63.7	31.3	6.0	62.7
Trucking	66.7	40.9	4.9	54.2
Direct sales	68.8	51.0	5.7	43.3
Home improvement	70.2	39.8	4.6	55.5
Other	72.5	45.0	4.1	50.7
Franchise operations	73.0	38.2	10.0	51.7
Other sales	74.1	48.2	4.7	47.1
Consulting	76.3	55.6	3.2	41.3
Entertainment	77.9	54.0	4.0	41.9
Real estate	89.5	75.1	4.7	20.2
Barber/beauty shops	90.0	73.3	6.7	20.0
Medical/health services	90.1	67.4	4.6	28.0
Exempt organizations	97.8	76.1	2.2	21.7
Insurance	98.3	89.9	4.0	6.2
All industries	76.2	48.2	4.9	46.9

Source: U.S. Congress (1979, p. 24).

more than half of payees reported none of their independent con-
tractor receipts. Also striking is the wide variation across industries
in the per cent of total compensation reported, ranging from just
43.5 per cent for taxicabs to 98.3 per cent for insurance. Certain
industries are clearly much more prone to income tax evasion than
others, even for a type of payment relatively vulnerable to evasion.

Indirect taxes on consumption are also subject to problems of
non-compliance. These include the provincial retail sales taxes (RST)
and the federal Goods and Services Tax, a form of value-added tax
(VAT). It has been widely argued that the RST format can be evaded
more readily than a VAT. The argument is that businesses purchasing intermediate inputs will always demand invoices in order to sub-
stantiate their credit claims for purchases under a VAT. But the
weakest link for an indirect tax is at the point of sale to final consumers, both by retailers of goods and suppliers of services to
households. Since the tax authorities do not audit purchase receipts

by households, firms can understate their final sales. Hence, both the RST and VAT can be evaded, at least in part, on sales to final consumers. This is particularly a problem with small suppliers in the informal sector, which is precisely the most troublesome area for income tax compliance. In practice, a VAT does appear to be somewhat less prone to evasion than an RST, but European experience with VATs has uncovered ingenious evasion methods.

Economic Theory of Tax Compliance and Enforcement

An extensive theoretical literature has been developed to examine the economics of tax evasion. Essentially, this theory is based on rational decisions by individuals about how much of their income to disclose to the tax authorities. The return to the individual from concealing a part of his or her income is the associated tax saving. The cost to the individual is zero if his or her evasion is not detected and the taxes plus a fine if his or her evasion is detected. The size of the fine and the probability of being caught are both determined by the tax administrative structure, and these in turn will influence the costs of evasion. Individuals are assumed to be averse to risk-taking, so that the optimal amount of evasion to undertake involves a balancing between the returns and the anticipated costs. This theory finds that increases in the probability of detection and/or the fine for evasion will decrease the amount evaded. However, increases in the tax rate may either increase or decrease evasion, depending upon the nature of the individual's attitude toward risk.

The basic economic theory of tax evasion has been elaborated in many dimensions to account for institutional details such as source withholding of taxes, labour market structures, and auditing strategies. One of the more policy-relevant of these elaborations has been to consider the economy as divided into a tax-compliant sector and a tax-evading sector. Some workers specialize in one sector, other workers in the other sector, but workers can move between the sectors in response to tax rate changes. All individuals consume products from both sectors and will substitute between the sectoral outputs in response to changes in their relative prices. In such a model, most or all of the gains from tax evasion are shifted into lower product prices for output from the evading sector. Hence, the main beneficiaries of income tax evasion may be purchasers of goods and services produced by evaders (as well as those workers who are particularly efficient at evasion). Moreover, in this model there is a more clear-cut finding that higher tax rates will increase the extent of evasion in the economy. This result appears to be supported by the limited, but somewhat weak, empirical findings on tax evasion.

Economic theory has also been applied to non-abusive tax avoidance behaviour, in which the participant believes that his or her actions are fully legal and acceptable to the tax authorities. Most of this theory has been applied to income taxes on financial assets rather than on labour earnings. In this case, the individual simply chooses those assets that maximize his or her net rate of return. For a fully taxable asset, the net return equals the gross return minus the associated income taxes. For a fully tax-exempt asset, the net return is identical to the gross return. Most legal tax shelters involve fast write-offs or tax deferrals, so that the effective tax rate is less than the individual's normal marginal tax rate. Financial markets will adjust to tax avoidance behaviour by equating the net rates of return on taxable and tax-preferred assets, at least for marginal holders of the tax-preferred assets. This diverts financial, and often real, resources into the tax-preferred sectors of the economy. Gainers are those individuals in the highest marginal tax brackets and those persons who held assets before they gained tax-preferred status.

Abusive tax avoidance behaviour involves some risk that the activity will be detected and its tax benefits disallowed or even penalized. Hence, it should be modelled in a way that combines the economic theory of non-abusive tax avoidance and the theory of ordinary tax evasion. This exercise does not appear to have been undertaken in the economic literature on tax compliance. The probability of detection, and the presence and size of fines – which may be simply tax penalties and interest charges – should act to raise the costs to the individual of undertaking abusive tax avoidance. For that reason, the same policy instruments are available to combat tax avoidance as well as tax evasion.

Finally, economic theory has addressed the issue of optimal tax enforcement strategies. Much of the literature has examined alternative audit strategies and the ways that potential evaders could learn about the audit methods and how to adjust their behaviour accordingly. The more interesting result, for discussion of tax policy, concerns the two principal enforcement methods. Governments can increase the probability of detecting evaders, although this is costly in terms of real resources such as personnel. For detected evaders, governments can increase the size of fines, thereby incurring no real resource costs. (We ignore the fact that larger fines will induce evaders to mount more costly defences and may also incur more costly prosecutions.) Because increasing fines is relatively costless, whereas raising detection probabilities is not, the efficient strategy is to have very high fines and accept lower chances of detection. The only practical limit to heavy fines is the common-sense notion of fairness – "the punishment must fit the crime."

Relevance of Compliance to Tax Fairness

Two dimensions are conventionally used by economic analysts in assessing the fairness of taxation: vertical equity and horizontal equity. As well, other notions of fairness may on occasion be invoked. An example is the relationship between tax burdens and the payers' use of or benefits from public goods and services. Such a "benefit" approach to taxation may be useful particularly with respect to the public supply of goods and services that compete closely with counterparts supplied in the market-place. For that reason, it is usually more of a guide to efficiency than to equity in taxation. Our treatment will focus on the vertical and horizontal dimensions of equity. Still, it should be noted that surveys and experimental studies have found taxpayers' compliance related to their perceptions of whether they are getting good value in public services for their taxes; this is very much a benefit view of taxation.

The vertical equity of the tax system may be compromised by non-compliance if such behaviour is disproportionately concentrated in higher-income classes. If non-compliance were uniformly distributed across the income scale, then tax rates generally would have to be higher to raise the same total revenues. But in that case, each income class would bear about the same total taxes as it would with full compliance and lower statutory tax rates. In setting the mix of taxes, tax rates, and tax bases including tax shelter provisions, legislators must have some idea of the resulting distribution of the tax burden across income classes. If they are aware of the extent and pattern of non-compliance, appropriate adjustments can be made in the choice of tax structure to achieve the desired effective progressivity. If the actual pattern of non-compliance departs from what the legislators believe, the results are also likely to diverge from the desired degree of vertical equity.

Evidence about the income pattern of non-compliance by taxpayers is fragmentary at best. Tax evasion on labour earnings is concentrated among the self-employed and business proprietors, but this still spans a broad range of occupations and industries, including both poorly paid and well-paid ones. Examples include painters, dentists, small merchants, prostitutes, artisans and crafts people, and auto mechanics. Evasion on incomes from business capital and financial assets most likely arises disproportionately at higher incomes, since wealth is concentrated at higher incomes. Likewise, both non-abusive and abusive tax avoidance are associated with wealth and therefore arise disproportionately at higher incomes. Avoidance of taxes through the creative use of non-taxable fringe benefits similarly would be associated most with business proprietors and highly paid employees.

The horizontal dimension of equity is more fundamentally involved in tax non-compliance, since any vertical inequities resulting from non-compliance can be countered by an appropriate adjustment of tax rates. But if compliance varies among taxpayers in the same income class, there is no easy remedy for the resulting horizontal inequities. Individuals with the same ability to pay tax end up paying different amounts of tax. Yet ability to pay tax is not necessarily the same as income under an income tax, or property value under a property tax, or total consumption under an indirect tax. For clarity, our discussion of this matter will focus on the personal income tax.

It is useful to distinguish among the possible reasons for variations in tax payments by persons at the same level of true economic income:

• definition of the tax base that omits certain elements of true economic income, such as home-produced services or some fringe benefits;
• special relief provisions included in the tax system (base and/or rates);
• special incentive provisions included in the tax system (base and/or rates);
• misunderstanding of or difficulty interpreting the tax provisions;
• intentional evasion of taxes;
• abusive tax avoidance.

The omission of certain elements from the tax base, usually for the pragmatic reason that they are too difficult to measure, is unavoidable. Although they may produce horizontal inequities, this cannot be characterized as non-compliance. Special tax provisions legislated for relief objectives are often an attempt to refine the proper measurement of ability to pay taxes (medical expense deductions, for example). Hence, they may actually improve the horizontal equity of the tax. Special tax incentive provisions will typically sacrifice horizontal equity; but their use by taxpayers does not constitute non-compliance so long as it is non-abusive ("legal" tax avoidance). All of the three remaining phenomena – misunderstanding, evasion, and abusive avoidance – constitute compliance problems and yield horizontal inequities.

An important aspect of horizontal equity is the durability of tax provisions over time. If the tax statutes or administrative procedures are subject to frequent change, then individuals whose economic circumstances are similar will be treated differently depending upon the timing of taxable events. For example, if special favourable provisions for taxing capital gains are enacted for some years but then abolished, some individuals will get the benefit of these provisions while others with equal gains that arise later will not. Similarly, if a government enacts estate, inheritance, or other death-related taxes, but the next governing party abolishes them, only the estates or bequests associated with deaths in that period will be affected. Hence, estates or bequests of the same magnitude will bear very different taxes depending on the exact timing of death.

If horizontal equity for people over time is an important objective, governments should avoid legislating major new taxes or changes in existing taxes unless these moves have sufficiently broad public support to survive the next change of governing party. Two additional reasons, based more in compliance responses, also dictate caution for governments in making many tax changes. First, tax changes that are not expected to last for many years frequently lead to tax-planning opportunities by which individuals or firms may avoid their impact, or even benefit from them. Second, unless the tax changes significantly simplify previously existing provisions, the very act of change leads to compliance problems. Taxpayers and intermediaries have to learn about the new provisions and interpret how they apply to their own circumstances. Tax administrators have to learn about the potential pitfalls of the provisions and act accordingly.

Compliance, enforcement, and administration of taxes involve social objectives beyond fairness. Foremost of these is the efficient allocation of resources. Economic efficiency involves the real resources consumed in the very process of administering, enforcing, and complying with the tax system. The materials and time used to operate the tax system are diverted from uses that could satisfy households' ordinary consumer needs or public-sector consumption needs. Given the amount of time required by taxpayers and intermediaries in compliance, these real resource costs are much larger than the published figures on public tax administration costs. Economic efficiency is also sacrificed by non-compliance behaviours such as evasion and avoidance (both "legal" and abusive). These actions divert resources to uses or sectors where their social payoff is not the highest. For example, a plumber operating in the underground economy, to evade taxes, will typically have a structure and scale of business that are less efficient than a plumbing firm with a store-front and several employees.

Alternative Approaches to Tax Compliance

Two alternative ways can be used to enhance the tax compliance of intermediaries and taxpayers. This goal can be pursued at the initial stage of designing tax policies or at the subsequent stages of devising administrative structures and legislative remedies to problems as they arise. One can hardly understate the value of careful analysis of the compliance and administrative aspects at an early stage of designing or reforming tax policies. Many tax concepts, such as income, are inherently fraught with difficult measurement problems (e.g., accruals, depreciation, imputed values, and inflation). These problems have persuaded a large contingent of modern tax economists to favour cash flow, consumption, or expenditures as the basis for direct personal taxation. Moreover, the efficacy of source withholding of taxes in combating evasion has induced some to favour a flat-rate schedule for personal taxes, perhaps supplemented by a higher tax rate at upper incomes. Other analysts believe that these proposals sacrifice too much in the way of equity and seek remedies more in the legislative, administrative, and enforcement areas.

Many problems of non-compliance stem from the complexity of tax provisions. Complexity itself may be required in trying to adjust the measure of ability to pay taxes for a wide range of individual circumstances. It is ironic that some such provisions, which attempt to improve horizontal equity, may actually create inequities through the resulting problems of understanding and variable application of the provisions. Most complex tax provisions result from attempts to limit the availability of tax expenditure benefits and to prevent a variety of non-compliance responses including abusive avoidance and evasion. All of these consequences merely reinforce the importance of taking care in designing the fundamental basis of the tax system. They also suggest that simplicity – with relatively few and simple tax expenditures and refinements in the measure of ability to pay – may facilitate both compliance and horizontal equity.

The other approach to enhancing tax compliance relies upon frequent ad hoc legislative changes and administrative rulings to overcome problems as they arise. Some of this process is unavoidable under any tax system, but the lack of clear, easily generalized tax concepts is often at the root of the problem. Administrative procedures for collecting taxes and enforcement are closely linked to the design and structure of the tax system. When the tax system has numerous exceptions and refinements to its basic rules, collection and enforcement become correspondingly complicated. In the process of designing a tax system or planning reforms, the nature of the information to be gathered in administering and enforcing the real-world operation must be carefully considered. Are the required items of information easily observed and measured, or are difficult imputations involved? Which agent will do the observing and reporting of the information, and what are the opportunities and incentives of the agent to furnish inaccurate information? What kinds of cross-checks can be used to confirm the reliability of information? And what are the costs to private agents as well as to the government in this process?

Application to Selected Ontario Tax Issues

The preceding principles and discussion can be applied to selected tax issues that are relevant to the mandate of the Ontario Fair Tax Commission. Our brief treatment here will point out some of the compliance, enforcement, and administrative aspects of both existing tax provisions and contemplated new taxes. These will be related back to the various fairness objectives as well as other taxation goals. For most existing taxes and tax provisions, the treatment will address principally administrative methods of improving tax compliance. For the contemplated new taxes, more direct consideration will be given to compliance as a fundamental aspect of tax design.

As part of the discussion, some suggestions will be made about useful areas of research for the commission to undertake.

Unintentional Non-Compliance

Many horizontal inequities result from unintentional non-compliance – misunderstanding of either the tax provisions or the tax administrative rules. The primary remedies must be sought in improved drafting of legislative provisions and information brochures and in simplified administrative procedures. In many cases, a rethinking of the underlying objectives of the tax policy is also needed to achieve acceptable simplifications. Problems with income assistance delivered through the tax system, tax provisions directed toward the situation of women and families, and other tax expenditures frequently fall into this category. Policy design and legal drafting have to balance the need for tight definitions (to minimize the use of beneficial tax provisions by non-targeted groups or circumstances) against the need for simplicity and clarity (to ensure high participation rates by targeted groups and circumstances).

Enforcement: Detection and Fines

Combating evasion and abusive avoidance requires effective detection and penalties. It is not commonly appreciated how large the fines must be in areas of non-compliance where the detection probabilities are small. To illustrate this point, consider a recent pilot project by Canada Customs to toughen enforcement against cross-border smuggling. At selected border points in British Columbia and Ontario, undeclared tobacco and alcohol products are subject to seizure in addition to fines (formerly, smugglers could get their goods back after paying taxes and fines). Let us assume that a 24-pack of beer costs $12 in the United States and $24 in Canada and that the fine per pack is F. Then, to deter prospective smugglers who are risk-neutral (will enter into a fair bet), the expected costs from smuggling must exceed the expected gains from smuggling. Let P denote the probability of a vehicle being searched, and assume that every search of a smuggler's vehicle will detect the contraband. Then, for each pack of beer, a fair bet for a prospective smuggler would be:

$$(1 - P) \times \$12 = P \times (\$12 + F)$$

The expected gain is one minus the probability of being caught multiplied by the savings from buying cheaper American beer ($24 − $12). The expected cost is the probability of being caught multiplied by the sum of the cost of the seized beer and the fine per beer pack.

The actual fine per 24-pack of beer in the pilot project is $F = \$12$, which would be an effective deterrent against smuggling only if P exceeded one-third. That is, Canada Customs would have to search more than one out of every three cars to eliminate the incentive for beer smuggling even under their trial policy of seizure plus $12 per pack fine. The equation can also be solved for the size of fines that would be needed to accompany more realistic detection probabilities. If one out of every 20 cars is searched ($P = 0.05$), a fine of $216 per beer pack is needed. If only one out of every 50 cars is searched ($P = 0.02$), the fine must be $576 per pack. These figures are much higher than many observers might expect would be needed to deter evasion. In fact, lower fines may suffice for the majority of the population because they are at least somewhat risk-averse (unwilling to enter into fair bets where there is a small chance of a large loss) or would not contemplate smuggling.

The foregoing example illustrates the problem of enforcement in many areas of tax evasion and abusive avoidance where the prospects of detection are rather small. Very large fines may be needed to deter non-compliance behaviour. The requisite fines may be so large that they are deemed unfair by the general public given the magnitude of the crime. Imposing these fines may also produce horizontal inequities, in that only a small percentage of offenders are penalized. One approach is to raise the probabilities of detection, or at least probabilities that are perceived by the taxpaying public. The policy problem is to achieve this in a way that is not overly costly in real resources (for the government, intermediaries, or taxpayers) and that is not perceived as excessively intrusive in personal or business matters. This can be done by targeting enforcement campaigns on particular industries or occupations where evasion is known to be widespread. Similarly, surveillance can be focused on those industries and investment strategies where tax avoidance is thought to be common. The publicity given to these campaigns and the resulting prosecutions can be effective in changing the perceived risks to non-compliance.

Improved Information Reporting

It was noted earlier that information reporting and/or withholding of taxes at source are important in achieving high rates of tax compliance. If the reporting is done by an intermediary party that has no direct interest in falsifying the information and is not easily bribed by the taxpayer, then the detection probabilities for non-compliance can be sharply increased. One type of income that is not currently reported by intermediaries to the Canadian tax authorities is capital gains on securities and real estate transactions. In the United States, intermediaries in these transactions are obliged to file information reports to the government and the taxpayer. The taxpayer must then append copies of the Forms 1099-B and 1099-S to his or her tax return, and the sums of the proceeds reported on these forms must tally with the proceeds reported on his or her statement of capital gains. This still leaves room for fraudulent statements about the cost basis of assets, but the existence of the transactions is revealed to the government, and audits can pick up problems in the computation of capital gains. The costs and benefits of this kind of information reporting in the United States are worth studying for possible application in Canada. Ontario may wish to encourage the federal tax authorities to pursue this step given the two jurisdictions' common interest in the outcome.

Extended Source Withholding

The most vexatious areas of non-compliance do not lend themselves easily to information reporting or source withholding. These are transactions between households and businesses rather than inter-business transactions. When the transactions are between business entities, the purchaser has an interest in documenting it for tax deduction purposes, so that the seller may be reluctant to conceal its existence. Final consumers do not get tax deductions for most of their household purchases (except for medical expenses and in-home offices or businesses). They have little incentive or reason to document their purchases, so that sellers may feel relatively secure in concealing these incomes from the tax authorities. However, they may also have to operate in the irregular economy in order to ensure lesser visibility.

For large purchases, such as major home repairs or renovations (over a set dollar limit), one could require the household purchaser to act as a tax intermediary. This approach has been done in Australia, where households purchasing renovation or repair services over a set limit must withhold and remit to the tax office a specified percentage of the gross contract payment. If the household fails to withhold the taxes, and this is detected, the household itself is liable for those taxes. The Australian experience with this approach might warrant study to determine its costs and benefits. However, this approach raised public resistance when implemented in Australia, and it may also be deemed too meddlesome in the Canadian social context. In addition, it is a method that could not readily be extended beyond the cited industry that is characterized by large dollar sales and high visibility – namely, the need for building permits and the presence of building crews and trucks. One should recall further the finding of economic theory that the benefits of tax evasion in the irregular economy are shifted mainly to the consumers. Hence, measures to combat evasion in a sector will primarily raise the market prices faced by consumers.

Linkages between GST and Income Taxes

Replacement of the federal Manufacturers' Sales Tax with the value-added-type Goods and Services Tax opens opportunities for improved tax administration and enforcement. Sales and purchases documented by a firm for the GST can be compared with the figures it claims on its business income tax return (corporate or unincorporated). Firms that claim substantial input credits for GST will have to report corresponding receipts from sales, with norms based on the firm's industry. Otherwise, any attempts by firms to evade their taxes will be detected more readily by the tax authorities. The use of invoices with GST registration numbers on all transactions will further expose firms to risks when failing to report business receipts. Despite these potential gains in tax compliance and administration that have accompanied the federal GST, it is not obvious that any further gains of these kinds would arise from Ontario joining in the GST.

Harmonization of Ontario RST with the GST

The principal gains from Ontario harmonizing its retail sales tax with the federal GST would be reduced costs of tax administration and compliance. (For present purposes, we ignore the gains in economic efficiency that would result from removing taxes on business capital and intermediate inputs arising under the Ontario RST.) A combined Canada–Ontario GST should involve total administrative costs that are not much larger than those of the federal GST alone. Hence, most of the costs of administering the Ontario RST would be saved. Similarly, the tax compliance costs of firms under the Ontario RST would be completely eliminated with little increase in their compliance burdens under a combined federal–provincial GST as compared with the federal-only GST. The only addition to administrative or compliance complexity if Ontario were to join the GST relates to the need to distinguish businesses' interprovincial purchases and sales; these would be treated like imports and exports for purposes of the Ontario portion of the GST.

The downside for compliance if Ontario joins the GST is the availability of a broader coverage of services than that which currently obtains under the existing provincial RST. Small firms are more predominant in the service sector than in the goods-producing sector, and they are also more prone to evasion based on their lesser visibility and the lesser tangibility of their output. Converting the Ontario RST into additional tax points on the GST reduces the taxation of most goods but increases the taxation of most services. The effective total tax rate on services is increased, which will raise incentives for tax evasion by those firms that are most prone to and able to evade. Offset against this is the GST invoice method, which may serve to increase the income tax compliance of firms. Research on the experience in this area by European countries and New Zealand might be helpful to the commission.

Taxing Visible or Registered Items

One way to get at the pocketbooks of flagrant tax evaders and avoiders is to impose or increase taxes on the purchase or use of major commodities that are hard to conceal. Examples include real property, cars, and larger boats. The need to register these items with public authorities (land title, auto, or boat registry) makes it particularly easy to enforce the collection of taxes on the purchase or the ongoing use of these items. These taxes can be graduated also in their rates so that only higher-valued items face significant taxes. Note that this approach may have appeal also as a method of increasing the vertical equity of the tax system.

In 1991, the U.S. federal government implemented new excise

taxes on certain "luxury" goods – high-value cars, boats, airplanes, jewellery, and furs. These include some items that must be registered as well as others not subject to public registration. A jurisdiction such as Ontario could consider taxing a broader range of luxury goods than those that must be registered. However, because it is a lower jurisdiction in a federal country, Ontario would be limited in the rates that it could apply to such goods before consumers would be induced to make their purchases in other provinces. Since most luxury goods are of high value per weight or volume, they are easily carried or shipped across provincial boundaries. If Ontario did wish to pursue taxes on luxury good purchases, a dual-rate provincial GST might be an attractive vehicle for implementing them (assuming that the federal government would accept such a variant under a harmonized tax). Still, most analysts of value-added taxes caution against using multiple rates on account of the added administrative costs and compliance problems.

Wealth and Death Taxation

Taxes on wealth, net worth, intangible assets, inheritances, and/or estates are often attractive to those seeking greater vertical equity in taxation. Even if they do not raise large revenues, these taxes may be regarded as a useful supplement to progressive income taxes for vertical equity. Yet before proceeding along this path, Ontario should carefully consider compliance problems that may afflict these kinds of taxes, particularly when applied at a subnational level. No other Canadian province has a significant tax of these kinds besides real-property taxes. Therefore, Ontario would have to draft its legislation carefully to prevent the shifting of assets or asset ownership to entities located outside the province. If it were successful in this, and if the effective rates of tax were very high, Ontario would risk driving out its wealthier residents. For these reasons, taxes of these kinds are usually more appropriate for application at the national level.

Even setting aside the jurisdictional issue, taxes on wealth and death suffer from special problems of durability over time. Because these taxes target a small part of the population – and a disproportionately influential group at that – they eventually succumb to political pressures for legislative changes to weaken their impact. Since they seldom provide a large enough portion of total revenues to matter, one government or the next caves in to these pressures.

Sometimes this results in the abolition of a tax, but more often it results in growing avoidance devices that are not countered by effective legislation. This outcome yields horizontal inequities for individuals over time, depending upon the timing of taxable events. Experience in Europe, where taxes on wealth and/or death are fairly common, reveals the secularly declining revenue yields of these kinds of taxes relative to the much more important income, consumption, and payroll taxes.

Separate Ontario Personal Income Tax

Unless the political support for wealth or death taxes is strong and durable, governments are likely to serve tax fairness better by strengthening the equity of their direct personal taxes and other major revenue generators. To the extent that Ontario cannot achieve this goal under its Tax Collection Agreement with the federal government, it may be impelled to operate its own personal income tax despite the higher administrative and compliance costs. The most prominent equity deficiencies in the Canadian personal income tax relate to its definition of the tax base. If it is judged that the worst defects can be remedied by a short list of additions, subtractions, and changes to components in the federal definition of taxable income, then Ontario taxpayers could begin with their federal taxable income calculation and have little additional compliance needs. (A similar approach is used by many states in the United States.) The administrative burdens of such a separate Ontario tax would depend upon what cooperative arrangements could be reached with the federal government in areas such as audits and enforcement. Administrative and compliance needs of alternative designs should figure prominently in any research the commission might undertake on an Ontario personal tax.

Policy and Research Agenda

Compliance, enforcement, and administrative aspects of the tax system are vital to the attainment of tax fairness. Non-compliance can undermine both vertical and horizontal dimensions of equity. It is essential to consider these factors at the time of designing new tax instruments and reforming existing policies – as well as in the day-to-day administrative and regulatory actions needed to enforce taxes. New forms of taxes often appear attractive to policy-makers and politicians largely due to the known weaknesses of more familiar taxes. Inevitably, non-compliance and associated inequities also will accompany almost any conceivable new form of taxation. Estimates of the overall extent of non-compliance are limited in availability and reliability. However, considerably more weight can be placed on estimates of industries, occupations, and asset types that are particularly prone to tax abuse. Findings of this kind can be particularly useful in the design of tax reforms and new tax policies.

Numerous piecemeal reforms to existing taxes may be worth pursuing for enhanced equity. Most tax expenditure provisions warrant scrutiny to determine whether their complications, and resulting uneven compliance and inequities, justify their continued operation. Possible extensions to the system of information reporting and source withholding may yield benefits that outweigh any incremental costs. Comparative experience with similar provisions in other countries can provide useful input into the assessment. Also, cross-national experience with taxes on wealth, inheritances, property transfers, and other bases lacking in Ontario may be useful in appreciating their potential and practical limits. A study of countries that have coordinated their value-added taxes with their direct taxes may also reveal how a Canadian province can benefit from merging its retail sales tax with the federal GST.

No single model can be used to guide future research on a problem like tax compliance. The behaviour encompassed by non-compliance is as diverse as the choice to work "off the books" or as a self-employed plumber or drug dealer and the choice of whether to shelter or conceal investment incomes. Useful insights will be generated from a wide range of methodologies – economic theory, field surveys, statistical studies, administrative findings, sociological methods, audit results, and accounting and legal studies. Still, the economic perspective does remind researchers that, if even a subset of the population approaches the compliance choice in a rational gambling manner, the probabilities of apprehension or the effective penalties need to be sharply stiffened to make non-compliance much less pervasive than it is at present. Attempts to add new taxes on top of existing, significantly deficient taxes may be a less promising tack than reforms to improve the existing major taxes.

Note

This paper was prepared for the Ontario Fair Tax Commission and completed in August 1992.

1 Because of its non-technical nature, this paper does not cite references except where tabular statistics are provided. However, a listing of sources upon which this paper draws is provided in the Bibliography.

Bibliography

Allingham, Michael G., and Agnar Sandmo. 1972. "Income Tax Evasion: A Theoretical Analysis." *Journal of Public Economics* 1: 323–38

Alm, James, Roy Bahl, and Matthew N. Murray. 1990. "Tax Structure and Tax Compliance." *Review of Economics and Statistics* 72: 603–13

Alm, James, Gary H. McClelland, and William D. Schulze. 1992. "Why Do People Pay Taxes?" *Journal of Public Economics* 48: 21–38

Clotfelter, Charles T. 1983a. "Tax Evasion and Tax Rates: An Analysis of Individual Returns." *Review of Economics and Statistics* 65: 363–73

– 1983b. "Tax-Induced Distortions and the Business-Pleasure Borderline: The Case of Travel and Entertainment." *American Economic Review* 73: 1053–65

Cordes, Joseph J., and Harvey Galper. 1985. "Tax Shelter Activity: Lessons from Twenty Years of Evidence." *National Tax Journal* 38: 305–24

Cowell, Frank A. 1990. *Cheating the Government: The Economics of Evasion.* Cambridge, MA: MIT Press

Cowell, Frank A., and James P.F. Gordon. 1988. "Unwillingness to Pay: Tax Evasion and Public Goods Provision." *Journal of Public Economics* 36: 305–21

Feinstein, Jonathan S. 1991. "An Econometric Analysis of Income Tax Evasion." *Rand Journal of Economics* 22: 14–35

Gaertner, Wulf, and Alois Wenig, eds. 1985. *The Economics of the Shadow Economy.* Berlin: Springer-Verlag

Kesselman, Jonathan R. 1989. "Income Tax Evasion: An Intersectoral Analysis." *Journal of Public Economics* 38: 137–82

– 1990. *Rate Structure and Personal Taxation: Flat Rate or Dual Rate?* Wellington, New Zealand: Victoria University Press for the Institute of Policy Studies

– 1993. "Evasion Effects of Changing the Tax Mix." *The Economic Record* (June)

Lindsey, Lawrence B. 1987. "Individual Taxpayer Response to Tax Cuts: 1982–1984: With Implications for the Revenue Maximizing Tax Rate." *Journal of Public Economics* 33: 173–206

Long, James E. 1984. "Tax Rates and Tax Losses: A Preliminary Analysis Using Aggregate Data." *Public Finance Quarterly* 12: 457–72

Long, James E., and James D. Gwartney. 1987. "Income Tax Avoidance: Evidence from Individual Tax Returns." *National Tax Journal* 40: 517–32

Poterba, James M. 1987. "Tax Evasion and Capital Gains Taxation." *American Economic Review* 77: 234–9

Roth, Jeffrey A., John T. Scholtz, and Ann Dryden White, eds. 1989. *Taxpayer Compliance*, 2 vols. Philadelphia, PA: University of Pennsylvania Press

Stiglitz, Joseph E. 1985. "The General Theory of Tax Avoidance." *National Tax Journal* 38: 325–37

Tanzi, Vito, ed. 1982. *The Underground Economy in the United States and Abroad.* Lexington, MA: Lexington Books

U.S. Congress. 1979. *Independent Contractors.* House of Representatives, Committee on Ways and Means, Subcommittee on Select Revenue Measures, 96th Congress, first session, 20 June, 16–17 July

U.S. Internal Revenue Service. 1983. *Income Tax Compliance Research: Estimates for 1973–1981.* Washington, DC: Department of the Treasury

Vaillancourt, François. 1989. *The Administrative and Compliance Costs of the Personal Income Tax and Payroll Tax System in Canada, 1986* Toronto: Canadian Tax Foundation

Witte, Ann D., and Diane F. Woodbury. 1983. "What We Know about Factors Affecting Compliance with the Tax Laws." In *Income Tax Compliance: A Report of the ABA Section on Taxation, Conference on Income Tax Compliance,* ed. Philip Sawicki, 133–48. Reston, VA: American Bar Association

Woodbury, Stephen A. 1983. "Substitution between Wage and Nonwage Benefits." *American Economic Review,* 73: 166–82

3 Equity and Tax Mix
Theoretical Perspectives

JAMES B. DAVIES

Introduction

There are many important issues in tax equity, but one of the most fundamental is: What should be taxed? At present, provincial and municipal governments levy a wide array of taxes – corporate income tax (CIT), personal income tax (PIT), property tax, and sales tax to name but the most important. However, neglecting benefit taxation, academic discussions of tax equity often identify a single tax base as "ideal." One therefore needs to ask: Which, if any, real-world taxes are appropriate from an equity viewpoint? What steps can be taken to eliminate or reduce fundamentally inequitable taxes and rehabilitate others? The purpose of this paper is to investigate the theoretical basis for such an exercise.

Leaving aside benefit taxation, tax practitioners, economists, and policy analysts consider three major competing notions of an ideal equitable tax base: consumption, annual income, and lifetime income. The consumption tax approach does not rely simply on sales and excise taxes; it also refers to methods that can be used to transform income taxes into consumption taxes effectively. On the personal side, registered retirement savings plans (RRSPs) and registered pension plans (RPPs), with unlimited contribution limits, would do the job. On the corporate side, a "cash flow" version of the CIT would be used (see Davies and St-Hilaire 1987; Boadway, Bruce, and Mintz 1987; and Beach, Boadway, and Bruce 1988). The annual income tax approach is more familiar. It was vigorously advocated in Canada by the Carter Report. Finally, the lifetime income approach has a philosophy similar to the annual income approach, but tries to use a much longer time frame. RRSPs and RPPs are used in this approach to achieve lifetime averaging. Wages, gifts and inheritances, business cash flow, and above-normal returns on non-business assets would all be taxable under an ideal lifetime income tax, but a normal return on capital would be exempt.[1]

Seemingly, few Canadians would support exclusive reliance on consumption taxes. However, only a minority would likely be in favour of abolishing them completely. The same could be said for payroll taxes. Does this reflect an underlying belief that there is some redeeming merit in these taxes despite their bad press? And, if so, is it based on some valid intuition about tax equity? These are interesting and largely unexplored questions that deserve some attention.

The annual income tax approach appears to capture much of the popular orthodoxy on tax equity. The broad public seems convinced that the "buck is a buck" philosophy is correct, and politicians pay attention to this in their public utterances. The federal tax reform of 1987, for example, was partly couched in terms of closing loopholes in order to move closer to an ideal comprehensive income tax. However, sheltered retirement savings is also popular (and was enshrined and enhanced in the 1987 tax reform), despite the fact that it seriously violates the annual income tax approach.

These observations about what tax provisions are popular in Canada suggest to me that prevalent notions of what is equitable are based on a mixture of consumption, annual income, and lifetime income tax approaches. Rather than reject this as evidence of sloppy thinking, I believe we should respond by re-examining our analyses of the equitable choice of tax base. There may be some wisdom underlying these apparently paradoxical prevailing attitudes.

At this point it is important to comment on the relative significance of horizontal and vertical equity in this study. Horizontal equity holds when people with equal "ability to pay" bear equal tax burdens. The major challenge is to identify what correctly measures ability to pay, which is really the central issue addressed in this paper. Vertical equity receives less attention for two reasons. Vertical equity holds when people at different levels of ability to pay bear appropriately different tax burdens. It may be thought, for example, that taxes should be progressive in order to achieve vertical equity. The degree of progressivity judged appropriate depends on personal value judgments and therefore receives little attention in this paper. The other reason that vertical equity considerations are not of primary concern here is that once those tax bases that reflect ability to pay have been identified, one can obtain whatever degree of progressivity is desired through the selection of an appropriate tax schedule.[2]

To be more concrete, the consumption and lifetime income tax bases discussed in this paper would make use of both RRSPs/RPPs with generous contribution limits. Some people feel that current Canadian RRSPs/RPPs erode the progressivity of the personal income tax (see, for example, National Council of Welfare 1979). But such a statement is accurate only if the tax schedule is held constant. If PIT rates are made more progressive at the same time that RRSP/RPP contribution rates are increased, then the overall progressivity of the tax need not be affected by raising contribution limits (see Davies 1988). It may be felt that, in practice, such offsetting changes in tax schedules do not occur. Such political limitations on the scope of tax policy may well be important, but their analysis is beyond the scope of both this paper and the author's expertise.

The second section of this paper sets out the theoretical justification for the consumption tax and lifetime income tax approaches. These are to be found in the dynastic and life-cycle views, respectively, of household and individual decision-making. However, the justification for these approaches depends on assumptions of certainty and perfect capital markets. It is important to relax these assumptions. The third section introduces borrowing constraints – an important form of capital market imperfection – and shows how these may justify some use of annual income taxes. Private risk and uncertainty about earnings and rates of return are analysed in the subsequent section. The final section looks at aspects of intertemporal equity – the "remedial" motive for taxation – and issues of intergenerational equity.

Implications of Alternative Models under Certainty and Perfect Capital Markets

Economists do not find static models of household decision-making very interesting. People can generally borrow and lend. While there are important exceptions (discussed in the next section), their welfare is therefore not typically determined by their income today, this week, or even this month. A longer time frame is required. In fact, in much work done by economists today, a far longer time frame is used – the lifetime, or even the dynastic. Some people feel, perhaps justifiably, that these time frames go to the opposite extreme and are just as unrealistic as would be a 24-hour or 7-day time frame. Combined with the assumptions of certainty and perfect capital markets, however, analyses of consumer welfare in these time frames can be used to justify two of the three important alternative tax bases discussed in this paper. It is therefore important to understand how tax equity would be achieved using these time frames.

Dynastic Models

Dynastic models have been popular since the famous paper by Barro (1974), which said that government deficits will not stimulate the economy if people are concerned about their descendants' welfare. The cost to later members of the dynasty of dealing with increased public debt wipes out the apparent benefit to the current generation of lower taxes or higher expenditures.

Formally, the dynastic view says that the utility of the current generation depends on its own consumption, C_0, and that of all future members of the dynasty:

$$U = U(C_0, C_1, \ldots , C_n, \ldots) \tag{1}$$

where C_t represents the consumption of generation t. The dynasty may be regarded as attempting to maximize (1) subject to a dynastic budget constraint:

$$\sum_{t=0}^{\infty} \frac{C_t}{(1+r)^t} \leq \sum_{t=0}^{\infty} \frac{E_t}{(1+r)^t} + W_0 \tag{2}$$

where E_t represents the labour earnings of generation t, r is the interest rate (per generation rather than per year), and W_0 is the wealth of generation zero inherited from earlier generations. Equation 2 says that the discounted value of consumption over the lifetime cannot exceed the sum of initial wealth plus the discounted value of lifetime earnings.

From (2) it is clear that consumption and wage taxes with constant marginal tax rates are equivalent from a dynastic viewpoint, provided that the initial wealth, W_0, is also taxed under a wage tax.

Note that either tax would be horizontally equitable if levied at a flat rate constant for all time. If tax rates are to vary over time, however, different families will be affected differently by the consumption tax versus the wage tax. For example, families who will be doing well (that is, have high E_t) during a period of high taxes will be better off with a consumption tax than a wage tax. This situation raises issues discussed below.

The dynastic story may seem somewhat far-fetched, but it is the implicit basis for the pure consumption tax approach. When a critic says that consumption taxes are vertically inequitable since higher income groups save a larger fraction of their income, consumption tax advocates point out that the portion of income that is saved will be taxed in the future when the wealth built up is dissaved. Although some wealth will not be dissaved, descendants have a way of eventually consuming their patrimony. Thus, if a consumption tax is in place permanently, the part of income that is saved will be taxed when it (plus accumulated interest) is eventually consumed, possibly at some very distant date in the future. If the critic indicates scepticism about the tax always being in place, the consumption tax advocate may point out that a wage tax is equivalent, is not subject to this limitation, and so can be used instead of, or alongside, a consumption tax. One way of thinking about a wage tax is that it is a form of consumption tax "prepayment."

Finally, we should be a little more specific about the impacts of alternative tax structures. Systems with constant marginal tax rates are reasonably easy to deal with analytically. We will therefore discuss the impact of linear progressive taxes in a number of cases. Linear progressive taxes are a combination of lump-sum transfer – the "demogrant" – and a proportional tax. In the dynastic framework it is easy to see that neither a lump-sum transfer in every period, nor a proportional wage or consumption tax would cause any horizontal inequity. More generally, a progressive consumption tax with increasing rates would have the same property if all dynasties had identical homothetic intertemporal preferences.[3] In that case they all smooth consumption over the generations in the same way, and dynasties with equal dynastic resources would always pay the same tax. However, an increasing-rate progressive wage tax would cause inequities since it would impose a larger dynastic tax burden on families with greater variability in wages from generation to generation, or whose initial generations happen to earn more than the average generation.

In most of the remainder of this paper discussion will be confined to the impact of tax systems with constant marginal tax rates, because variable-rate taxes often lead to distracting complications. In some cases, for clarity, attention is further restricted to proportional taxes. (A proportional tax is, of course, just a special case of a linear progressive tax with a zero demogrant.) Where the results would not necessarily extend to linear progressive taxes, this will be noted.

The Life-Cycle Model

In the recent history of economics the life-cycle model (LCM) predates the dynastic approach. Its authors – Modigliani and Ando (1957); Modigliani and Brumberg (1954) – were interested in the idea that most saving was for retirement. (Precautionary saving as insurance against unemployment, medical expenses, and so on, and even saving for a fixed target bequest, can be grafted onto the model without changing its implications, but I avoid these complications here.) As initially developed, the model assumed that people would work for some period, retiring say at age R, and then would live on for a fixed period, dying with certainty at age T. In order to avoid some unrealistic features, however, it is better to allow the length of life to be uncertain. Instead of maximizing an intergenerational utility function like (1) above, people would try to maximize a utility function depending on consumption at different ages:

$$U = U(C_0, C_1, \ldots , C_{\bar{T}}) \tag{3}$$

where $\bar{T}$ is the biological maximum length of life. In the absence of an annuity market, utility would be maximized subject to a lifetime budget constraint:

$$\sum_{t=0}^{\bar{T}} \frac{C_t}{(1+r)^t} \leq \sum_{t=0}^{\bar{T}} \frac{E_t + I_t}{(1+r)^t} + E + I \tag{4}$$

where I_t is the amount inherited, or received as a gift, at age t, and E and I are the discounted streams of wages and inheritances, respectively. Accidental inheritances will be received because the lack of an annuity market forces people to hold their wealth in bequeathable form. Note that inheritances and wages of equal amount have the same consequences for the individual. Finally, as in the dynastic model, increasing-rate progressive consumption taxes, in addition to linear progressive wage or consumption taxes, would be horizontally equitable, whereas increasing-rate progressive wage taxes would not. The latter defect can be overcome, however, through the use of averaging devices – the simplest being "designated" or "registered" savings along the lines of an RRSP or RPP with no contribution or withdrawal restrictions (see Davies and St-Hilaire 1987 or Beach, Boadway, and Bruce 1988).

Using equation 4, one can see that constant marginal-rate consumption taxes are equivalent to wage taxes, in terms of their impact on individual welfare, provided that inheritances are taxed at the same rate as wages. As in the discussion of the dynastic model, the conditional nature of this equivalence is important.

The life-cycle model provides a conceptual basis for confining one's attention to a lifetime time frame. It differs from the dynastic model in providing an equity motivation for taxing inheritances in every generation. (The dynastic model calls for a tax on initial wealth only at the time the tax system is started up.) But, it is important to emphasize, neither framework provides any justification for taxing capital income. The dynastic model suggests the use of consumption taxes while the LCM provides a basis for lifetime income taxes. In order to provide some justification for using annual income taxes we must depart from the assumptions of certainty and perfect capital markets.

Implications of Capital Market Imperfections

In a perfect capital market agents can lend any amount, and can borrow up to the limit set by their capacity to repay in the future. In the real world there are a variety of capital market imperfections. Moral hazard and adverse selection are present. An equilibrium response is for credit to be rationed and for riskier borrowers to face both higher interest rates and stricter borrowing constraints. For simplicity, we concentrate here on the implications of strict borrowing constraints. No borrowing against future income is allowed. Throughout the discussion the LCM framework will be used and, for expositional convenience, for the most part two-period lifetimes and zero bequests will be assumed. Under these assumptions wage and consumption taxes are equivalent in terms of welfare impact for the taxpayer.[4]

In a world without capital market imperfections the basic requirements of horizontal and vertical equity are unambiguous. People with equal lifetime incomes should pay equal lifetime taxes, and this can be accomplished via any linear wage or consumption tax. People with equal pre-tax lifetime income and welfare will pay equal taxes and have equal after-tax welfare. Vertical equity can be achieved by adjusting the demogrant and marginal tax rate.[5] When there are borrowing constraints, matters are more complex.

When there are borrowing constraints, proportional wage or consumption taxes will still lead to equal lifetime tax burdens for people with equal lifetime incomes, irrespective of the discount rate used. However, this does not correspond to people with equal pre-tax welfare paying equal lifetime taxes, and the loss of welfare will be equal only under very special assumptions about utility functions. Figure 1 illustrates.

Figure 1 sets out the earnings and consumption opportunities of two individuals, Bob and Sue, over hypothetical two-period lifetimes. The individuals' "endowment points" plot their labour earnings in the two periods, E_0 and E_1. Budget constraints are drawn starting at these endowment points. The budget constraints show combinations of consumption in the two periods, C_0 and C_1, which can be achieved by saving part of E_0. The budget constraints are straight lines because the interest rate is assumed constant. The change in C_1, ΔC_1, is related to the reduction in C_0 by the relationship, $\Delta C_1 = -(1 + C_1) \Delta C_0$. In keeping with the economic theory of consumer choice, an individual will choose to locate at a point on his or her budget constraint that is on the highest available "indifference curve."[6] Two contrasting examples of such equilibria are presented by the cases of Bob and Sue in Figure 1.

In Figure 1 Sue gets all her wage income in the first period and chooses to save a substantial portion of this income. She is therefore not effectively borrowing-constrained.[7] Bob gets most of his wages in the second period, and would ideally like to do some borrowing. However he cannot; he is effectively borrowing-constrained. At the observed interest rate, Bob's lifetime earnings exceed Sue's significantly in present value. However, the borrowing constraint is sufficiently severe for Bob that they have equal pre-tax welfare.

Now, assume that Bob and Sue have identical homothetic preferences. Under a proportional wage or consumption tax their budget constraints and desired consumption points will all shrink toward the origin in equal proportion. Thus these two people with equal pre-tax welfare end up with equal after-tax welfare, which seems

FIGURE 1
Two-Period Example of Lifetime Tax Impacts: Homothetic Preferences

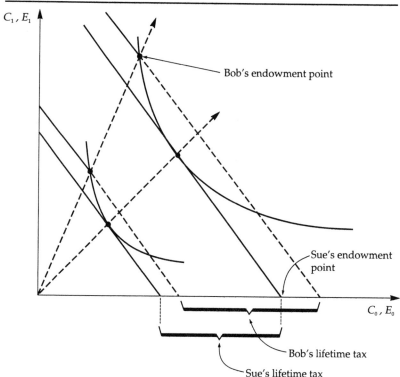

C_1, E_1

Bob's endowment point

Sue's endowment point

C_0, E_0

Bob's lifetime tax

Sue's lifetime tax

like a horizontally equitable result. But note that Bob pays taxes that, discounted at the observed interest rate, exceed Sue's. In other words, people who are disadvantaged because of borrowing constraints will pay more in tax than people with equal pre-tax utility but not subject to borrowing constraints. Does this seem horizontally equitable?

Note further that if Bob and Sue had identical non-homothetic preferences their utility losses due to proportional wage or consumption taxes would differ. Thus, in general there is inequality in utility losses under a proportional wage tax for people with equal pre-tax welfare.

An instructive form of non-homothetic preferences, which is still relatively easy to work with, is the quasi-homothetic form. Under quasi-homotheticity there is a minimum consumption level, $\underline{C}_i$, required for subsistence in a period t. Utility is gained from the excess of C_t over $\underline{C}_t$. Figure 2 illustrates some of the implications for equity of assuming that preferences take this form.

In figure 2 Bob and Sue again have the same pre-tax utility, but now their indifference curves are homothetic with respect to the point $(\underline{C}_0, \underline{C}_1)$, rather than the origin. (Note that $\underline{C}_0 < \underline{C}_1$ as drawn. This could reflect higher subsistence requirements in old age.) Thus preferences are quasi-homothetic. Now if proportional wage or consumption taxes are imposed, Bob suffers a greater loss of utility than Sue, moving to $U_{\text{after}}^{\text{Bob}}$, whereas Sue only falls to the utility level, $U_{\text{after}}^{\text{Sue}}$. An intuitive way of explaining why Bob suffers more is that he is pushed much closer to his subsistence level in the first period than is Sue.

How can the tax burden, measured in utility terms, be equalized between Bob and Sue? In this particular example this could be accomplished by levying a consumption tax with exemptions equal to $\underline{C}_0$ and $\underline{C}_1$ for the young and old respectively.[8] Similar arrangements could be made under a lifetime income tax. However, this approach would not work under an annual wage tax. (This is obvious from the fact that a second-period exemption would have no value for Sue under a wage tax here, since her second-period labour earnings equal zero. Therefore, an exemption would be worth much more to Bob, thus creating horizontal inequity.) What modification to a wage tax would equalize the loss of utility for Bob and Sue?

There are various ways of equalizing the utility loss due to wage taxes for Bob and Sue. These all involve finding some measurable indication of whether or not people are borrowing-constrained. One obvious indication is provided by whether or not they receive interest income. Thus we can clearly discriminate against Sue by taxing her interest income. This will increase her tax burden, bringing her loss of utility more into line with Bob's. The solution is given by the budget constraint AB in figure 2. The slope of this budget constraint equals $-[1 + r(1 - \tau_i)]$, where τ_i is the tax rate on interest income that is required to push Sue down to a post-tax level of utility equal to Bob's.

Figure 2 illustrates that there can be a theoretical argument for taxing interest income on the grounds of horizontal equity if borrowing-constrained individuals are present and the tax system is otherwise based on wage taxation. How relevant this theoretical argument is to tax policy clearly depends on two things: the fraction of taxpayers who are borrowing-constrained, and the severity of

FIGURE 2
Two-Period Example of Lifetime Tax Impacts: Non-Homothetic Preferences

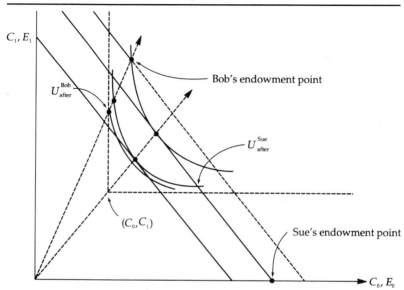

the constraints faced by this group. In addition, note that, as discussed above, any capital income tax will generate some horizontal inequity among the non–borrowing-constrained if they are heterogeneous in saving rates. The latter inequity has to be set against the improved equity between borrowing-constrained and unconstrained groups, which may be achieved by taxing interest income.

There are now a number of studies in North America that use a variety of data to estimate the extent to which consumption is borrowing-constrained (see, for example, Flavin 1981; Hall and Mishkin 1982; and Zeldes 1989). While the results of these studies do not always translate into a proportion of the population that is borrowing-constrained, the "stylized fact" from these studies indicates that about 20 per cent of households in the United States are borrowing-constrained. Whether such a fraction is large enough to justify taxing interest income in order to improve horizontal equity between the constrained and unconstrained is subjective. Some will think 20 per cent a small figure; others will consider it large.

How severe are the constraints faced by the borrowing-constrained group? To deal with this partially we can ask, for example, how large taxes on interest income would have to be, given

TABLE 1

Interest Income Tax Rates Required to Equalize Tax Burdens in Utility Terms for
Borrowing-Constrained and Unconstrained Individuals

A. $\tau_w = 0.3$

		$\underline{C}/E$	
E_0^c/C_0^u	.1	.2	.3
.05	.004	.010	.018
.10	.012	.027	.048
.15	.023	.053	.095
.20	.039	.091	.161

B. $\tau_w = 0.2$

		$\underline{C}/E$	
E_0^c/C_0^u	.1	.2	.3
.05	.003	.006	.010
.10	.007	.016	.027
.15	.131	.031	.055
.20	.023	.053	.095

C. $\tau_w = 0.4$

		$\underline{C}/E$	
E_0^c/C_0^u	.1	.2	.3
.05	.007	.017	.031
.10	.018	.043	.079
.15	.035	.084	.150
.20	.060	.141	.246

Source: Author's calculations.

plausible intertemporal preferences for taxpayers, in order to equalize welfare losses for the constrained and unconstrained. Tables 1
and 2 report the results of such an analysis.

The calculations reported in tables 1 and 2 are based on a two-
period version of the LCM and are meant to be exploratory and
illustrative only. Their starting point is the assumption of quasi-
homothetic preferences in which the utility function is of the constant elasticity of substitution (CES) form with respect to the origin
$(\underline{C}_0, \underline{C}_1)$. Unconstrained individuals receive all their labour income
in the first period. Suitable values are chosen for the taste parame-
ters, interest rate, and tax rates. The first stage in the calculations
is to find unconstrained utility, U^u, and the consumption plan that
would be followed by the unconstrained person, (C_0^u, C_1^u). For each

TABLE 2
Interest Income Tax Rates Required to Equalize Tax Burdens in Utility Terms for
Borrowing-Constrained and Unconstrained Individuals: Sensitivity Testing

A. Interest rate

E_0^c/C_0^u	r		
	.025	.050	.075
.05	.003	.010	.017
.10	.015	.027	.040
.15	.037	.053	.073
.20	.075	.091	.124

B. Time preference

E_0^c/C_0^u	ρ		
	.000	.025	.050
.05	.014	.010	.005
.10	.031	.027	.020
.15	.055	.053	.051
.20	.088	.091	.113

C. Intertemporal substitution

E_0^c/C_0^u	γ		
	1	2	4
.05	.007	.010	.017
.10	.015	.027	n.a.
.15	.026	.053	n.a.
.20	.039	.091	n.a.

Note: Except as indicated, parameters are the same as in the "central case" of the
middle column, table 1, panel A.
Source: Author's own calculations.

set of parameters, I consider four alternative, constrained individuals, differentiated according to the extent to which their first-period earnings, E_0^c, fall below C_0^u. The least constrained individual has E_0^c 5 per cent below C_0^u; the most constrained has a shortfall of 20 per cent. The constrained individuals are then awarded second-period earnings, E_1^c, sufficient to give them $U^c = U^u$, so that the situation corresponds to that of Bob versus Sue in figure 2. Both constrained and unconstrained individuals are then hit with a proportional wage tax – in the central case set at 30 per cent. The resulting utility losses are recorded, and, as explained above, it is found that the loss is greater for the constrained than for the unconstrained individuals. I then compute what alternative interest income tax rates would be required to make the utility losses of the constrained individuals equal to those of the unconstrained.

The central case parameter values are similar to those commonly used in tax policy simulation work. An important parameter is γ, which is the inverse of the intertemporal elasticity of substitution in discretionary consumption.[9] Values of γ greater than unity are generally assumed, in line with considerable evidence that intertemporal consumption choice is relatively inelastic. Here $\gamma = 2$. Next, the central case r is set at .05, indicating a pre-tax interest rate of 5 per cent in real terms. The central case rate of time preference, ρ, is set at .025. This implies a desired growth rate of discretionary consumption equal to 1.25 per cent per year if the rate of interest income tax is zero, and a growth rate of zero if interest income is taxed at a 50 per cent rate.

Next, what about the proportional wage tax rate, τ_w? If set according to the existing levels of payroll and income taxes falling on wages and salaries, τ_w might not be too high. In 1990, personal income taxes in Canada (both federal and provincial) totalled $99.7 billion, and CPP/QPP collected $10.1 billion. If 75 per cent of the PIT revenue were imputed to wages and salaries, the total wage tax bill from these two sources would be about $85 billion. This compares with aggregate wage and salary incomes of $377 billion. On this basis, the representative wage tax rate would be 23 per cent. However, there are other considerations: the consumption opportunities of the borrowing-constrained are reduced not just by taxes on wages and salaries, but also by other taxes (most obviously by sales and excise taxes, which are quite heavy in Canada). However, the PIT is progressive, so that total collections divided by total income overstate the average tax rate faced by the representative taxpayer. As a compromise between these considerations, $\tau_w = 0.3$ is used in the central case calculations. Alternative runs are done with $\tau_w = 0.2$ and $\tau_w = 0.4$.

Finally, the subsistence consumption level must be set in relation to lifetime earnings. In the central case it is set at 20 per cent of before-tax earnings. Whether or not this seems realistic depends on how strong one believes the demands of subsistence are. The mean family income in Canada is around $50,000 at present. Thus, the 20 per cent figure suggests that subsistence costs for the typical family might be about $10,000.

In order to take into account the position of low- and high-income families alternative values of $\underline{C}$ relative to E are considered in each panel of tables 1 and 2. These alternative values are based on subsistence requirements equal to 30 per cent and 10 per cent of income before tax.

In interpreting the $\underline{C}/E$ ratios considered here, it should be borne in mind that, even for families in the middle of the income distribution, there is a considerable gap between before- and after-tax income, so that the 20 per cent ratio on a before-tax basis translates into a considerably higher ratio of $\underline{C}$ to after-tax earnings; and that we will consider borrowing-constrained individuals who have an earnings shortfall of up to 20 per cent below what they would need to be unconstrained. For the borrowing-constrained, the $\underline{C}/E$ ratio, particularly on an after-tax basis, will therefore be quite high.

Turning now to panel A of table 1, we see that the level of interest income taxation needed to equalize the utility losses of the unconstrained and borrowing-constrained families depends very much on both the severity of borrowing constraints and the size of subsistence requirements. With the least severe borrowing constraint and lowest $\underline{C}$ an interest income tax rate of only 0.4 per cent is sufficient. However, with the most severe borrowing constraint, and $\underline{C}/E =$ 0.3, an interest income tax rate of 16.1 per cent is required. If $\underline{C}/E$ is highest for low-income groups this result has the interesting implication that the taxation of interest income compared with wages should be relatively heavier at lower income levels.[10] Vertical equity can of course be achieved by adjusting the wage tax schedule to achieve the desired degree of progressivity.

From panels B and C of table 1, the maximum interest income tax rate called for declines to 9.5 per cent if τ_w is reduced to 0.2, and rises to 24.6 per cent if τ_w is raised to 0.4. Thus as τ_w rises, the required interest income tax rate rises relative to τ_w.

Table 2 shows the results of some sensitivity testing. Experiments are performed with the interest rate, r, the time preference rate, ρ, and the intertemporal substitution parameter, γ. Higher values of each of these parameters increase the required interest income tax rate. Thus, if one believed that the average real before-tax interest rate exceeded 5 per cent, that the intertemporal elasticity of substitution was significantly less than 0.5 ($\gamma > 2$), that borrowing constraints were severe, and that subsistence consumption requirements were relatively high, then interest income taxes would have to be levied at a rate comparable with that on wage income in order to achieve an equal tax burden, in utility terms, between the unconstrained and the borrowing-constrained.

Note that, as pointed out earlier, the strength of the justification for interest income taxation advanced here depends on the proportion of the population that is borrowing-constrained, as well as on the severity of the inequities between a typical constrained individual and a typical unconstrained one. We must not forget that interest income tax creates horizontal inequities within the unconstrained population. Thus, there is a trade off, and a compromise has to be reached. If an interest income tax rate close to τ_w were required to equalize utility tax burdens between the constrained and the unconstrained, but only 5 to 10 per cent of the population were borrowing-constrained, then the compromise level of interest income tax would be less than τ_w.

Finally, it should be emphasized that the above argument for interest income taxation assumes that the basic tax system is an annual wage tax. It has not been demonstrated that borrowing constraints create equity problems that cannot be dealt with under a consumption tax or lifetime income tax. In fact, in the example investigated in this section it would be possible to avoid inequity between the constrained and unconstrained using these alternative tax bases.

Private Risk and Uncertainty

The role of wage, consumption, and income taxes in a life-cycle model with various sources of uncertainty has been analysed most recently by Ahsan (1989, 1990). There are two basic kinds of uncertainty to examine: risky earnings and uncertain rates of return.

We have already discussed the effects of fluctuations in earnings on horizontal equity under wage and consumption taxes. When the fluctuations are foreseen, there is no problem with horizontal equity under a consumption tax, but with an increasing-rate progressive wage tax there will be inequity in the absence of averaging arrangements. The latter problem is, of course, still present if the fluctuations are not perfectly foreseen. There is no advantage to imposing interest income tax. This form of taxation would not compensate for the possible inequities caused by a lack of averaging arrangements.

Let us turn to risky rates of return. For simplicity, let us adopt the two-period version of the life-cycle model, and suppose, initially, that different investors (Margaret and Janet) have access to assets with different degrees of riskiness. In particular, suppose that Janet has access only to a safe asset with rate of return r, while Margaret invests in a risky asset with expected return R, and a standard deviation of returns, σ. Janet and Margaret have the same preferences, have equal labour earnings (received only in the first period), and are both expected utility maximizers. For simplicity, assume that they have equal expected utility in the no-tax situation:[11]

$$U(C_0^J, C_1^J) = E\left[U(C_0^M, C_1^M)\right] \tag{5}$$

or, if utility takes the additive form and the risky asset has two possible payoffs, $\underline{R}$ and $\overline{R}$, which occur with probabilities π and $(1 - \pi)$, respectively:

$$u(C_0^J) + \frac{u(C_0^J)}{(1+\rho)}$$

$$= u(C_0^M) + \frac{1}{(1+\rho)}\{\pi u[(E_0 - C_0^M)\overline{R}] + (1-\pi)\, u[(E_0 - C_0^M)\overline{R}]\} \tag{6}$$

This will require that $R > r$, in order to compensate Margaret for holding the risky rather than the safe asset.[12]

Now suppose that we impose a proportional consumption tax at rate τ_c. If $u(\cdot)$ has the popular constant elasticity form, Janet and Margaret will suffer the same decline in expected utility as each other, and will simply cut back planned consumption in all periods/ states of the world by the fraction τ_c. (With other utility functions matters will be more complicated. For the purposes of this section, however, those complications will be ignored.) Also note that *ex post* Janet and Margaret will have borne lifetime tax burdens proportional to their actual consumption. Thus, there is a strong case that horizontal equity is achieved to a reasonable approximation with uncertain rate of return using a consumption tax, without any need for supplementary taxes. Note that in our present tax system registered assets – i.e., those held under RRSPs and RPPs – receive consumption tax treatment, and so are handled appropriately if they have risky rates of return.

The situation with a wage tax, or with non-registered assets (which effectively receive wage tax treatment), is different. For Janet, who is not exposed to risk, an equal-present-value-yield wage tax is fully equivalent to a consumption tax. For Margaret this is not true. The reason is that the difference in timing of wage and consumption taxes alters their impact on risk exposure. In the simple example we are dealing with, wages are known with certainty and wage taxes will, correspondingly, be non-stochastic. Under the consumption tax how much tax you pay in the second period (and therefore over the lifetime) depends on whether $\underline{R}$ or $\overline{R}$ is received. If the low payoff is received, taxes will be lower, and conversely if the high payoff is received. This means that the government shares risk with the taxpayer. Moving to a wage tax eliminates this sharing, so that even if the wage tax burden is equal in expected present value to the former consumption tax burden, the taxpayer will be worse off.

Ahsan (1989, 1990) establishes that a theoretically simple (but practically difficult) adjustment is sufficient to make the wage tax fully equivalent to a consumption tax. This adjustment is therefore sufficient to remove any horizontal inequity under a wage tax between people who face different levels of risk. The solution is to tax above-normal returns on assets as if they were labour income. In our example, this would mean taxing $(E_0 - C_{\underline{0}}^M)(\underline{R} - r)$ or $(E_0 - C_{\underline{0}}^M)(\overline{R} - r)$ at rate τ_w.

Note that, since $\underline{R} < r$ is certainly possible, the tax system will, in some states, allow a deduction for below-normal rates of return. Clearly, in any actual tax system this aspect would have to be strictly controlled. Still, because $R > r$, on average investment income tax revenue would be positive.

The theoretical desirability of taxing above-normal returns on non-registered assets, which I will refer to below as the "Ahsan proposal," has been recognized by many consumption tax proponents. The older argument was often couched in terms of *ex ante* versus *ex post* equity. In the example we are discussing, a consumption tax gives both *ex ante* and *ex post* equity since burdens are proportional to expected and actual consumption. However, a wage tax leads to a problem of *ex post* inequity, since those who reap $\overline{R}$ do not have higher lifetime tax liability. (There is no *ex ante* equity problem in the example since *ex ante* both investors are equally well off.) An obvious solution is to tax people on above-normal returns. Discounting at r, *ex post* lifetime consumption must equal the present value of wages plus these abnormal returns. Thus, the Ahsan scheme would provide both *ex ante* and *ex post* equity.

In practice it is generally considered infeasible to tax above-normal returns on non-registered assets. For this reason, consumption and lifetime income tax advocates concerned about the *ex ante* versus *ex post* equity problem have generally argued that people should be allowed to hold most of their assets in registered form. They contend that there should be a generous exemption for interest income, but that other income on non-registered assets should be fully taxed (see, for example, Beach, Boadway, and Bruce 1988 and Economic Council of Canada 1987). The latter provision would encourage people to hold assets in registered form, and would also ensure that above-normal returns did not go untaxed.

The Ahsan scheme also relates to the proposals made by the Queen's University school of public finance economists in Canada to tax business income on a cash-flow basis. As discussed in Boadway, Bruce, and Mintz (1984), cash-flow business taxes are equivalent to taxes on pure economic profit or "rent" – that is, on above-normal returns in business. Thus, for non-corporate business income the Ahsan proposal can be achieved simply by taxing business income on a cash-flow basis under the PIT. If CIT is retained, and is implemented in cash-flow form, then attention to corporate-source income is required only under the PIT in order to correct the tax rate – that is, to achieve "integration."[13]

It is interesting to ask how the existing taxation of investment income compares with what would be recommended under the Ahsan scheme. To answer this question fully would require a very detailed inquiry into the effects of both CIT and PIT with reference to business and investment income. Here, I can only scratch the surface.

Even leaving aside CIT, the taxation of capital income under the Canadian income tax system is complex. Different assets and taxpayers are taxed at widely varying rates. At one extreme, a large accumulation of assets is now held in registered form – that is, in RRSPs and RPPs, which effectively receive consumption tax treatment. At the opposite extreme, interest income is now fully taxed – both on its real and purely inflationary components.[14] This is in contradiction to the Ahsan scheme, since interest essentially represents the safe return, r, which would not be taxed under this scheme. What of other forms of capital income? Corporate-source income is given special treatment in two ways: via the dividend tax credit and provisions for capital gains taxation. The latter include the lifetime capital gains deduction, deferral, and preferential rates of capital gains tax.

In terms of equity, the issue with these various forms of capital income taxation is whether the effective tax rates imposed are greater or less than those required under the Ahsan scheme, that is,

$$\frac{\tau_w\,(R-r)}{R}\;.$$

In cases where corporate income tax is not in fact being paid, say due to excessive CIT incentives, the relief from the dividend tax credit and lifetime capital gains deduction is likely too great. However, this does not seem to be the representative situation. Where corporate income tax is being paid, the total burden on capital income can easily exceed that required by the Ahsan scheme even with a generous dividend tax credit and lifetime capital gains deduction.

There is one area in which a quantitative comparison of existing tax rates with those suggested by the Ahsan scheme can be readily and interestingly made. This uses the methods explored by Glenday and Davies (1990) for computing accrual equivalent marginal tax rates (AEMTRs) on personal capital gains.[15] The effective burden of capital gains taxes is reduced both by deferral, and by the 25 per cent exclusion of such gains from taxable income. The value of deferral is affected by the rate of return on the investment and the holding period. By making a range of alternative assumptions on these parameters, it is possible to get an idea of the range of AEMTRs on personal capital gains in practice. This can be compared with the effective tax rates that would be imposed under the Ahsan scheme.

Table 3 compares the tax rates on investment income that would be dictated by the Ahsan scheme with AEMTRs on capital gains under the current Canadian PIT, assuming an ordinary marginal tax rate of 0.5. (The burden of other taxes – for example, CIT – is ignored.) It is assumed that $r = .05$, and that there is no inflation. (The implications of changing r can be easily computed if one wishes to make an alternative assumption on this parameter.) Alternative realized or *ex post* rates of return on capital income, and alternative holding periods are assumed. AEMTRs are computed as explained in Glenday and Davies (1990, 192–4), taking into account the fact that, since 1990, 75 per cent of net capital gains are taxed.

Table 3 indicates that the effective tax rate on investment income called for under the Ahsan scheme rises with the realized rate of return on the risky asset, whereas the AEMTR given by actual taxes generally declines with the realized return. Another feature to note is that, as is well known, AEMTRs decline with the length of the

TABLE 3
Accrual Equivalent Marginal Tax Rates on Personal Capital Gains under Canadian
PIT and Marginal Tax Rates under "Ahsan Scheme"

	Realized Rate of Return				
Term (yrs.)	.025	.050	.075	.100	.150
A. Current system					
1	.375	.375	.375	.375	.375
5	.364	.353	.342	.332	.314
10	.350	.326	.304	.284	.250
20	.323	.278	.240	.210	.165
30	.297	.237	.192	.159	.117
B. "Ahsan scheme"					
	−.500	.000	.167	.250	.333

Note: Calculations assume an ordinary marginal tax rate of 0.5, a rate of return of
.05 on the riskless asset, and zero inflation. Under the current system only 3/4 of
capital gains are taxed. Accrual Equivalent Marginal Tax Rates are computed as explained in Glenday and Davies (1990).
Source: Author's own calculations.

holding period, reflecting the increasing deferral benefit. When the realized return is less than r, the Ahsan scheme calls for a negative effective tax rate, whereas the actual system produces AEMTRs fairly close to the statutory rate of 0.375 (75 per cent of the ordinary marginal tax rate of 0.5). At the other extreme, when the realized return equals 0.15, the effective tax rate under the Ahsan scheme is 0.333, whereas an AEMTR of this magnitude is reached only for holding periods of less than four years. If the realized return equals 0.1, the AEMTR equals the effective tax rate under the Ahsan scheme when the holding period is 14 years.

The conclusion from this exercise is that, if we ignore corporate income taxes and the lifetime capital gains deduction, the taxation of capital gains is at about the "correct" level from an equity view-point when returns are high relative to the return on a safe asset and holding periods are not too long. Existing capital gains taxes are too heavy when returns are either not much above the safe return, or are actually below it; and they are too low when both returns and holding periods are high. Thus existing capital gains taxes are a fairly poor substitute for the equitable form of taxation I have referred to here as the Ahsan scheme, even if we neglect the complications of CIT and lifetime capital gains deductions.

Intertemporal Equity

Two intertemporal equity issues will be discussed here. The first relates to what might be termed "remedial" taxation for individuals who have not paid sufficient tax in the past; the second concerns intergenerational equity.

Remedial Taxation

It can be argued that a good tax system would tend to make up for past errors. Some people have accumulated wealth partly with the help of inappropriately low tax payments in the past. In other words, part of their current wealth represents unpaid taxes. I will refer to this component below as "unpaid tax wealth." It would seem desirable, on both horizontal and vertical equity grounds that this wealth, or the income it produces, should be taxed to some extent, even if this comes at the cost of taxing the normal return on legitimate wealth. In other words, there is an equity motive for wealth or capital income taxes that may be referred to as the desire for "remedial" taxation.

Suppose that one attempts to implement the Ahsan scheme, but for some reason gifts and inheritances are excluded from the tax base. The normal return on taxpayers' wealth, including their unpaid tax wealth, would never be taxed. This defect can be removed by making sure that gifts and inheritances are also taxed, so that remedial taxation will occur once a generation. However, if, as in Canada today, there are no capital transfer taxes, there is an equity argument for other taxes to be imposed to attack unpaid tax wealth.

The desire for remedial taxation may be an important part of the reason why we have such a range and variety of taxes, the implicit reasoning being that "if you don't get caught by one, then you'll at least get hit by some of the others." The public may take some comfort from the knowledge that even clever real estate speculators, who may benefit from a variety of income tax shelters, have to pay GST and PST on personal consumption expenditures. It may also take comfort from the notion that, although there are loopholes, the attempt to tax capital income at corporate and personal levels attacks unpaid tax wealth to some extent.

The remedial taxation argument provides fairly strong equity grounds for favouring income taxes over the Ahsan scheme if gifts and inheritances are not taxed. However, note that it provides a

TABLE 4
Intertemporal Equity Example

	Period	E	C	S	W	T
A. Joe						
	0	$90	$45	$36	$0	$9
	1	10	41	−36	36	5
	Lifetime	100	86	0	−	14
B. Bob						
	0	$10	$45	$−36	$ 0	$1
	1	90	9	36	−36	45
	Lifetime	100	54	0	−	46

Note: E = earnings
  C = consumption
  S = saving
  W = wealth at beginning of period
  T = tax

weaker argument against switching from income to consumption taxes. Ultimately, wealth gets consumed – if not by this generation, then by the next, or the next. Thus, in the end, a consumption tax hits unpaid tax wealth and imposes remedial taxation. Moreover, it does this without imposing an inappropriate burden on legitimate wealth.

Intergenerational Equity

An argument that is frequently made for an annual, as opposed to a lifetime, income tax is that the demand for, and provision of, government goods and services changes over time, and does so in a fashion that is not entirely predictable. From this it is suggested that people should pay tax according to how well off they are today, rather than over the lifetime. This position can lead to some curious results, as can be shown by the simple example set out in table 4.

  Consider a society with two members (Joe and Bob) in each birth cohort, and look at just two time periods. Assume that the only source of income is wages (so that $r = 0$); that the government budget must balance in every period; and that people attempt to smooth their consumption perfectly over time. Joe earns $90 in the first period and $10 in the second; Bob earns $10 in the first period and $90 in the second. In the first period government expenditure equals $10; a tax rate of 10 per cent is levied; and both Joe and Bob, expecting their lifetime after-tax income to be $90, consume $45. When the second period is reached, government expenditure increases sharply to $50. A proportional income (or wage) tax of 50 per cent is required for budget balance. Joe is lucky – he earns only $10 in the second period and so gets off with a $5 tax payment, bringing his lifetime taxes to just $14. Bob, however, is required to pay a $45 tax payment in the second period, and pays a total of $46 over his lifetime. Joe's and Bob's lifetime tax burdens are extremely unequal, despite the fact that they have equal lifetime income and may have benefited equally from government expenditures.

If the proposal to tax "lifetime income" were taken literally, as suggested by Vickrey (1947), a record of Joe's and Bob's past earnings and tax payments would be kept by the tax authority, and when the second period was reached Bob would have received a refund of $15 and Joe would have been asked to contribute $25, so that each would end up paying $30 in lifetime taxes. This arrangement would follow Vickrey's proposal for lifetime cumulative averaging. There are a couple of important points to make about this:

• If Joe and Bob benefit equally from government expenditure in both periods, then the Vickrey solution seems entirely equitable and the annual income tax approach distinctly inequitable.
• The proposals for "lifetime income" taxes, which have been made in Canada (for example, by Davies and St-Hilaire 1987 and the Economic Council of Canada 1987), would not implement the Vickrey scheme.

Theoretically, if there were no limits on RRSP contributions, and negative balances were allowed, people could achieve full averaging and replicate the situation under the Vickrey scheme. However, given imperfect tax planning and the uncertainties taxpayers face, as well as restrictions on RRSP contributions, such perfect averaging will not be achieved. Thus, with a real-world lifetime income tax, Bob would still suffer as a result of having most of his wages received when tax rates were high, and Joe would still benefit from the opposite. The differences in lifetime tax burdens would not be as extreme, however, as under a pure annual income or wage tax.

Why does the lifetime income tax approach not seem equitable to some when expenditure levels are fluctuating over time? In part, it may be felt that benefits do not accrue to different income groups equally. Suppose higher-income groups benefit more. Then, in terms of the above example, Joe will benefit less from government expenditure over his lifetime since, when he is a high earner (period 0), expenditure is low. In contrast, Bob does very well since he is in a position to reap large benefits when expenditures are high. The only problem with this argument is that it is not clear that, overall, people with high current income receive greater benefits than others from government expenditure.[16]

Alternatively, there may be some concern about people who do not anticipate fluctuations in their incomes properly, that is, those who do not save adequately against the threat of a rainy day. In our example, suppose that Joe mistakenly believes that his high income is going to go on permanently. He does not save in the first period, and so has only his wages of $10 to consume in the second period. If the tax rate has gone up to 50 per cent he will pay taxes of $5 and be in a miserable situation. This situation would be made totally intolerable if he were presented with a total tax bill of $21 to bring his lifetime taxes up to the level required by the Vickrey scheme.

But nobody is suggesting that lifetime taxes à la Vickrey should be implemented in Canada. Lifetime averaging only enters to the extent that people save via RRSP/RPPs. Thus, if Joe did not think there was any need to save, he would have only his wage income of $10 on which to pay tax in the second period. If he had deposited $10 or $20 in an RRSP in the first period, on the other hand, he would of course have to pay tax on this in the second period. However, the tax would not be punitive or impossible to pay. It would be based on the resources that Joe actually had available to spend in the second period.

My conclusion, therefore, is that criticisms of lifetime income tax proposals on the grounds of possible intergenerational inequities relative to annual income taxes are based on an erroneous comparison. This mistaken comparison is between annual income taxes and something like Vickrey's lifetime cumulative averaging scheme, which would indeed create problems, but which is not the form of lifetime income tax that people have been proposing for Canada.

An important point emerging from this discussion is that registered savings vehicles spread people's taxable income over the lifetime so that the taxes they pay in a period are based roughly on the resources they have available for consumption at that time. If registered saving opportunities were absent, one consequence would be that the taxable income of retired persons would be much smaller than that of younger people. We are living in a period of quite generous public services to the elderly. Being able to tax the retired on their entire withdrawals from registered saving, rather than merely on their interest or investment income means that their tax burdens are much more in line with the value of the services that they are receiving, and which future generations may not receive on such a lavish scale when they themselves are old.

Conclusion

The purpose of this paper has been to ask whether modelling real-world factors like capital market imperfections, uncertainty, non-steady states, and "non-ideal" taxes justifies the use of multiple tax bases to achieve tax equity. With perfect capital markets, certainty, a steady-state economy, and access to ideal taxes, horizontal and vertical equity can be achieved via either a consumption tax (if we take a dynastic view), or a lifetime income tax (if we view each generation's life cycle in isolation). Practical implementation of either approach requires the use of a "personal income tax" with generous RRSP/RPP contribution limits, supplemented by cash-flow business taxes. In the case of a lifetime income tax, gifts and inheritances would be included in the "PIT" base. Additional taxes could be levied as user fees in some cases, or in order to combat externalities (as in the cases of gasoline, alcohol, and tobacco).

Leaving aside benefit taxes, and charges motivated by externalities, there is still a remarkable mixture of different taxes in Canada. To some extent this may be explained by an ambivalence between a dynastic outlook (which may help to explain why we do not tax gifts and inheritances) and a life-cycle viewpoint (possibly explaining why our PIT is not replaced by a personal consumption tax). However, neither the dynastic nor the life-cycle viewpoint calls for capital income taxation under ideal conditions. One of the main challenges in this paper, therefore, has been to see whether adding real-world complexities provides a rigorous basis for elements of capital income taxation.

It is sometimes thought that when economies are not in steady state, say because government expenditures vary widely and perhaps unpredictably over time, one must tax annual income (including capital income) to achieve intergenerational fairness. However, it is possible that a lifetime income tax of the kind that has been actively proposed in Canada would do a better job of ensuring that each generation foots a tax bill commensurate with the benefits it reaps from government expenditure. The kind of lifetime income tax that has been seriously proposed in Canada is not a lifetime cumulative averaging scheme, which would create problems; it relies, instead, on the self-averaging of the RRSP/RPP system. This means that people are not taxed at today's rates on income they earned and consumed years ago. Instead they are taxed in relation to the resources they have available for current consumption.

The failure to use ideal tax bases may result in the need to impose "remedial" taxation in order to get at wealth accumulated from unpaid taxes. Under some circumstances we have seen that this provides a "second-best" argument for taxing capital income. For example, if there are practical or political difficulties in taxing gifts and inheritances, but it is believed that they should be taxed, capital income taxes may compensate to some extent for their non-taxation.

We have seen also that the existence of risky investments, as well as pure economic rent, motivates some taxation of capital income. Under either an ideal personal consumption tax or lifetime income tax there would be cash-flow taxation for both corporate and non-corporate businesses, and taxation of above-normal returns on non-business assets (for example, on houses or collectables). It has been argued here, however, that these forms of taxation are approximated only very crudely by existing taxation of capital income under our combined CIT-PIT system.

Finally, the implications of borrowing constraints were investigated. A stylized fact from U.S. studies is that as many as 20 per cent of households may be borrowing-constrained. Taxes that would otherwise be horizontally equitable may impose a greater burden in utility terms on constrained than unconstrained individuals. An example is an annual wage tax. It has been demonstrated here that significant taxation of real-interest income could be conceivably required to avoid the horizontal inequity between constrained and unconstrained individuals that could be created under such a tax. However, it has also been pointed out that it may be possible largely to avoid such inequity under consumption tax or lifetime income tax approaches. This is an area that requires further study.

In conclusion, this paper has found an equity basis for some important broad features of tax mix in Canada, but has disputed the equity foundations for other elements of the mix. In particular, the equity rationale for various aspects of capital income taxation has been questioned. The arguments for capital income taxation examined here are all of the "second-best" variety. The best approach to both horizontal and vertical equity lies in a personal consumption tax if one takes the dynastic view, or a lifetime income tax if the life-cycle framework is favoured.

Notes

1 See Davies and St-Hilaire (1987). A variant that does not call for the taxation of gifts and inheritances, and was meant to be practically implementable, was proposed by the Economic Council of Canada (1987).

2 It may be objected that, in practice, there are limits on the tax rates that can be applied to particular tax bases. To tax the rich adequately, for example, some might feel that an annual wealth tax is required since it would be politically difficult to raise the top marginal income tax rate much above its current value. The present paper makes no attempt to deal with such considerations. The political economy of taxation is not studied here.

3 A dynasty would have homothetic intertemporal preferences if, in the absence of taxes, its relative consumption in different generations did not vary with dynastic wealth. A doubling of the dynasty's wealth, for example, would result in a doubling of every generation's consumption.

4 The taxes will generally not be equivalent in terms of their impact on saving.

5 If a rising marginal rate is desired, then annual wage or consumption taxes may generate horizontal inequity, as discussed in the last section, due to a lack of averaging. In general, if a rising marginal tax rate is desired, then lifetime averaging is required for complete horizontal equity.

6 All the points on an indifference curve correspond to a particular level of "utility." The slope of the indifference curve here tells us about an individual's intertemporal preferences.

7 Like Bob, under the assumptions used in this section, Sue could not borrow if she wanted to. However, she does not want to borrow, and the borrowing constraint is accordingly said to be "ineffective."

8 This arrangement resembles the Carter Report's recommendation not to tax "non-discretionary income," except for the fact that the Carter Report was dealing with income, rather than consumption taxation. An

income tax, even with exemptions $\underline{C}_0$ and $\underline{C}_1$ would not solve the problem here, as discussed in the text.

9 The intertemporal elasticity of substitution in discretionary consumption equals the per cent rise in the ratio, $(C_1 - \underline{C}_1)/(C_0 - \underline{C}_0)$, which would occur as a result of a 1 per cent increase in the intertemporal price ratio, $1 + r(1 - \tau_i)$. It is a measure of the sensitivity of intertemporal consumption plans to changes in the interest rate.

10 This runs directly counter to the former \$1000 exemption for interest (and some other forms of investment income in certain years) in force under the Canadian PIT from 1974 to 1987. That exemption fully sheltered interest income for many low- and middle-income taxpayers.

11 The assumption that individuals attempt to maximize expected utility (where the term "expected" is used in its mathematical sense) is the conventional way of modelling consumer choice under uncertainty. The axioms under which persons will choose to behave in this way were first formulated by Von Neumann and Morgenstern (1953). For an informal explanation see Layard and Walters (1978, ch. 13.)

12 Sandmo (1970) and Dreze and Modigliani (1972) established conditions under which savings will decline as risk increases in this setting. The substitution effect of increased risk is for savings to decline whenever the investor is risk-averse. However, the income effect may go in either direction. Thus, the conditions are rather complex. It is not clear whether Margaret will consume more or less than Janet in the first period, especially since the fact that her expected rate of return is higher than Janet's opposes the substitution effect created by the risk she faces.

13 If there were a single CIT rate of, say, 40 per cent, but personal marginal tax rates varied from zero to 50 per cent, then some system to provide credits for CIT paid and to apply the PIT marginal rates is required. There are several ways in which this can be done.

14 Formerly, the Canadian tax system allowed a reasonably generous exemption for interest income. The \$1000 interest income deduction introduced in 1974 would be worth about \$3200 in today's dollars – enough to shelter the interest on at least a \$30,000 GIC.

15 An AEMTR is the marginal tax rate that, if applied to capital gains on an annual accrual basis, would impose the same burden on the taxpayer, in present value terms, as do actual capital gains taxes.

16 While high-income people benefit more (for example, from airports, police protection, higher education, and the like), we do have very sizeable transfer payments and social welfare expenditures that are aimed at the other end of the income distribution. Also, those forms of government expenditure that benefit higher-income groups may do so

more in relation to people's permanent rather than current income (likely the case for education). Thus, for the sake of equity, one would still want to tax on the basis of lifetime rather than on current income.

Bibliography

Ahsan, Syed. 1989. "Choice of Tax Base under Uncertainty." *Journal of Public Economics* 40: 99–134
– 1990. "Risk-Taking, Savings, and Taxation: A Re-examination of Theory and Policy." *Canadian Journal of Economics* 23: 408–33
Barro, Robert J. 1974. "Are Government Bonds Net Wealth?" *Journal of Political Economy* 82: 1095–1117
Beach, Charles M., Robin W. Boadway, and Neil Bruce. 1988. *Taxation and Savings in Canada.* Ottawa: Economic Council of Canada
Boadway, Robin, Neil Bruce, and Jack Mintz, 1984. "The Role and Design of the Corporate Income Tax." *Scandinavian Journal of Economics* 86: 286–99
– 1987. *Taxes on Capital Income in Canada: Analysis and Policy.* Canadian Tax Paper No. 80. Toronto: Canadian Tax Foundation
Canada. Royal Commission on Taxation. 1966. *Report* (Carter Report). Ottawa: Queen's Printer
Carter Report. See Canada, Royal Commission on Taxation.
Davies, James B. 1988. "Incidence of Tax Expenditures in a Lifetime Framework: Theory and an Application to RRSPs." In *Tax Expenditures and Government Policy*, ed. Neil Bruce, 339–67. Kingston: John Deutsch Institute, Queen's University
Davies, James B., and France St-Hilaire. 1987. *Reforming Capital Income Taxation in Canada: Efficiency and Distributional Effects of Alternative Options.* Ottawa: Economic Council of Canada
Dreze, J.H., and F. Modigliani. 1972. "Consumption Decision under Uncertainty." *Journal of Economic Theory* 5: 308–35
Economic Council of Canada. 1987. *Road Map for Tax Reform, The Taxation of Savings and Investment.* Ottawa: Economic Council of Canada
Flavin, Marjorie A. 1981. "The Adjustment of Consumption to Changing Expectations about Future Income." *Journal of Political Economy* 89: 974–1009
Glenday, Graham, and James B. Davies. 1990. "Accrual Equivalent Marginal Tax Rates for Personal Financial Assets." *Canadian Journal of Economics* 23: 189–209
Hall, Robert E., and Frederic S. Mishkin. 1982. "The Sensitivity of Con-

sumption to Transitory Income: Estimates from Panel Data on House-holds." *Econometrica* 50: 461–82

Layard, P.R.G., and A.A. Walters. 1978. *Microeconomic Theory*. New York: McGraw-Hill

Modigliani, F., and A. Ando. 1957. "Tests of the Life Cycle Hypothesis of Saving: Comments and Suggestions." *Bulletin of the Oxford University Institute of Statistics* 19: 99–124

Modigliani, F., and R. Brumberg. 1954. "Utility Analysis and the Consumption Function: An Interpretation of Cross-Section Data." In *Post-Keynesian Economics*, ed., K.K. Kurihara, 388–436. New Brunswick, NJ: Rutgers University Press

National Council of Welfare. 1979. *The Hidden Welfare System Revisited*. Ottawa: National Council of Welfare

Sandmo, A. 1970. "The Effect of Uncertainty on Saving Decisions." *Review of Economic Studies* 37: 353–60

Von Neumann, John, and Oskar Morgenstern. 1953. *Theory of Games and Economic Behavior*, 3rd ed. Princeton, NJ: Princeton University Press

Vickrey, William. 1947. *Agenda for Progressive Taxation*. New York: The Ronald Press Co.

Zeldes, S. 1989. "Consumption and Liquidity Constraints: An Empirical Investigation." *Journal of Political Economy* 97: 305–46

4 What Is the Appropriate Tax Unit for the 1990s and Beyond?

MAUREEN A. MALONEY

Introduction

One of the most perplexing issues for any tax reformer is the choice
of tax unit. There is no easy answer to the question, although some
answers are more obviously wrong than others. In considering an
appropriate tax unit for the 1990s, this paper attempts to unravel
some of the complexities of the issue, to discuss some options, and
to propose tentative solutions to the problem.

At the outset, it is important to recognize that no tax reform
takes place in isolation from the larger socioeconomic and political
context of its time – a subject somewhat beyond the scope of this
paper. Any proposal concerning the appropriate tax unit must take
into account a number of contextual factors, such as changing family
structures, the increasing participation of women in the waged outside workforce, and the alarming disparities of both income and
wealth (Maloney 1991) among taxpayers. Moreover, each of these
trends must be considered from the perspective of different groups
in our society, in view of their particular needs and resources. Specific tax reforms must also be assessed in conjunction with other
aspects of the tax system. The distributive impact of a tax change
can be properly understood only in relation to the tax system as
a whole, including property taxes, school and municipal taxes, tobacco and alcohol taxes, import/export tariffs, and sales taxes. This
analysis should also factor in the distributive effects of any licensing
or user fees and, particularly in light of the 1992 Ontario budget,

lotteries and gambling operations. Many of these changes are likely to be regressive in their overall impact. An analysis of these contextual factors is, unfortunately, beyond the scope of this paper. The purpose of identifying them here is only to highlight them as important issues that obviously require further study and consideration.

A Framework for Evaluation

I will use the common tax evaluative criteria – equity, economic efficiency, neutrality, and administrative simplicity – as a loose framework for discussion. All of these are interpreted through my own particular "lens." One further criterion, equality, is also used here. How then are these to be defined?

Definitions

Equity. All measures should be equitable – both horizontally and vertically. Horizontal equity is achieved if the measure treats like cases alike. Vertical equity is achieved if the measure gives appropriately different treatment to cases that are not alike. The latter proposition is traditionally used to support the notion of progressive taxation.

Economic Efficiency. All tax measures must be assessed with respect to their effect on economic activity. The following questions must be asked: Will the introduction of such a measure aid or hamper productivity and efficiency? And, if so, to what extent?

Neutrality. All tax measures should be neutral in their impact. That is, they should neither distort the allocation of resources in the market for labour or capital, nor influence individual choices about economic or social relationships. This criterion, perhaps more than all the others, embodies the liberal paradigm. Tax systems should not impede the individual choices or decisions of free and autonomous people. The flaw, of course, lies in the assumption that all individuals are free to make social and economic choices. In particular, the neutrality principle conveniently ignores the reality of a pre-tax world in which income and wealth are unevenly distributed.

Administrative Simplicity. All tax measures should, as far as possible, be easy to understand and apply in order to facilitate compliance and enforcement.

Equality. This criterion was first introduced as a tax-policy objective in a 1987 report for the Advisory Council on the Status of Women (Maloney 1987). Equality demands more than equity; it requires that all tax measures be evaluated in terms of their impact on different segments of society, particularly disadvantaged groups. While current interpretations of equity, both vertical and horizontal, may catch class biases, they do not go far enough because the need for equity is generally recognized with respect only to the distribution of income, and even then with very limited effect. A truly progressive tax system would help bring about substantive equality by reducing the vast disparities of income, and even more so wealth, that exist in Canada. Furthermore, the existing concept of equity does not address other dimensions of social disadvantage. Equality demands that tax laws be analysed to determine whether they prejudice particular groups in society such as women, aboriginal peoples, racial and ethnic minorities, people with mental and physical disabilities, and gay and lesbian persons.

Very little analysis of this type has been done except with respect to the differential impact of the tax system on women. One of the major obstacles hindering this research is the lack of adequate information and statistics on these different groups to permit accurate assessment of the impact upon them of certain tax measures. Such analysis is needed to ensure that tax measures promote not only formal equality, but also substantive equality by redressing the historical and current social and tax mistreatment of certain groups and by ridding both the tax system of its systemic biases and enacting measures that help ensure the equal treatment of disadvantaged groups in our society.

Although the criteria set out above provide a useful framework to evaluate different tax measures, they are not without difficulty. The criteria are not necessarily compatible with each other. Indeed, unless economic efficiency is equated with neutrality (which some economists do argue), a clash will occur whenever measures are introduced that distort the market in the name of economic efficiency. Similarly, there are obvious potential clashes between the concepts of neutrality and economic efficiency on the one hand and equity and equality on the other. Where such conflicts occur, however, equality must be the overriding criterion. Economic efficiency must not be maintained or fostered at the expense of disadvantaged groups. If certain measures are deemed necessary to improve economic efficiency, they can be introduced provided appropriate transfers are made to compensate for the disparate impact such provisions may have on certain groups. With these objectives in mind, I will now examine the various options available when considering the tax unit.

The Choices of Tax Unit

The available options for the appropriate tax unit are deceptively few and simple. Three choices are usually trotted out as the potential candidates: the individual, the marital/partnership unit, and the family unit. Other units could be devised (for example, communes or cooperatives). In this paper, I will concentrate primarily on the individual and marital/partnership units. The marital/partnership unit has been selected because this is potentially the strongest candidate for a joint or collective tax unit and certainly the one that is the most serious rival of the individual taxation unit currently utilized in the Income Tax Act (The Income Tax Act, Revised Statutes of Canada 1952). In this paper, unless otherwise stated, the term "marital unit" has a broader definition than that of a "legally married couple." Included within the marital unit are common-law relationships, be they heterosexual, gay, or lesbian. At the moment, the Income Tax Act, for the most part, takes into account only legal marriages. The 1992 federal budget proposed a broader definition of "spouse" to cover common-law partnerships, which took effect on 1 January 1993. However, the act remains heterosexist. If federal human rights legislation is introduced, prohibiting discrimination on the basis of sexual orientation, the current discrimination in the act would presumably be repealed. There is no justification for the continued heterosexist bias of the tax system.

The pros and cons of the individual versus the marital unit, especially as they affect women, are examined below at some length. However, at the end of this exposition it will become apparent that there is no clear answer as to what should constitute the optimum tax unit. The answer does not lie in the adoption of one option for all purposes; rather, the tax unit must vary depending on the specific provision at issue, with the guidance of some overarching rules or principles that will help ascertain the correct tax measure in a particular case. Different types of living arrangements must always be factored into these calculations. Tax measures that still relate to patriarchal notions of the "traditional family" (meaning a legally married woman and man with children, where the woman works only in the home) are outdated and do not capture the full texture of modern-day living arrangements.

The Individual Tax Unit

Advocates of the individual tax unit argue that tax should be levied on an individual without regard to the domestic or personal arrangements of that person. The tax base includes only those items of income accruing to – and, more rarely in our current system, the wealth owned by – that individual. Progressive rates of tax are applied to the total tax base of the individual, and liability for any taxes owing rests with that individual.

Such a system has much to commend it. It can, if properly designed, promote equity among individuals – both horizontal and vertical. More important, it does not inquire into the individual's personal relationships, living arrangements, family income, or wealth. This accords with the neutrality criterion in that no tax preference exists for one type of relationship over another. It also advances the equality objective (at least formally) since it treats gay and lesbian persons the same as it does heterosexuals.

For women, individual taxation may be crucial. Marital or partnership taxation disadvantages women in relationships, particularly those who do not share incomes with their partners. If the existing tax system expressly required women to pay higher marginal tax rates than men, there would be an outcry at the unfairness of the system. However, the fact that certain measures in our tax system – for example, the spousal tax credit and unused credit transfers – have exactly this effect appears to pass largely unnoticed. A simple illustration may help: If, in 1992, Olive Oyl worked only in the house and received no outside income, her husband, Popeye, would have received a tax credit of $915 against his taxable income. If Olive began to work outside the home, earning in excess of $5000, Popeye's tax credit would have started to disappear until he lost the entire $915 tax credit (increasing his taxes by this amount). It is Olive's entry into the waged workforce that caused Popeye to pay the additional $915 in taxes. From the household income perspective, Olive is penalized when she starts work because it has the effect of raising her spouse's tax by $915. Obviously, if Olive is able to secure only low-wage employment, this may have a considerable effect on her when she decides to enter the waged workforce. And this is only one of a panoply of measures that take into account joint income. The others will be discussed in more detail below.

The tax system, as it stands, is unfair. It reveals a governmental preference for women to stay in the home and thereby plays an important ideological role as well as a fiscal one. Formal equality alone demands that women be treated not as appendages of partners, be they male or female. Women who wish to work only in the home should, of course, have every right to do so. This is not the point. Women who work only in the household economy should not be given preferential treatment by the tax system – especially not by credits granted to their husbands. Conversely, women who work outside the home should not be penalized by the tax system for doing so. Obviously, the taxes levied on waged work outside the home directly reduce the financial returns from engaging in such work. For women who can command only low wages – a reality for too many women – this situation is particularly troubling. To choose to work outside the home may not be feasible when these tax costs are added to the increased costs already associated with entering the paid labour force (such as travel, clothing, food, and, if the woman is also a mother, child care). This factor alone – ignoring for the moment the complex issue of imputed income and the value of household production – is enough to favour the individual unit of taxation and the repeal of those provisions that, in recognizing marriage, have these invidious effects.

Economic efficiency experts also argue against any system that provides disincentives for women to enter the outside workforce (Boulet and Lavallée 1984; Leuthold 1978; and Killingsworth 1983). These pressures will increase as baby boomers retire and more workers are needed in the market-place. The theory is that women in marital relationships tend to be secondary earners. In addition, women in general can obtain only low wages in the outside workforce. Putting these two factors together, researchers inferred, and subsequently verified by empirical research, that the choice of a secondary worker to be employed outside the home is far more elastic than that of the primary earner who is usually the husband (see Leuthold 1978; Killingsworth 1983; and Kiker and de Oliveira 1990). The woman for whom this scenario is most true is the young mother with a partner and small children. The reasons for this are outlined by Stiglitz (1988, 467):

> There are, moreover, some grounds for expecting females to be quite sensitive to changes in after-tax wage. When the married woman does not work outside of the home, she is still being productive; it is only that her services are not monetized, and therefore not taxed. Frequently, when she goes to work, the family will have to replace those services in one way or another. It may hire someone to do the cleaning or cooking; it may rely more on frozen dinners or eat out more often (effectively purchasing the cooking services that the wife previously supplied). Thus the net gain to the family is much less than the gross income of the wife.

The reasons for the elasticity of women's labour outside the home are complex and deeply rooted in our social, economic, and political framework (Breton 1984 and Boothby 1986.) However, it is clear that any additional barriers to entering or re-entering the outside labour force will have far greater impact on women than it will on men. Therefore, disincentives in the tax system will have a major impact on women's decisions to work inside or outside the home, and it is crucial that such disincentives be removed. Indeed, depending on the degree of elasticity of women's propensity to enter the outside workforce, some would argue that there is a good case for providing tax incentives in the form of lower-income tax rates, tax credits, and other advantageous tax treatments. However, as a society, we should be clear why this is appropriate and necessary.

In particular, it is important to examine the different assumptions underlying the secondary worker theories. In the past, there has been an unspoken assumption that women do not have to enter the workforce if they do not wish to, and only do so in order to earn extra money for family luxuries: the infamous "pin money." Or, perhaps, women enter the outside workforce, as one of the leading judges (Lord Denning 1974) of this century patronizingly pointed out, to amuse themselves: "Many a married woman seeks work. She does so when the children grow up and leave the house. She does it, not solely to earn money, helpful as it is: but to fill her time with useful occupation, rather than sit idly at home waiting for her husband to return. The devil tempts those who have nothing to do."

A few statistics may help to highlight the fallacy of these assumptions. Of the women in the labour force, 39.4 per cent do not have husbands or partners; and 18.5 per cent of this group of women are single parents (see Connelly and MacDonald 1990, 13). Even for those women who do have partners or husbands, the financial situation of most families with double incomes is far from rosy. More than one-third (34.1 per cent) of such women had husbands or partners whose total income in 1985 was less than $20,000 and 60.1 per cent had husbands or partners whose income was less than $30,000 (Connelly and MacDonald 1990, 7). Many women work outside the home because of economic necessity. For example, by the late 1980s, two full-time workers in Ontario earning minimum wage would be unable to raise their joint incomes to the poverty line for a family of four in an urban area. All forms of family units saw their incomes drop between 1980 and 1985. Only those family units in which both partners worked managed to retain equilibrium. Those in single-parent families lost the most; the average income of single female parents dropped to 51 per cent of the average family income in 1985 (Rashid 1989). With the exception of elderly families, the incidence of low income increased among all family groups. This is not a situation of economic stability and security in which people are able to make choices.

There is a similar myth that women tend to take part-time waged work only because of their home-centred responsibilities. This assumption can also be dismissed with a few facts. The incidence of part-time work among women has indeed increased from 29 per cent of paid women workers in 1970 to 32.6 per cent in 1985. Two-thirds of all part-time workers in 1985 were women. The number of women in part-time jobs (32.6 per cent) greatly exceeds that of men (12.8 per cent). Of these part-time workers, two-thirds of the women worked in clerical, sales, or service occupations. Almost half (47.9 per cent) of all women who worked in sales jobs were part-time. In 1985 a labour force survey questioned women about their reasons for working part-time. The results were interesting: a full 27.8 per cent (including almost 25 per cent of married women) said they could find only part-time work. Only 20 per cent of married women gave "personal or family responsibilities" as their reason for working part time (see Rashid 1989).

To complete the picture, it is necessary to add that not all women who work only in the home do so by choice. Women experience higher unemployment rates than men. In 1986 the unemployment rate for women was 11.2 per cent compared with 9.6 per cent for men. Approximately one-fifth of unemployed women are seeking re-entry into the workforce. Moreover, those women who choose to work in the home often do so for only short periods of time. One of the most interesting aspects of the 1984 family history survey was its examination of work interruptions of one year or more. The survey concluded: "Population estimates from the survey show that 86.2 per cent of women have been regularly employed. Of these women, 42.1 per cent have had no interruptions of one year or more and 42.0 per cent have had one such interruption. Only 15.9 per cent had two or more interruptions. The evidence does not support the idea that women enter and leave the labour force, take one extended leave and return, or leave permanently" (Butch 1985, 30). The survey also showed that of the 1.7 million women not in the paid labour force with children at home, only 19 per cent had never been employed and 56.6 per cent of these were over 45 years of age.

These studies cast serious doubt on the notion that most women are secondary workers. Those women who are secondary workers are so not because they are hoping to earn spare cash for the family, but because the poor salaries paid to many women in the outside waged force is too small to compensate for the productive work that will be forgone in the home or purchased outside because the wife is working in the outside workforce. Accordingly, the elasticity of women's labour is a direct result of the market wage discrimination that faces most women, and this should be explicitly acknowledged as the reason for the favourable tax treatment of women. There are two reasons why favourable treatment should not be based on economic efficiency grounds of the secondary worker: First and foremost, the secondary worker syndrome arises out of the inequitable wages and working conditions that women face in the market-place. Second, women who do not have the option of working in the home (an increasing number as we have seen above) face the same inequities on a daily basis.

To conclude, my contention is that the secondary worker theory is predicated on a belief that the optimal tax system is one that is economically efficient. Increasingly, this is the only criterion by which new tax measures and budgets are judged. This should not be the case. The main functions of the tax system should be to raise revenues for government programs in a manner that redistributes income and wealth fairly and enhances, insofar as possible, the opportunities and choices of citizens. One method of achieving these goals is to make it easier for people, and particularly for women, to enter and remain in the waged labour force. An economic efficiency analysis may be used to bolster equity and equality arguments in favour of reducing the barriers faced by women in the waged workforce. However, it should not be used as the primary justification for such policies, because of its reliance on paternalistic notions of women's reasons for working outside the home, and the assumption that they have a choice when doing so. These very assumptions are partly responsible for the significant differential between men's and women's wages. It is a striking failure of the market economy and economic efficiency concepts that even in 1992, women still earn only 60 cents for every dollar a man earns. This is the justification for favourable tax treatment.

One novel solution would be to recognize the current undervaluation of women's work by taxing them at 60 per cent of the rates applicable to their male counterparts. In my opinion, this appears to be a quick and relatively simple way of alleviating, to some extent, the continuing discrimination perpetrated against women on a daily basis in the labour market. However, as someone who believes deeply in the eradication of poverty, I have difficulties in advocating that the tax rate on a well-paid professional woman be in effect the same as, or less than, that on a poorly paid, unskilled male labourer. Nevertheless, the concept is an intriguing one that will be explored a little more fully in the section on recommendations.

Focusing solely on the benefits of the individual unit and the detriments that result from using the marital unit is only one side of the story. Choice of tax unit is a complicated issue that mirrors many of the hard choices facing our society today. The liberal insistence on individual rights and obligations clashes with the pursuit of collective and communitarian goals. Many feminists are rightly sceptical of the notion of a collective good that has, until now, meant the surbordination of women for the collective good of men. However, the misapplication of concepts in the past is no excuse for creating future and further inequities by replacing an initially flawed concept with one that is equally flawed, albeit in a very different way.

There are definite difficulties with using the individual tax unit for all purposes. The individual unit of tax does not, and cannot, take into account all the relevant circumstances of an individual's life. If there is to be a genuine attempt at calculating a taxpayer's ability to pay, several factors that fly in the face of individual taxation must be taken into account. For instance, if economic and other savings are achieved by a mutual sharing of income between couples, among family members, or other identifiable groups, this increases a taxpayer's ability to pay. Conversely, if the taxpayer is economically responsible, morally or legally, for people who are wholly dependent on the taxpayer for economic support, such support will decrease her or his ability to pay. Yet, to the extent that the responsibility for dependants and other such commitments are allowed to enter the calculation of ability to pay, the notion of individuality and independence are being eroded. How is such a conflict reconciled? Some commentators believe that the answer lies in the adoption of the marital or family unit for taxation purposes.

The Marital/Partnership Unit

As mentioned in the introduction, the marital unit is defined broadly in this paper. It encompasses couples of any sexual orientation who meet the definitional criteria for common-law spouses set out under current family law legislation respecting length of cohabitation and/or parental status. Other stable communities could be included in this category, but the logistical and practical difficulties of defining them would be considerable unless such groups were willing to identify themselves. The common theme of all of these units is the economic mutuality of the home environment. Proponents of a marital tax unit typically give two rationales for such a system, both of which are predicated upon this economic mutuality. First, it is said that double or group living gives rise to economies of scale that increase those individuals' collective ability to pay. Since tax levels should increase with ability to pay, these economies should be factored into the tax equation. Second, there is an assumption, often unstated, that individual members of a marital unit share their incomes and, perhaps, their wealth.

How would the marital unit work for tax purposes? It could work in one of two ways, each having a very different tax result. Under the first system, referred to here as the "cumulative model," the income of a couple is aggregated to ascertain their collective ability to pay. Tax liability is then determined on a joint basis using a higher progressive rate scale than that applied to an individual living alone. The net result is that the couple ends up paying more tax cumulatively than they would have done had they been taxed as individuals. (England used such a system until quite recently.)

Another possibility would be to aggregate the two incomes and then split the total equally between the two people. This latter system, the "income-splitting model," is extremely preferential to couples. Furthermore, the advantage grows in direct proportion to the disparity in incomes between the two people, the greatest advantage being obtained by the high-income earner who lives with someone without income. The income-splitting model is blatantly preferential toward marriages in which women remain in the home. It has few, if any, legitimate benefits and will not be considered in any detail. The only possible justification for it is one based on a mutual sharing of incomes. As discussed below, this justification is extremely weak, as there is insufficient evidence to support the assumption that sharing occurs. Before leaving this option, however, I should point out that it is employed in the United States with the addition of separate rate schedules.

If marital unit taxation were to be introduced, the only type that could be justified is the cumulative model, in which income is aggregated and progressive rates are applied to result in higher, joint-income taxes. I agree ultimately with those who argue that such a system would be unfair, but it should be acknowledged that there are some good reasons for advocating it.

The main advantage of adopting a marital tax unit is to reflect accurately the economic well-being of taxpayers. Couples are said to be the logical economic unit based on the two theories noted above, namely, that they share income and wealth, and that joint living produces considerable economic savings. The merits of these two theories will now be explored.

Couples are able to make economies of scale that increase their ability to pay vis-à-vis the lone individual. For example, only one home need be rented or bought (though possibly larger), and one vacuum cleaner, one fridge, one stove purchased, and so on. One study (Rea 1984) has estimated the savings of marriage to be between 32 and 35 per cent of the expenditures of two people living alone. In addition, account must be taken of the valuable (and currently untaxed) household labour that many women (and some men) perform. The amount of household production increases dramatically when one spouse (usually the woman) does not work outside the home. If this is ignored, families in which the wage earners have disparate incomes – as well as individuals – will be treated inequitably.

An example may help illustrate the points that have been made thus far. Two couples – Alex and Pat, Reg and Scott – both have household taxable incomes of $60,000. In the first household, Alex earns the entire $60,000 and Pat works in the home. In the second household, Reg and Scott both earn $30,000 each. The additional tax liability for the first couple based on 1992 Ontario tax rates (ignoring surtax) is $4099. For the second household, this is a significant saving, which might be considered inappropriate if, in fact, both couples share the income equally. Based on this scenario, it has been argued that families, not individuals, should be the appropriate tax unit on which the tax base is calculated and progressive tax rates applied. The Carter Report recommended family taxation for these reasons: "We believe firmly that the family is today, as it has been for many centuries, the basic economic unit in society. Although few marriages are entered into for purely financial reasons, as soon as the marriage is contracted it is the continued income and financial position of the family which is ordinarily of primary concern not the income and financial position of the individual members."

However, the assumption that husbands and wives share income, and perhaps property, appears to be fallacious, and this is a major stumbling block for proponents of the marital unit. The empirical evidence suggests there is no consistent pattern of sharing between spouses. For example, in an Australian study, Meredith Edwards (1984) found that low-income couples were more likely to share incomes than two high-income earners. Women who worked only in the home were unlikely to have much control over major spending items except in poorer families. Research (Pahl 1989) in England shows much the same pattern. There is no extensive research on this in Canada, although one Manitoba study (Cheal 1991) supports similar though not as pronounced differentials in income-sharing and control by family type in Winnipeg. Especially in view of falling marriage rates in our society and the emergence of different family structures, marital unit taxation cannot be justified on the assumption that resources are shared. Can marital unit taxation be justified solely by reference to the economic savings gained from joint living arrangements?

There are, undoubtedly, economic and psychological savings that result from shared accommodation. In addition to the hard cash savings resulting from the economies of scale outlined above, there are considerable imputed savings. Chores can be shared and thus reduced proportionately per individual. More important, returning to the simple example given above, the second couple, Reg and Scott, had to give up a great deal of leisure (or more accurately valuable household production) in order to earn the same cash income amount as the first couple. They will either have to do household work in addition to their outside jobs or purchase them in the outside market. Indeed, one study (Lazear and Michael 1990) revealed that although two-income-earner couples had approximately 20 per cent more income than a similarly situated one-income-earner couple, the two-income couple required 30 per cent more money income to achieve the same living standard of the one-income-earner couple. Viewed from this perspective, the additional tax payable by the first couple may be justified by the extra outside work that the second couple had to perform in order to earn their income and maintain their household. However, the tax savings realized by the two-earner couple will vary arbitrarily depending upon the income disparity between them. Accordingly, this is not a fair way to compensate people for the additional work. In any event, if we do not take into account the greater leisure capacity of someone who earns $25,000 in interest income without any physical or mental effort, why should we do so simply because someone lives with a person who chooses to work in the home?

The real difference that should be counted is not leisure – although an optimum tax system should presumably take leisure into account – but the unrecognized value of household labour. The second couple will either have to work longer hours, or more likely purchase such labour in the market, which will decrease their ability to pay taxes. Should we then tax the imputed income received by the first couple in the form of Pat's household labour?

Valuing Imputed Household Production

A serious flaw in the tax system is the refusal to value, pay for, and, subsequently, bring into the tax base the imputed income that arises from the performance of work in the house. This type of work is often described as housework and, more tellingly, as "women's work." Accordingly, it can be made invisible and dismissed. It must not be; household production is extremely valuable and must be acknowledged as such. (For an excellent discussion on this, see Waring 1988.) And the tax system, as one of the major economic laws in our society, is an extremely important place wherein it could be given recognition. The refusal to tax imputed income results in perpetuating women's economic dependence on men. O'Kelly (1985) observes that most non-working (sic) spouses are women, who are economically dependent on their husbands. Furthermore, what is in form a gender-neutral favouritism of home production may in fact be a form of sex discrimination that tends to keep women economically dependent on men. There is also the possibility that the refusal to tax imputed income may be as much an ideological statement as a pragmatic one, helping to reinforce the myth that the proper role for women is in the home.

Various suggestions have been made regarding the method of valuing and taking into account household production and reproduction. I do not propose to reiterate the various alternatives in any detail here. (For a fuller discussion of the alternatives, see Maloney 1989.) From an administrative perspective, the easiest, though not the fairest, way is to give each household a refundable tax credit of a certain amount that can be put toward the cost of hiring someone to perform the services or, alternatively, that can be taken as some financial recognition of the services performed and taxed accordingly. Child-care expenses could be treated in a similar manner. This approach solves the problem of where to get the money to pay the taxes on the imputed income.

Implementing this or some such system would also recognize the changing role of household production in our economy. Interestingly, the outside market-place and workforce are making increasing incursions into the home. As computers and fax machines allow more and more people to perform "outside" types of work in the home, the distinctions between outside and inside work may start to collapse. Moreover, the distinctions between income and imputed income may also start to disintegrate and other types of imputed income may be brought into the tax base such as imputed rent from property.

Finally, it is important to note that by perpetuating the myth that work in the home is not productive, the income tax system reinforces a stereotype that has important repercussions elsewhere in the law. For instance, the value of housework is an important factor in determining many personal injury awards as well as maintenance and alimony settlements. Traditionally, women have been, and continue to be, undercompensated by judicial awards in these areas because of the low value placed on work in the home (see Cassels 1992).

The foregoing has been a brief outline of the pros and cons of individual and marital taxation. I shall turn now to the existing personal income tax provisions.

The Existing Provisions

The current federal personal income tax system, which forms the basis for the Ontario income tax through the tax collection agreements, uses the individual as the tax unit. Individuals are required to complete tax returns, and tax liability, for the most part, remains with the individual. Several provisions exist to ensure that taxpayers cannot avoid or abuse the system. In particular, the attribution rules (see the Income Tax Act, sections 56(4), 56(4.1)–(4.3), 74.1–74.5, and 75.1) attempt to prevent income splitting designed to reduce taxation. In a system of individual income tax, there are considerable tax savings to be realized if a higher-income earner is able to transfer some of her or his income to a lower- or non-income earner in the family group. This person is usually the taxpayer's spouse or minor children (although attribution can apply to certain other transfers as well).

Although the attribution rules are in many ways complex, the basic mechanism used to prevent income splitting is quite simple. The rules do not prevent property or income rights from legally passing from one spouse to another or to minor children. However, any income arising from the property or right is deemed, for income tax purposes only, to belong to the spouse who transferred the property or right. (Parenthetically, it should be noted that only legally married spouses are presently subject to the attribution system although the 1992 federal budget has proposed to extend the rules to cover heterosexual common-law couples.) The legal entitlement to the property or right, and any income arising therefrom, remains with the spouse or minor child to whom the property was transferred. The act allows any increase in the value of property to be taxed after it has been transferred to the minor child. This exception for capital gains does not apply to property transferred to a spouse, unless the couple has separated and has elected to have the attribution rule not apply. If a couple divorces, all attribution ceases automatically. It should be noted that the act was amended in 1987 to exempt from these rules transfers of property between spouses at fair market value. This amendment helps reinforce the individualistic framework of the Income Tax Act, at least insofar as spousal transactions are predicated on market concepts.

These rules have been reasonably effective in ensuring that the concept of individual taxation remains whole. They are, however, far from perfect. For example, they remain ineffective in dealing with the transference of shareholdings and other interests in family corporations. Provided some consideration is given for the shares issued by a corporation or for property subsequently transferred to it, many opportunities exist for income to be siphoned off by using shareholdings in corporations. This is true particularly in light of the recent Supreme Court of Canada ruling in the case of *The Queen v. McClurg*.[1] Accordingly, there is a case for tightening up the rules, which could be done realistically only at the federal level.

Concerns have also been raised that the attribution rules are detrimental to women's aspirations by providing a disincentive for families to share incomes and property. In particular, the attribution rules create disincentives for wealthy husbands to pass property and income to their less wealthy wives during marriage. Accordingly, a difficult decision may have to be made to determine whether the attribution rules should remain because they serve a sufficiently important purpose. I believe that they do. Abolishing the attribution rules would help only wealthy families to reduce their tax bills. Moreover, it is not certain that this would be, in itself, of any real help to the women in these wealthy families. Assuming their husbands could, in fact, be induced to transfer some assets, such women would at least have legal title to the property in the event of a marriage breakdown. However, there is evidence to suggest that they would not exercise decision-making powers or control over the property during the existence of the marriage despite their legal ownership. Even if they could obtain de facto control over the property, I am still not convinced, based on equity considerations, that we should abolish attribution. If a choice has to be made, I would prefer to collect the additional tax revenues and distribute them to even more economically disadvantaged women.

If a decision is made to eliminate the attribution rules, the effect would be to allow the income-splitting model of the marital unit for wealthy families. In fairness, if the attribution rules are repealed, the act should be amended to adopt income-splitting marital-unit taxation for all couples, regardless of income.

While the attribution rules attempt to preserve the integrity of the individual tax unit, there are, at the same time, a number of other provisions that belie the principle of individual taxation. Increasingly, the personal income tax system is recognizing the economic mutuality of families, especially the economic dependence of some family members on others. In reviewing and analysing the list of these provisions, as I shall do below, it will become apparent that they are not linked by any overarching rationale.

Provisions That Recognize a Marital Unit

In order to provide some analysis of the eclectic group of provisions that recognize – indeed, in some cases insist on – the marital unit, I have attempted to group them under categories. The categories are my own, with some of the provisions falling into more than one group. Where this is the case, I have acknowledged the duplication. As I shall discuss later, the groupings may be a useful tool for deciding what interests, if any, may justify infringing upon the principle of individual taxation. The groupings are:

- affirmative-action provisions;
- dependency provisions (marriage and home labour preference);
- economic mutuality provisions (marital preference);
- loophole or tax avoidance plugs (and, accordingly, unfavourable to the marital or family unit); and
- welfare measures – equity provisions.

Affirmative-Action Provisions

The provisions in this category help to address, or at least to recognize, the discrimination that women encounter by entering the outside workforce. There is presently only one such provision: the child-care expenses deduction (see the Income Tax Act, section 63). There is also one affirmative-action provision that benefits men: the alimony and maintenance deduction.

Child-Care Expenses Deduction

The notion of family income is built into the child-care expenses deduction in that its availability is restricted, in most cases, to the parent with the lower income. This restriction can be justified as a revenue-saving measure; because the child-care expense is given as a deduction, it is worth more to a higher-income earner than a lower-income earner. However, at the symbolic level (and perhaps in its practical effect), this deduction can be characterized as an economic efficiency or affirmative-action measure. That is, it potentially encourages and helps mothers, who are usually the lower-income earners in their families, to enter or re-enter the paid labour market.

This explanation does not, however, justify the use of a deduction that gives the greatest subsidy to the women who earn high incomes. One possible reason for allowing the provision to remain a deduction would be that women who can obtain higher wages for the work they perform are perceived to be more productive, and the government has the greatest interest in encouraging these women into the workforce. I would welcome watching the spectacle of a government attempting to sell this to the public.

The only credible argument to justify the use of a deduction is that child-care expenses should be treated in exactly the same way as business expenses, on the basis that they are incurred for the purpose of earning income and are directly referable to the income-earning process. Should governments fail to invest substantially more money in improving access to daycare, this argument may become more compelling. For the moment, it is premature. Under the current system, the women who most need assistance are receiving the least. This deduction, at the very least, should be changed into a refundable tax credit available to either parent, or divisible between them. The effect on revenues would be negligible, and the change would have two beneficial effects: first, it would alleviate the bias of the current provision toward high-income earners by giving the same tax savings to all and, second, it would be truer to the principle of individual taxation. The fairest option would be to increase the amount of the refundable credit as income decreases, ensuring that those who need assistance the most receive the most benefit.

If a government wished to address the need for affirmative action directly, the tax credit could be made available to women only regardless of whether they have a partner or whether or not that partner works outside the home. In my view, it should be available also to men who are single parents. It is possible that such a provision might not withstand a challenge under the equality provisions of the Charter of Rights and Freedoms. However, I doubt that this would be a problem in view of the specific exception in subsection 15(2) of the Charter for affirmative-action programs.

The Alimony and Maintenance Deduction

This deduction allows spouses or former spouses paying alimony or maintenance (usually men) to deduct the entire amount of these payments in computing their incomes (see the Income Tax Act, sections 60(b)(c), (c.1), 56(b), (c), and (c.1). The payee (usually the woman) has to include the full amount of these payments in her income for tax purposes, even if they are made not for her individual benefit, but for the benefit of the couple's children. Husbands are not allowed to deduct the full amount of maintenance income given during marriage, so it is extremely difficult to see why they are allowed to do so when the marriage is over. The notion of one spouse's legal responsibility to support the other cannot justify the deduction/inclusion system, since no such system applies during the life of the marriage. Indeed, the attribution rules specifically prohibit the income splitting in this manner. Nor does an ability-to-pay rationale make sense; one study (Weitzman 1985) found that men's standard of living increases by an average of 42 per cent following divorce while women's falls by 73 per cent. The Department of Justice's evaluation of the Divorce Act (Department of Justice 1990) found that almost 50 per cent of divorced women lived below the poverty line. The only other possible rationale is that the deduction encourages men to make these payments. Given that the delinquency rate on support payments hovers in the 80 per cent range (Burtch, Pitcher-LaPrairie, and Wachtel 1980), this affirmative-action program is not working (see also Bala 1988 and Smith 1988). Since deductions are not allowed to "encourage," let us say, the payment of speeding tickets, other fines, or personal legal responsibilities, it is difficult to see why we should do so for alimony payments, particularly when it is to the poorer spouse's disadvantage. It has been estimated that the federal and provincial tax subsidy amounts to approximately $250 million annually. Even if the deduction is allowed to stand for the ex-spouse's support, there is absolutely no way to justify the deductibility of payments made to support a child, and even less to justify including such payments in the mother's income. A government that is truly committed to affirmative action to redress women's poverty would repeal the deduction/inclusion system as its first order of business. Indeed, there is no excuse for not doing so considering that such a change would likely have a positive effect on revenues, given the higher average marginal tax rate of those who pay support.

Dependency Provisions (Marriage and Home Labour Preference)

These provisions all reflect a popular image of "family" in which the woman (typically) is dependent upon the man. They all operate to reduce the couple's aggregate tax liability, presumably in recognition of the economic burden that is supposed to be entailed by such dependency. Their effect is to give preferential treatment to families in which one spouse works only in the home. There are several such provisions.

Transfer of Unused Credits to Spouse

A taxpayer is, in many cases, allowed to transfer unused credits to a spouse, possibly a recognition of the economic mutuality of couples, or more likely the notion of dependency – usually of the woman on the man – although this is never expressly stated (see the Income Tax Act, section 118.8). The act allows the transfer of unused pension credits, educational credits, and dividend tax credits. These are not welfare measures because they are unrelated to family income; they are related only to the degree of economic dependence of the woman on the man. The sole criteria are that one spouse earn little or no income and the other earn a sufficiently high income to utilize some of the transferred credits.

Deductibility of Spousal RRSP Premiums

According to the Income Tax Act, section 146(5.1), spouses are permitted to contribute to each other's registered retirement savings plans (RRSPs) and certain other deferred-income plans. These might have been considered welfare provisions if they were subject to a maximum family or individual income. They are not, although the benefit, in theory, accrues to spouses who have such little income in the year that the RRSP savings are withdrawn. If this provision does benefit women in this manner, it could fall within the affirmative-action section provision as a measure recognizing that women do not receive equal pay in the labour market from which to make RRSP contributions. Such a grouping would be fraught with difficulty because the provision serves only to encourage transfers of income after the fact – that is, after the husband has been able to accumulate more in the discriminatory market – and then only on the voluntary initiative of the man. In reality, the greatest benefit accrues to the high-income earner (the husband), who receives considerable tax savings; this benefit increases with his income since the tax benefit is given as a deduction rather than a credit. Moreover, as I mentioned earlier, it is unlikely that many wives will obtain decision-making power over assets transferred to them legally, and I suspect this is especially true when the transfers are made as a tax-planning device.

Spousal Credit

The spousal tax credit – see the Income Tax Act, section 118(1)(a) – is the most obvious dependency provision. The credit is given only if the woman has little or no income. If this credit reflected a public recognition of the productive household services performed by the spouse who works in the home, then it would be more acceptable. If so, it should be given directly to the person on whom the household is dependent: the "homeworker." To do this would, of course, compound the preferential treatment of one-income-earner couples. The universal refundable tax credit system discussed earlier would be a far more equitable way of recognizing the value of household production.

Household Work

The non-recognition of the imputed income arising from household production, already mentioned in connection with the spousal tax credit, is perhaps the most fundamental (albeit unnoticed) recognition of women's dependency on men in our present income tax system.

Economic Mutuality Provisions (Marital Preference)

These provisions are also founded on the popular image of "family," but they focus on a somewhat different aspect: the idea that a normal couple has one mutual economic life, in which all assets, income, and expenses are shared. More accurately, this vision attributes the economic position of the man to the woman, and treats her interests as subsumed by those of her husband. Rather than grant an absolute reduction in the couple's aggregate tax burden, these provisions tend to operate by deferring any tax consequences resulting from transactions between spouses. The non-recognition of such inter-spousal transactions is thought to be appropriate since their economic fate is so tightly bound up together. Some of these provisions could also arguably be located in the "dependency" category, and, like the dependency provisions, their effect is to create a tax preference for marriage.

Inter Vivos Transfers of Property of Spouse etc. or Trust

The spousal roll-overs, both *inter vivos* (see section 73), and on death (see section 70(6)), are perhaps the clearest example of the economic mutuality provisions. These roll-overs exempt spouses from the normal rules requiring the payment of capital gains, the recapture of capital cost allowances and, conversely, taking capital losses or any terminal loss on depreciable property. Although roll-overs are for the most part advantageous, they are also important provisions to prevent artificial tax avoidance schemes that could be effected by transfers between spouses. This function is secondary, however, as the attribution rules already curtail the most obvious abuses.

Disposal of Principal Residence to Spouse or Trust for Spouse and Where Principal Residence Is Property of Trust for Spouse

The provisions – the Income Tax Act, section 40(4)–(5) – that preserve the capital gains tax exemption for principal residences, transferred by a taxpayer to a spouse, or spousal trust, are another recognition of the economic mutuality that is supposed to exist within marriage. The cost of the house, the size of the gain, and the amount of the spouses' joint incomes are all irrelevant in determining the availability of the exemption. It should be noted that these provisions are partly intended to complement the rule that permits only one principal residence per family (a disincentive to marriage).

Preferred Beneficiary

Contrary to the general rule – see section 108(1)(g) – the recognition of spouses as preferred beneficiaries allows a trust to avoid taxation of accumulating trust income. The payment of tax is deferred until such time as the income is actually distributed to the spouse.

Inheritances

Perhaps one of the most important, yet invisible, preferences flows from the non-taxation of inheritances. The repeal of the federal inheritance and estate tax, and of provincial succession duties, provided tremendous benefits to spouses and even greater benefits to children and other family beneficiaries, since spouses often received generous exemptions under such legislation. Political resistance to a re-introduction of inheritance taxes is often expressed in terms of the economic mutuality of the family.

Moving Expenses

The provisions – see the Income Tax Act, section 62(3) – that allow the taxpayer to deduct job- or school-related moving expenses also permit the deduction of expenses incurred by the spouse in such a move. Like the others, this rule reflects a notion that marriage results in one mutual economic existence, but it differs from the others in providing an absolute tax reduction to the couple rather than just a deferral.

Pension Transfers

Since 1987 spouses have been able to divide benefits under the Canada Pension Plan. As a result, such pension transfers have been exempted from the application of the attribution rules.

Loophole or Tax Avoidance Plugs (and, Accordingly, Unfavourable to the Marital or Family Unit)

These provisions recognize the possibility of using the family transactions to avoid payment of tax. Although they arguably impose some disadvantages on those who marry, they also draw upon and reinforce assumptions about the economic mutuality of couples. They imply that transfers of property to a wife, for example, do not involve any real change of control over or enjoyment of the property.

Attrition Rules

The attribution rules (see sections 56(4), 56(4.1)–(4.3), 74.1–.5, and 75.1), discussed in some detail above, are the clearest example of the need to recognize that individual taxation may give rise to opportunities for tax avoidance. Parenthetically, it is also a recognition that at least some families do or will share property and income, if only to save taxes.

Superficial Loss

The prohibition against deducting superficial losses is extended by section 40(2)(g)(i) beyond the taxpayer to her or his spouse, who re-acquires the property disposed of by the taxpayer within the limited time period – see section 54(i).

Tax Liability Re Property Transferred Not at Arm's Length

Spouses are also jointly and severally liable for payment of their partner's tax under section 160, where property has been transferred between spouses.

Business Carried On by Spouse or Controlled Corporation

The required roll-over of the cumulative eligible capital of a business proprietorship on a transfer of the business to a spouse, or to a controlled corporation, denies a deduction to the unit. In an arm's-length transaction, this event would result in a deductible loss – see section 24(2).

Welfare Measures – Equity Provisions

The contribution to a spousal RRSP, allowance of spousal moving expenses, and a few other provisions mentioned above could have qualified for this category if there had been some correlation between the tax expenditure and family income. Welfare provisions are based on an explicit correlation between the amount of the tax benefit provided and the income of the marital or family unit in question. This takes the form of an income ceiling above which the tax benefit is restricted or disallowed, with the intention of targeting the benefit only to those deemed to be in need. For this reason, they can be seen as an extension of the welfare system. What follows is a list of the provisions of this nature currently in the act.

Child Tax Credit

In 1992 the refundable child tax credit started to disappear when joint spousal income reached $25,921. However, the provision was substantially revamped commencing 1 January 1993. The intention was to collapse the family allowance, child credit, and the refundable child tax credit into a single child tax benefit payable monthly, in most cases to the mother. The basic benefit will be reduced at a rate of 5 per cent of family net income over $25,921 for families with two or more children, and a lower rate of 2.5 per cent for families with one child. In addition, a new federal earned-income supplement increases the new benefit by up to $500 for low-income working families with children. This is an affirmative-action program to encourage low-income families into the outside workforce. It is based on the questionable and dangerous assumption that low-income people choose not to work. The supplement will not be received, for example, by those squeezed out of the labour force as a result of high rates of unemployment and the massive structural changes occurring in industry.

Sales Tax Credit

The introduction in 1990 of a revamped sales tax credit, which is now refundable (section 122.5), was designed to offset, for low-income earners, the concurrent increase in federal sales tax rates with the introduction of the Goods and Services Tax (GST). This credit also diminishes above $25,921 of aggregated spousal income.

Ontario Welfare Measures

The following is a brief outline of some credits that could qualify as welfare measures in Ontario.

Property Tax Credit

This credit reduces the income tax payable by people with low or moderate incomes and thus qualifies as a welfare measure. The amount of the credit depends on the amount of rent or property tax paid and aggregate family income.

Sales Tax Credit

This credit also helps reduce the tax burden on people of low or moderate incomes based on a maximum fixed amount per adult ($100) and per child ($50), depending on combined family income.

Ontario Home Ownership Tax Credit

This credit is also limited to one per couple. The intention here is to benefit first-time homebuyers and the construction industry. The provision limits the amount of people who can claim it based on couple status. Because it is aimed at increasing access to home ownership for those not yet in the market, this credit can arguably be characterized as a welfare measure. However, it might also be grouped with the anti-avoidance provisions because of the one-per-couple restriction.

The Effect of the Existing Provisions

The effect of these provisions varies greatly, depending on the marital status and income of the family in question. Currently, the major difference is between legally married couples and unmarried couples. Due to the 1992 federal budget, the critical difference will be between opposite-sex couples who have lived together for more than 12 months or have parented a child ("spousal status"), and those who have not met either of the latter two requirements, or those who are gay or lesbian couples regardless of the longevity of their relationship ("non-spousal status").

Generally speaking, the current system favours legal marriage for a one-income couple, but common-law status for a two-income couple with children – both can claim the personal tax credit and one can also claim the equivalent-to-married credit for one child. It is more or less neutral with respect to childless, two-income couples.

This simple summation does not tell the whole story. Gay and lesbian couples are disadvantaged if they are a one-income couple with or without children. If they are a two-income couple they are probably better off, particularly if one or both are low-income earners, as they will not have to aggregate their incomes to determine eligibility for the child tax benefit and sales tax credit. Similarly, any low-income couples who are legally married are worse off by these provisions. This is made clear by the fact that the government has estimated that it will collect a projected $965,000,000 in additional revenue between 1993 and 1997 simply as a result of widening the definition of "spouse" to encompass common-law couples. Indeed, it has been estimated that if all married couples had remained unmarried and without spousal status, they would have received $4.7 billion more federal and provincial government transfer payments in 1989 (Morrison and Oderkirk 1991). The relative disadvantage of marital status stems from the welfare provisions rather than from the taxes levied. In contrast, the net tax savings for married couples amounted to $1.2 billion in 1992. Accordingly, low-income couples suffer most from spousal status, and high-income, one-earner families benefit most from the current system. However, to the extent that the woman in this family does not participate in or share income, she is probably worse off if she wishes to enter the waged workforce. Given this overview, what changes, if any, should be made to the existing structure?

Changing Family Structures

In any decision to alter taxes, Canada's changing demographics should be borne in mind. There has been a growing diversification in the forms of Canadian families (see Ram 1990). Single-parent families are growing far faster than two-parent families – indeed, at three times the rate. Other trends are also apparent from the statistics. For instance, there are growing numbers of two-working-parent families and smaller families. The number of childless families is quite startling. Only two-fifths of all Canadians live with a child or children under 15, and, when broken into age categories, only half of all persons aged 20 to 39, and less than one-third of those aged 40 to 59, live with one or more children under 15 years. As a result, there is no longer any form of family configuration that can be described as typical. Also, as a result of the trend toward smaller families, the support system represented by extended families in the past is no longer present as a source of child care or other forms of assistance.

Given these facts, it is not surprising that the 1986 census showed an increase in the number of private family households with an annual growth of three per cent per annum from 1951. There were nine million private households in 1986 (see Burch 1990 and Ram 1990, 14), and the types of living arrangements within them had changed markedly. Certainly the number of non-family households has grown and continues to grow. The largest increase was in single-person households, accounting for 12.7 per cent in 1986, up from 7.4 per cent in 1951. Many of these single households were occupied by seniors: 17 per cent of men over 65 years and 40 per cent of women over 65 years lived in single-person households. Presumably these figures will increase with the rising life expectancies and the disintegration of traditional families that we are witnessing.

The movement toward single living is in part accounted for by the increasing individualization of society. For example, studies (Shanas 1979) show that most single seniors prefer to live alone rather than with relatives. A small but still significant number of people also live in nursing homes or in similar living arrangements – 5.4 per cent of men and 9.1 per cent of women in 1986. Again, it is anticipated that these numbers will grow substantially as baby boomers reach their twilight years.

Interestingly, it is not simply independent seniors who are swelling the ranks of the single-person household. Young adults are also living alone more frequently. This is attributable to a number of factors: people are marrying later and less frequently; divorce rates are high and remarriages later and less frequent. Other factors are also important: more money brings independence and there is a far greater variety of accommodation, especially suitable for single people, now available. However, the most recent evidence suggests that this trend is stabilizing and perhaps even reversing as more young people are choosing (or are forced because of fiscal restraints) to live with their parents. Studies (Heer, Hodge, and Felson 1986) show that this is related to unemployment rates among the young rather than a desire of young people to stay in the home with their parents or other family members.

We are also witnessing an increase in longevity, which has led to an increased overlap between generations. Of particular importance to women, I believe, is the fact that both the number and proportion of ageing adults with living parents and grandparents have grown. For instance, "in 1921, there were 53 persons over age 65 for every 100 persons in the 45–54 age group; by 1986, the corresponding figure was 106. Over the same period, the ratio of the over-80 age group to the 60–64 age group rose from 24 to 48" (Ram 1990, 14). These figures will increase in the future as the baby boomers reach their senior years. This trend will be of concern to women, who undoubtedly will end up bearing the brunt of care-giving for elderly parents, in-laws, aunts, uncles, and so on. This situation will be exacerbated by the current trend to save on health costs by placing an increasing burden on home care rather than on institutional care. Obviously, if this move is accompanied by good support services and systems, it will be welcome.

The suspicion, however, is that increasing demands for cost-cutting in health and other care services will have the effect of privatizing the costs onto women relatives. This might mean the revitalization of extended families living in the same home. It may also decrease outside workforce participation. The tax system will certainly have to be sensitive to this, as it may have considerable impact on women's ability to enter the waged workforce. Some form of relief or benefits to cover care-giving expenses will have to be available for women working outside the home.

Not surprisingly, Ontario, given its large population, is very reflective of the general trends and patterns in Canada as outlined above. Ontario demonstrates similar characteristics in nearly every category: family size, divorce rates, lone parenting, and solo living. The main differences are that Ontario has lower rates of births to single women, and a lower propensity of couples to enter into common-law unions than is observed nationally. In addition, Ontario's wives and married mothers had one of the highest provincial labour force participation rates in 1986.

Recommendations for a Tax Unit

What Are We Trying to Achieve?

Our objectives should include the following:

- To treat men and women equally – at least formally and, preferably, substantively. The latter would require positive action provisions to rectify historical and current inequities – primarily economic ones – and this would accord with the equality goal set out in an earlier section.
- To avoid discriminating in favour of any type of relationship; in particular, not to reinforce patriarchal and heterosexist stereotypes and norms. This provision would fulfil both the equity and neutrality criteria.
- To take into account the fact that people do have financial responsibility for children. Presumably, we think children are essential and that society should share the costs of their upkeep. This measure would accomplish a social objective and, insofar as it recognizes a decrease in ability to pay, would aid the equity criterion.
- To recognize, if possible, the saving realized by people sharing

income compared with those who do not have these advantages. This would help achieve vertical equity.

- To redistribute wealth among the appropriate units. Such redistribution would aid the equality objective.
- To take into account the value of household labour or production. To some extent this can be done by extending the child-care deductions (which should be transformed into credits) for women who choose to provide it themselves. The difficulty here, of course, is that such a system encourages working in the home environment as it will add costs to the choice to work outside.

Given the changing family structures in our society, it would be unwise to attempt marital unit taxation in preference to the individual unit. However, the question still arises: To what extent, if any, should a personal relationship be taken into account by the tax system? As we have seen, there are a large number of tax provisions that utilize marital or couple taxation. It is impossible to devise the perfect system. Accordingly, the least imperfect one will have to suffice. I believe the easiest way to achieve most of the objectives outlined above is to categorize the particular provision into one of the five groups identified earlier: affirmative-action provisions; dependency provisions (marriage and home labour preference); economic mutuality provisions (marital preference); loophole or tax avoidance plugs (and, accordingly, unfavourable to the marital or family unit); and welfare measures – equity provisions.

Affirmative-action provisions should be encouraged. Accordingly, if marital units need to be used in order to prevent revenue leakage when affirmative-action provisions are enacted, then this is acceptable. In the vast majority of cases, however, the act should simply be explicit in its affirmative-action thrust, which would usually vitiate the need to bring in marital status. The affirmative-action program must, of course, be one that can be justified. Alimony and maintenance deductions do not pass this threshold. The deduction of child-care expenses is currently inequitable, and should at least be changed to a credit that, preferably, is refundable.

Dependency provisions should be eliminated. These provisions undermine the important contribution that women working in the home make to the economy. Equally important, they raise the costs of entering the workforce for women, thereby distorting their choices and undermining their autonomy. Dependency provisions also treat women less favourably than men by effectively taxing them at marginal tax rates that are initially higher than those of their husbands.

The economic mutuality provisions are more troubling. My initial reaction is that they should be repealed. These provisions provide preferential treatment on the basis of joint living. Joint living already results in considerable economic and imputed savings, so it is difficult to see why the income tax system should compound the advantages. On the other hand, if there is a real economic mutuality that could be shown to exist between the couple, these provisions might be appropriate. They also do not affect women's waged workforce participation. Ideologically, however, these provisions reinforce women's dependent status as part and parcel of the man's estate. Therefore, these provisions should not be allowed to continue.

Anti-avoidance provisions should definitely be allowed to continue. The income tax system employs a plethora of anti-avoidance techniques to stop unfair schemes resulting in tax evasion and the reduction of revenue. Any close relationship, business or personal, provides opportunities for collusion to avoid taxes. The income tax system has a legitimate need to close any such loopholes. Therefore, family or personal relationships can be legitimately taken into account in such circumstances.

The most difficult decision has to be made with respect to welfare provisions. These provisions are tax expenditures given to alleviate poverty. Family income is used to prevent revenue leakage by ensuring that only one of two people with low incomes can claim the benefits. Not to do so would be enormously expensive and, in the current economic and political climate, not feasible without drastic cuts being made to the size of the programs or the amount of the benefits. Furthermore, these provisions are essentially no different from other direct subsidies – like welfare payments – that are handed out by provincial governments. Accordingly, unless the criteria for these direct subsidies are changed, there is no reason why payments delivered through the tax system should be treated differently.

Basing welfare payments on joint incomes can, however, be very unfair. Indeed, as this system has the effect of disadvantaging many women, it may be contrary to the Charter. The fact that the benefits are based on aggregated household income rather than individual income discriminates against women who will be less likely to receive such benefits if their financial position is considered with that of a (usually better-paid) man. In those cases where couples do, in fact, share income, the aggregation of household income may be acceptable discrimination. There is some evidence to the effect that low-income earners tend to share income more than higher-income earners. However, if couples, or indeed certain couples, do not share income, it not only is unfair but presumably compounds the poverty trap of individual women to use a marital unit in setting income ceilings. Not only will joint living result in reduced benefits, but the aggregated incomes will constitute a formidable barrier for women who consider entering the outside workforce. These provisions, therefore, strike at the heart of women's autonomy and self-determination. At the very least, these provisions might require a reformulated definition of spousal unit based on intention to share income and the permanency of the relationship. A one-year common-law relationship, as the federal budget proposes to introduce, is far too over-inclusive and will result in unfairness and hardship (or tax evasion tactics) for many women. To the extent that the federal government does not change these guidelines, the province of Ontario should add a further tax credit for people caught unfairly by the provision. For example, at the very least, common-law relationships should parallel the Ontario Family Law Act, which requires three years of cohabitation or a child (see Statutes of Ontario 1986, c.4, sections 1(1) and 29). If this requirement is the criterion, then a credit can be introduced to compensate for any loss of benefit based on the existence of a relationship that does not meet this criterion. A further earned credit could be added for women caught by the provisions to ameliorate the penalty for work outside the home that these welfare provisions, determined on family income, create.

Units Based on Systemic Disadvantage

Women are more likely to be poor than men. In 1987, 1,515,000 women lived in poverty as compared with 1,067,000 men. Single parents, especially women, are disproportionately poor and many have wealth of under $4000. In 1984, 24 per cent of single-parent families headed by men reported wealth of less than $5000, and 15.6 per cent reported wealth of less than $1000. Of single-parent families headed by women, 50.5 per cent reported wealth of less than $5000 and 39.7 per cent reported wealth of less than $1000.

Women also own very little property compared with men. Of the total of 8,991,670 households in the 1986 census, 6,436,845 were "maintained" by men and 2,554,830 were "maintained" by women. Of the households maintained by men, 70 per cent were privately owned (see Census of Canada 1986a).

Aboriginal women and disabled women are in even worse financial straits. A larger proportion of aboriginal people have no income at all, and those who do earn income earn significantly less than the Canadian average. In the 1986 census, the average Canadian income was determined as $18,188. The average income for single "North American Indians" was $10,538: $12,302 for men and $8574 for women. Their median income was $7591 (see Census of Canada 1986b).

The plight of people with disabilities is also appalling. There are approximately 3.3 million persons with disabilities in Canada. Only 40 per cent of adults with disabilities report any work-related income and, in 1985, 56 per cent of all people with disabilities had a total annual income (including income related to their disability) of less than $10,000 (see Statistics Canada 1987). Women with disabilities fare even worse. Of men with disabilities with incomes, 50 per cent receive less than $10,000 per year, and the same is true of 76 per cent of women with disabilities with incomes. The comparable figures for the total population are 30 per cent for men and 55 per cent for women (see the National Council of Welfare 1990).

The hundreds of thousands of people represented by these statistics are not making choices about whether to work inside or outside the home. The vast majority are either in the outside workforce, working for appallingly low salaries, or are unable to enter the workforce based, in part, on sexism, racism, or "ablism." Increasingly, those with economic power will be called upon to justify and subsequently ameliorate the extremely uneven distribution of wealth and income in society. It is no accident of fate that women, people with disabilities, and aboriginal people are significantly over-represented at the bottom end of the income strata. Correspondingly, no act of fate is likely to right the situation. Positive action must be taken and could commence in the income tax system. This could best be achieved by more creative and expansive tax deductions specifically aimed at these disadvantaged groups.

The Tax Collection Agreement between Ontario and the Federal Government

Most of the measures outlined here would be best implemented by the federal government. To the extent that they are not, Ontario would have to consider introducing and administering its own personal income tax system. This would allow far greater flexibility and progressivity. The disadvantages are increased bureaucracy, heightened taxpayer frustration, and further costs. However, if real change is to be undertaken, this is the only feasible alternative.

If the decision is made to stay within the present fiscal arrangements, ad hoc adjustments, some of which have been outlined above, can be made in the form of personal tax credits, where appropriate. Under the tax collection agreement, the federal government will allow provinces to enact personal tax credits, provided they comply with the criteria established in 1981. Ontario was the first province to enact credits in 1972 and has maintained tax credit programs since that time (Conklin and St-Hilaire 1990). Generally speaking, the credit should not alter the basic progressivity of the tax system. More specifically, the tax credit must be rebatable from other taxes actually paid; open to all residents of the province, whether taxpayers or not; and easily administered.

The federal government will waive, and has waived, one or more of the preconditions. It has also refused to enact some credits. Accordingly, caution has to be exercised.

Conclusion

The issues raised when examining the appropriate tax unit are some of the most complex in tax policy reform. There are no easy solutions. It is essential to prioritize the objectives that the reform hopes to achieve. In this paper, the greatest emphasis has been placed on women's autonomy and substantive equality for disadvantaged groups. These decisions mean some families will occasionally be treated inequitably vis-à-vis other families and, to the extent that this results in poverty or unwarranted disadvantage, it will be taken into account.

Some of the ideas proposed in this paper are quite novel, and some will be easier to implement than others. The grouping of the marital unit provisions according to their effect or objective helps to identify clearly those types of provisions that allow the use of joint incomes and partnership status and those that do not. Hopefully, these suggestions will be acted upon promptly to ensure full and unimpeded participation of women in the waged workforce.

The more radical and progressive reform would be one that differentiates among different groups in our society. Novelty should not bar this proposal from further consideration. Society is in flux, and the demographics are changing more rapidly and drastically than ever before. There is no longer any particular group that qualifies as the typical family: women are entering the waged workforce in increasing numbers, and disadvantaged groups are becoming increasingly disadvantaged. All these changes must be factored into the income tax system since it mirrors, more than any other piece of legislation, the social and economic trends and objectives of its day. Our current system is failing in that challenge. It is time that it became more reflective of the economic, social, and political realities facing taxpayers.

Note

I would like to thank my colleague, Lisa Phillips, for excellent editing and helpful commentary on an earlier draft of this paper. The earlier draft also benefited from the insightful comments of Allan Maslove and an anonymous reviewer. All remaining errors and inaccuracies are, of course, mine.

1 *The Queen v. McClurg.* 1990. 3 SCR 1020: 1991. 1 CTC 169. While section 74.4 of the Income Tax Act attempts to prevent the most obvious means of splitting income through corporations, it is quite limited in scope and many avoidance opportunities remain. Indeed, section 74.4 appears designed to encourage some of these activities, for example, by exempting "small business corporations" [s.74.4(2)(c)].

Bibliography

Bala, Nicholas. 1988. *Family Law in Canada and the United States Different Visions of Similar Realities in National Themes in Family Law.* Toronto Carswell
Boothby, Daniel. 1986. *Women Re-entering the Labour Force and Training Programs.* Ottawa: Economic Council of Canada, Minister of Supply and Services

152   Maureen A. Maloney

Boskin, Michael J. 1974. "The Effects of Governmental Expenditures and Taxes on Female Labor." *American Economic Review* 64: 252
Boulet, Jac-André, and Laval Lavallée. 1984. *The Changing Economic Status of Women*. Ottawa: Economic Council of Canada
Breton, Albert. 1984. *Marriage, Population, and the Labour Force Participation of Women*. Ottawa: Economic Council of Canada, Minister of Supply and Services
Burch, Thomas K. 1990. *Families in Canada*. Ottawa: Minister of Supply and Services
Burtch, Brian, Carol Pitcher-LaPrairie, and Andy Wachtel. 1980. "Issues in the Determination and Enforcement of Child Support Orders." *Canadian Journal of Family Law* 3: 5
Butch, Thomas K. 1985. *Family History Survey.* Ottawa: Statistics Canada
Canada. Royal Commission on Taxation. 1966. *Report* (Carter Report). Vol. 3: 143. Ottawa: Queen's Printer
Carter Report. See Canada, Royal Commission on Taxation
Cassels, Jamie. 1992. "Damages for Lost Earning Capacity: Women and Children Last!" *Canadian Bar Review* 71(3): 445
Census of Canada. 1986a. *Dwellings and Households Part 1*. Cat. 93-104, table 11-1. Ottawa: Statistics Canada
- 1986b. *Profile of Ethnic Groups*. Cat. 93-154, tables 2-39 and 1-64. Ottawa: Statistics Canada
Cheal, David. 1991. *Family Finances: Money Management in Breadwinner/Homemaker Families, Dual Earner Families, and Dual Career Families*. Winnipeg Area Study, Research Report No. 38
Conklin, David W., and France St-Hilaire. 1990. *Provincial Tax Reforms: Options and Opportunities*. Institute for Research on Public Policy, 91
Connelly, M. Patricia, and Martha MacDonald. 1990. *Women and the Labour Force*. Ottawa: Minister of Supply and Services
Department of Justice. 1990. *Evaluation of the Divorce Act – Phase II: Monitoring and Evaluation*. Ottawa
Edwards, Meredith. 1984. *The Income Unit in the Australian Tax and Social Security Systems*. Melbourne: Institute of Family Studies
Heer, David M., Robert W. Hodge, and Marcus Felson. 1986. "The Cluttered Nest: Evidence That Young Adults Are Living with Their Parents: Who Are They?" *Journal of Marriage and the Family* 48: 107-12
Income Tax Act, Revised Statutes of Canada 1952, c. 148 as amended (hereafter referred to as the act)
Kiker, B.F., and M. Mendes de Oliveira. 1990. "Estimation and Valuation of Non-Leisure Time." *Oxford Bulletin of Economics and Statistics* 52: 115

Killingsworth, Mark K. 1983. *Labor Supply*, 29–43. Cambridge: Cambridge University Press

Lacasse, Françoise D. 1971. *Women at Home: The Cost to the Canadian Economy of the Withdrawal from the Labour Force of a Major Proportion of the Female Population*, No. 2. Ottawa: Studies of the Royal Commission on the Status of Women in Canada

Lazear, Edward P., and Robert T. Michael. 1990. "Real Income Equivalence among One-Earner and Two-Earner Families." *American Economic Review* 80: 203

Leuthold, Jane. 1978. "The Effect of Taxation on the Hours Worked by Married Women." *Industrial and Labour Relations Review* 31: 520

Lord Denning. 1974. In *Langston v. A.U.E.W.*, 980. All ER 987

Maloney, Maureen A. 1987. *Women and Income Tax Reform*. Ottawa: Canadian Advisory Council on the Status of Women

– 1989. "Women and the Income Tax Act: Marriage, Motherhood, and Divorce." *Canadian Journal of Women and the Law* 3: 182

– 1991. "The Case for Wealth Taxation in Canada." *Canadian Journal of Public Administration* 34: 241–59

Morrison, Richard J., and Jillian Oderkirk. 1991. "Married Couple and Unmarried Couple: The Tax Question." *Canadian Social Trends* (Summer): 15–20

National Council of Welfare. 1990. *Women and Poverty Revisited*, 115. Ottawa

O'Kelly, C. 1985. "Tax Policy for Post Liberal Society: A Flat-Tax-Inspired Redefinition of the Purpose and Ideal Structure of a Progressive Income Tax." *Southern California Law Review* 58: 727–60

Pahl, Jan. 1989. *Money and Marriage*. London: MacMillan

Ram, Bali. 1990. *Current Demographic Analysis: New Trends in the Family*. Ottawa: Minister of Supply and Services

Rashid, A. 1989. *1986 Census of Canada: Family Income*. Ottawa: Minister of Supply and Services

Rea, S.A. 1984. "Taxes, Transfers and the Family." *University of Toronto Law Journal* 34(314): 322

Shanas, Ethel. 1979. "Social Myth as Hypothesis: The Case of the Family Relations of Old People." *The Gerontologist* 19: 3–9

Smith, Bud. 1988. "The Attorney General's Page: Family Maintenance Enforcement Program." *The Advocate* 46: 873

Statistics Canada. 1987. *Disabled Persons in Canada*. Cat. 82-602, pages x, xi, and table 3

Statutes of Ontario. 1986, c.4, sections 1(1) and 29

Stiglitz, Joseph. 1988. *Economics of the Public Sector*. New York: Norton

Waring, Marilyn. 1988. *If Women Counted: A New Feminist Economics.* New York: HarperCollins

Weitzman, Lenore J. 1985. *The Divorce Revolution The Unexpected Social and Economic Consequences for Women and Children in America,* 362. New York: The Free Press

5 The Macroeconomic Impacts of Harmonizing the Ontario Retail Sales Tax with the Federal GST

Simulations with the Focus-Ontario Model

PETER DUNGAN

Introduction

The purpose of this paper is to examine the possible impacts that harmonization of the Ontario retail sales tax (RST) and the federal Goods and Services Tax (GST) would have on the Ontario macro economy – that is, on the aggregate levels of output, prices, employment, and related indicators for the Ontario economy. To conduct the study we have used a macroeconometric model of the Ontario economy developed and maintained at the Institute for Policy Analysis, University of Toronto.

The methodology below describes in detail how we determined the impacts of harmonization with the model, while the following section presents and discusses the results. The remainder of this introduction puts the present study in the context of earlier work, and sets out the main issues behind the analysis.

This paper and the simulation work conducted for it are based on earlier work performed for the retail sales tax/Goods and Services Tax working group of the Fair Tax Commission, and is summarized in its "Working Group Report" submitted to the Treasurer of Ontario in April 1992. That report looked at various possibilities for partial harmonization, and also at alternative tax-credit schemes and possible fiscal offsets (whereby revenue losses from a lower harmonized RST rate would be partly made up by increases in corporate or personal income taxes). The current paper considers only a complete harmonization with the GST, and it also ignores possible tax credits. The basic simulation assumes that revenues equivalent to

the RST must be collected from the harmonized system alone, and
not from other tax sources – that is, we assume that harmonization
must be "revenue neutral." One alternative is presented in which
the harmonized rate is set so as not to increase consumer price
inflation; this results in a revenue shortfall (of approximately $1.7
billion in 1995) that is made up by an increase in income taxes.

Finally, the present study begins with the RST rate and base as
they existed after the Ontario provincial budget of May 1993. In
this budget the RST base was widened to include most insurance
(except personal life and health insurance) and a variety of much
smaller items; the budget estimated that this base widening would
increase tax revenues by $835 million on a full-year basis (Ontario
Ministry of Finance 1993, 36). As insurance is not part of the GST
base, any full harmonization would have to set a revenue-neutral
harmonized rate to make up this revenue added in the May 1993
budget.

Issues

Harmonizing the RST with the GST will change the sales tax burden
across the major categories of expenditures and possibly will alter
the total tax take. From these points spring the three principal issues
that concern us in modelling the macroeconomic impacts of
harmonization.[1]

The first issue is the extent to which removing the sales tax
burden from investment goods and exports will improve the productivity and international competitiveness of the Ontario economy.
Presently, the RST is paid partly or totally on a number of business
purchases and, as a cost, it is passed through into the prices of
many exports and investment goods. But, under the GST, this tax
burden on business would be removed and the prices of exports
and investment goods would fall somewhat. Cheaper exports can
affect Ontario's competitiveness in international markets, while
cheaper investment goods should encourage more investment and,
therefore, a higher capital stock for Ontarians to work with, thereby
improving their productivity. In the long run, therefore, harmonization would add to Ontario's GDP (but not necessarily employment) by expanding productivity and competitiveness, and we use
the macroeconometric model to determine the extent of this
expansion.

The second issue, which relates to impacts on consumer prices, and the third issue, which concerns "revenue neutrality," are closely related. If tax is being removed from exports and investment goods, then either revenue will be lost (harmonization is not "revenue neutral," but in fact lowers revenues), or other taxes must be raised, or the harmonization sales tax burden on consumption and residential investment must be increased. If the last, then harmonization will show up as an increase in consumer prices (the CPI) and a corresponding reduction in purchasing power. Unfortunately, a rise in the CPI means at least a temporary increase in the rate of inflation. We need to be careful in defining how the Bank of Canada will react to this extra inflation, and to consider how a rise in the measured cost of living may be passed through into wage demands, touching off a (limited) wage–price spiral. The macroeconometric model can help us disentangle these effects and gauge their size.

Finally, if revenue neutrality is the goal, then we can use the model to tell us the "revenue-neutral" rate for the provincial part of the harmonized tax, or to ask how much other taxes might have to be raised to achieve neutrality, and with what macroeconomic consequences.

Method: How the Impact of Harmonization Is Modelled

This study was conducted using the FOCUS model of the Canadian economy and the Focus-Ontario model of the Ontario economy.[2] The national model is required, even though harmonization is Ontario-specific, because the policy switch is likely to have effects on such national variables as the exchange rate and interest rates. We will concentrate on describing how harmonization was modelled in the Ontario model, noting now that parallel changes are required in the national model.

We begin with a projection or base case for the national and Ontario economies through the 1990s in which it is assumed that the RST system continues as at present.[3] Then, beginning arbitrarily in 1995, we alter the equations of the models to change the Ontario sales tax base from its current form to the federal GST base. An appropriate tax rate is selected and some assumption is made about the Bank of Canada's response to any inflationary impact of harmonization, and a new simulation is run from the year 1995 to the year 2001. The differences between the two model simulations, in terms of GDP growth, employment, inflation, the deficit, and other key indicators, are due solely to the introduction of harmonization at the selected tax rate, and represent our estimate of the macroeconomic impacts of harmonization.[4]

First, how does the tax base change under harmonization? In aggregated models like FOCUS and Focus-Ontario we make use of the principle that, although some sales taxes are paid (and often rebated) on intermediate inputs by business, eventually all sales taxes can be understood to be paid by the different categories of final demand. For example, under the RST the sales tax on cars is obviously paid by the final consumer. Under the GST, car manufacturers pay GST when they buy steel or glass, and auto retailers pay GST when they purchase from auto manufacturers, but each of these tax payments is rebated; so again it is the final consumer who really pays the GST on cars. If a firm producing investment goods (like machine tools) or goods for export pays RST for some of its inputs (like office supplies, computers, or health insurance) then these costs under open competition must eventually find their way into the prices of the investment goods or exports and the tax is "paid" in reality by the purchasers of these final demands. Using input-output tables and associated industry and final-demand tax data from Statistics Canada, we can assign weights to the categories of final demand reflecting the extent to which they are taxed under the RST and the GST. The weights we used are shown in table 1. In modelling harmonization, the model switches from the RST to the GST weights by final-demand category, although, of course, a different tax rate may be applied depending on revenue needs or other policy considerations. Note that for the final demand category of government expenditure we assume that tax rates and arrangements will be such that there is no change in the total amount of tax collected. This is, in fact, the way the GST system was established, with partial rebate rates that were meant to equalize the federal government's average tax take from the different levels of government.

Next, we must select the harmonized sales tax rate. As it turns out, the effect of changing the tax base weights, as in table 1, would be to increase sales tax revenues slightly at the current 8 per cent Ontario sales tax rate. A rate of approximately $7^2/_3$ per cent yields no change in the provincial deficit in the first year of harmonization (including the effects of somewhat reduced tax revenues across the board due to negative impacts on Ontario real output). This is the rate used in the first simulation presented below (simulation I: "Sales Tax Revenue Neutrality").

TABLE 1
Tax Base Weights – RST and GST

Final Demand	RST	GST
Consumer durables	.965	1.000
Consumer semi-durables	.790	1.000
Consumer non-durables	.459	.459
Consumer services	.227	.531
Residential investment	.460	.750
Investment – Non-residential structures	.370	0.0
Investment – Machinery	.541	0.0
Exports	.051	0.0
Government expenditure	(Equal tax revenues)	

Of course, these combined changes in rates and tax base do not simply affect revenue collection. By changing the rate and base weights in the model, we also change the prices associated with the different final demand categories in the model. For example, lowering the base weight to zero on investment goods and exports reduces their prices and encourages demand. Raising the base weights on the consumption categories (especially services) raises their prices and reduces demand. The rise in individual consumer prices also increases the CPI.

Before running the impact simulation, it is necessary to make some assumption about the Bank of Canada's response, especially because in simulation I we presume there will be positive initial impacts on the CPI. We have assumed that the Bank of Canada will maintain its inflation targets – that is, that it will act so that no change is permitted in the CPI inflation rate from base-case levels. However, the Bank has indicated that it will permit initial impacts of indirect tax changes to pass through into CPI inflation, although it will not validate any wage–price spiral from attempts to pass cost-of-living increases through to wages. Therefore, in our simulation, the Bank permits the CPI inflation rate to increase in the initial year (1995) only, and only by the amount of the initial shock. Thereafter, monetary policy maintains the CPI inflation rate at base-case levels, although the CPI price level is permanently increased by harmonization.

As we noted above, when the Bank of Canada has to fight to contain secondary inflationary pressures, as in simulation I, a loss of output results. This period of negative output and employment impacts could be significantly mitigated by setting the harmonized RST rate so that there is no net change in the CPI, and then raising the revenue required for revenue neutrality in some other way. Simulation experiments determined that a tax rate of about 6.5 per cent resulted in no change in the CPI inflation, and the model was then instructed to increase the provincial personal income tax rate in 1995 so as to make up for the resulting revenue loss. The PIT rate increase is then continued through the remaining years of the simulation. The PIT rate increase required is about 5.5 percentage points (as applied to the basic federal tax), which is a signficant increment yielding just over $1.7 billion in 1995. For comparison, the May 1993 Ontario budget raised the basic provincial PIT rate by 3 percentage points (actually 6 percentage points for July–December 1993).[5] The combination of a 6.5 per cent harmonized rate and increased PIT revenues results in simulation II below ("No CPI Change; PIT Increase").

Results

Finally, we turn to the results of the two model simulations. Key Ontario and Canadian indicators for simulation I ("Sales Tax Revenue Neutrality") are shown in table 2, and results for simulation II ("No CPI Change – PIT Increase") are in table 3. Each table shows results in the form of changes from the base case, whether in levels form (e.g., unemployment rate up 0.3 percentage points) or as a percentage of the base (e.g., real GDP down 0.3 per cent of base).

Simulation I ("Sales Tax Revenue Neutrality")

Briefly, simulation I is a story of short-term and long-term gain. By removing the sales tax burden from investment goods and from exports, competitiveness and productivity are both improved. The latter takes some years to cement in place as stronger investment gradually builds up a bigger capital shock. In the short run, there is a more transitory increase in labour productivity caused by a surge in wages, as will be discussed below. But by the seventh year of the simulation virtually all indicators are positive: output is up, employment is up (very slightly), labour productivity is up, and real wages are poised to rise above base case. Inflation is not increased (although the CPI level is up slightly due to the temporary inflation increase in 1995). The one disappointment is that the provincial government balance is down by about $600 million in the seventh year (that is, the deficit is worse by $600 million). This is partly due to the pain caused to the economy in the earlier transition years to harmonization; lower GDP and employment decreases revenues, which adds to debts and hence to interest on the debt in future years. But the deficit increase is also the result of switching the sales tax base away from exports and investment goods and toward consumption under a base-case projection in which it is exports and investment that will be the growth leaders in the 1990s, with consumption lagging behind. By switching to a tax base that grows less quickly and at a rate that is revenue-neutral in 1995, the harmonized sales tax actually loses revenue slightly over the subsequent years relative to the non-harmonized case. However, the loss of revenue is not severe compared with total revenues and could be offset by relatively small tax increases or expenditure cuts elsewhere. Note that, as expected, there are some significant shifts in the categories of final demand: expenditure on non-residential investment is above base throughout the simulation; expenditure on consumption is down but recovers near the end, as is reflected also in the behaviour of real disposable income. There is a strong shift in consumption away from services and to goods.

While the long-term gain is relatively clear, there is still a significant period of some short-term pain. As can be seen from table 2, Ontario GDP is 0.3 per cent below base in the first two years of harmonization (losing almost $1 billion 1986 dollars relative to base in each year). Positive GDP gains do not begin until the fourth year. Employment declines until the seventh year, and by a maximum of just over 70,000 jobs (in the third year). There are increases in the deficit of not only the provincial government, but also of other levels of government as well (note the results for the "Consolidated Government Balance").

There are at least two reasons for the short-term loss in GDP and employment. First, it takes longer for investment and exports to respond to the positive opportunities made available by harmonization than it does for consumption and residential housing to react (negatively) to the relative price increases that harmonization causes for these categories. Second, and more important, is that the CPI shock caused by shifting the indirect tax burden to consumption under harmonization leads to attempts to raise nominal wages in response. Workers are only trying to maintain the real purchasing

TABLE 2
Focus-Ontario Model – Institute for Policy Analysis
RST–GST Harmonization Simulation I – Sales Tax Revenue Neutrality

	1995	1996	1997	1998	1999	2000	2001
(Impacts are percentage changes unless otherwise indicated)							
Real Output and Components							
Real Gross Domestic Product	−0.3	−0.3	−0.2	0.3	0.5	0.3	0.8
Consumption	−1.0	−1.0	−0.8	−0.3	−0.2	−0.3	−0.1
Goods	−0.8	−0.9	−0.8	0.1	0.5	0.4	0.8
Services	−1.3	−1.2	−0.8	−0.8	−0.9	−1.0	−1.0
Investment							
Residential construction	−1.2	−2.4	−2.4	0.0	0.9	0.1	1.1
Machinery and equipment	1.9	2.8	2.6	3.3	3.9	3.4	3.5
Non-residential construction	0.9	1.9	2.5	3.0	2.5	1.8	1.9
Exports	0.1	−0.1	−0.2	0.0	0.2	0.4	0.6
Consumer Price Index	0.9	0.8	0.6	0.4	0.4	0.4	0.4
Ontario GDP deflator	0.1	0.0	−0.2	−0.4	−0.4	−0.5	−0.5
Unemployment rate (% pts)	0.4	0.7	0.8	0.2	0.0	0.1	−0.2
Employment (000s)	−34.7	−65.1	−73.7	−24.9	−2.7	−13.4	16.0
Wages – private sector	0.2	0.2	0.2	0.3	0.3	0.3	0.4
Real wages – private sector	−0.7	−0.6	−0.3	−0.2	−0.1	−0.1	0.0
Labour productivity	0.4	0.9	1.2	0.8	0.5	0.6	0.6
Consolidated government balance ($ Bill)	−0.5	−1.3	−1.6	−0.7	−0.5	−1.2	−0.4
Provincial government balance ($ Bill)	0.0	−0.2	−0.4	−0.3	−0.4	−0.7	−0.6
Ratio: Prov Debt / GDP (%)	0.1	0.1	0.2	0.2	0.3	0.4	0.4
Real personal disposable income	−1.0	−1.0	−0.8	−0.3	−0.2	−0.2	−0.1
Impacts on Canada:							
Real GDP – Canada (% ch)	−0.2	−0.3	−0.2	0.1	0.2	0.1	0.3
Exchange rate (US $/Cdn $)	0.0	0.2	0.3	0.0	−0.3	−0.4	−0.6
Levels Changes ($86 Million) – Ontario GDP and Components							
Real Gross Domestic Product	−781	−853	−488	922	1394	1100	2706
Consumption	−1449	−1497	−1171	−502	−258	−439	−106
Goods	−532	−668	−584	84	441	329	683
Services	−916	−829	−587	−586	−699	−768	−789
Investment							
Residential construction	−207	−445	−471	−1	184	17	255
Machinery and equipment	586	940	961	1314	1693	1593	1758
Non-residential construction	68	149	211	263	235	176	191
Exports	77	−116	−286	15	451	732	1108

power of their earnings – note in table 2 how nominal wages rise
somewhat, but real (purchasing power) wages still fall. To employers,

however, there is no corresponding price increase to match against the higher nominal wage demands (note that the Ontario output deflator holds steady and actually falls slightly in the longer term). In response, they cut back output and reduce their workforce relative to the base case. Moreover, the Bank of Canada is following a policy of only validating the initial impact of tax shift on the CPI (about 0.9 per cent for Ontario and 0.4 per cent for Canada as a whole). Therefore, in the face of rising wage and price pressures, the Bank permits interest rates to rise slightly and the exchange rate to appreciate (by 0.2 per cent to 0.3 per cent in the second and third years), further suppressing aggregate demand (this is why exports do not appear to respond to improved competitiveness in 1996 and 1997). Reduced demand and output, in turn, means additional job losses and increases in the unemployment rate. However, after several years of higher unemployment, workers accept the real wage losses inherent in raising indirect taxes on consumption, and base-case employment levels can be restored with no additional inflationary pressures. With a lag (in years after those shown in table 2), labour will also begin to enjoy real wage gains based on improved labour productivity from the higher induced capital stock.

Simulation II ("No CPI Change – PIT Increase")

Simulation II (see table 3) represents an approach to harmonization that attempts to mitigate the short-term pain resulting from the initial CPI shock and its subsequent effects on wages and on monetary policy. In this simulation the harmonized rate is set at 6.5 per cent. This is sufficient to raise approximately the same amount of indirect tax revenue from consumption as under the RST, although there will still be a relative shift from consumer services to goods.

There is still a negative effect of harmonization on GDP in this simulation, but it lasts only one year in the present case, instead of three years under simulation I. The longer-term positive impacts, therefore, come sooner and are generally stronger. Paralleling the GDP, the initial employment losses are also much smaller and less prolonged.

Within the GDP it should be noted that simulation II is not particularly kind to consumption. While the overall sales tax burden on consumption is not increased in this simulation, there is, nevertheless, a hefty increase in personal income taxes that actually reduces real disposable income and consumption more than in simulation I. Offsetting the greater decline in consumption is a stronger positive impact on investment and exports than in simulation I; targeting for no CPI change therefore tends to yield better long-term results for productivity and international competitiveness. There is also less of a negative impact on the provincial deficit and debt in simulation II. This is partly because there is less lost output in simulation II, and, therefore, less erosion of revenue and buildup of debt in the earlier years. The relative improvement in the deficit also results from the fact that the personal income tax base grows more strongly in the base case than does consumption, and in simulation II both bases are being tapped for revenues, not just consumption as in simulation I. However, it is also important to note that even in simulation II the impact of harmonization on the deficit is still negative – again, because the fastest-growing elements of the economy (investment and exports) are being removed from the tax base.

Despite these differences in the initial several years of harmonization, it is also clear from tables 2 and 3 that both harmonization simulations are tending to much the same longer-term results. The more favourable results for the transition period offered by simulation II would have to be set against the potential competitive costs of higher income tax rate (but a lower indirect tax rate on consumption).[6] The longer the time horizon one takes, the less important the transition costs can become.

A final comment: simulation II argues that there is at least a short-term advantage in introducing a harmonized RST at a rate lower than what would be revenue-neutral, and then making up the revenue by raising the PIT. Arguments for fairness might actually push in the opposite direction. As we noted several times, harmonization requires increasing the tax burden on consumption and, all else being equal, this will increase the tax burden on low-income individuals, even if it increases the burden on higher-income individuals as well. An immediate remedy often suggested is to increase low-income PIT credits and make up for the lost revenue by increasing the harmonized sales tax rate. Indeed, in part, this was what was done with the federal GST. The model we have used would suggest this is a poor solution, since raising the harmonized rate even higher than the revenue-neutral level would worsen price–wage pass-through and increase the transition costs still further. Instead, it should be noted that setting the harmonized rate so that there is no increase in the CPI will itself greatly reduce any adverse impacts on low-income individuals, and therefore lessen

TABLE 3
Focus-Ontario Model – Institute for Policy Analysis
RST–GST Harmonization Simulation II – No CPI Change – PIT Increase

	1995	1996	1997	1998	1999	2000	2001
(Impacts are percentage changes unless otherwise indicated)							
Real Output and Components							
Real Gross Domestic Product	−0.2	0.1	0.5	0.5	0.5	0.4	0.5
Consumption	−1.1	−1.0	−0.7	−0.8	−0.8	−0.9	−0.9
Goods	−0.8	−0.5	0.0	0.0	−0.1	−0.3	−0.4
Services	−1.5	−1.6	−1.5	−1.6	−1.6	−1.6	−1.5
Investment							
Residential construction	−0.9	−0.7	0.5	0.8	0.3	−0.2	−0.3
Machinery and equipment	2.1	3.5	3.8	4.0	3.7	3.7	3.9
Non-residential construction	1.1	2.3	2.9	2.6	2.4	2.4	2.7
Exports	0.1	0.2	0.4	0.6	0.6	0.6	0.6
Consumer Price Index	0.0	0.0	0.0	0.0	0.0	0.0	0.0
Ontario GDP deflator	−0.6	−0.7	−0.8	−0.8	−0.8	−0.9	−0.9
Unemployment rate (% Pts)	0.3	0.2	−0.2	−0.2	−0.1	0.0	0.1
Employment (000s)	−26.4	−21.7	13.0	17.8	10.9	−3.6	−7.5
Wages – private sector	0.0	0.0	0.0	0.1	0.2	0.2	0.3
Real wages – private sector	0.0	0.0	0.1	0.1	0.2	0.2	0.2
Labour productivity	0.3	0.5	0.3	0.2	0.3	0.5	0.6
Consolidated government balance							
($ Bill)	−0.5	−0.4	0.2	0.2	0.1	−0.3	−0.4
Provincial government balance ($ Bill)	0.0	0.0	0.0	0.0	−0.1	−0.3	−0.4
Ratio: Prov. debt / GDP (%)	0.2	0.2	0.1	0.1	0.2	0.2	0.3
Real personal disposable income	−1.1	−1.0	−0.7	−0.8	−0.8	−0.9	−0.9
Impacts on Canada:							
Real GDP – Canada (% ch)	−0.1	0.0	0.2	0.3	0.2	0.2	0.3
Exchange rate (US $/Cdn $)	0.0	0.0	−0.4	−0.6	−0.6	−0.6	−0.6
Levels Changes ($86 Million) – Ontario GDP and Components							
Real Gross Domestic Product	−517	170	1372	1413	1376	1303	1537
Consumption	−1589	−1487	−1074	−1140	−1277	−1510	−1564
Goods	−552	−380	30	38	−67	−289	−352
Services	−1037	−1107	−1103	−1177	−1210	−1220	−1213
Investment							
Residential construction	−161	−122	97	156	64	−46	−67
Machinery and equipment	629	1158	1409	1574	1599	1735	1911
Non-residential construction	81	181	241	231	225	238	272
Exports	158	264	646	998	1158	1146	1155

or eliminate the need for new low-income sales tax credits. Further, the increase in the PIT that is required can, if desired, be structured to spare low-income individuals through the use of low-income credits and high-income surtaxes.

Conclusions and Caveats

The principal conclusions I would draw from the model work on the macroeconomic implications of harmonization are as follows:

1. Over a longer period, harmonization of the provincial sales tax with the federal GST will increase Ontario's GDP in a non-inflationary fashion by expanding the capital shock and improving international competitiveness.
2. If the harmonized provincial sales tax is to yield approximately the same revenues as the RST (after the May 1993 Ontario budget) then the required tax rate is about $7^2/_3$ per cent. This method of achieving revenue neutrality will shift the tax burden to consumption and cause temporary CPI inflation. While the Bank of Canada might be expected to permit the "first-round" CPI inflation impact, it is unlikely to permit indirect inflationary impacts through attempted wage pass-throughs. The result is some short- to medium-term loss in Ontario GDP and employment.
3. If the harmonized rate were to be set at about 6.5 per cent, there would be no initial new tax burden on consumption and virtually no impact on inflation. However, revenue neutrality would require an increase in personal income taxes (or an increase in other taxes, or a cut in expenditure) of about $1.7 billion in 1995 (and some-what more in succeeding years). The necessary increase in the provincial PIT rate is about 5.5 percentage points. The absence of an initial inflation shock and of subsequent wage pass-through would significantly reduce (but not eliminate) the negative impacts on Ontario's GDP and employment as harmonization began, and would permit the positive impacts on GDP to appear sooner.

Naturally, as with any study of this sort, the conclusions must be tempered with caution based on the assumptions made and the features of the model used to conduct the analysis. The most important of these cautions, or "caveats," are as follows:

1. The first caution has to do with the impact of harmonization on improved productivity and competitiveness. In aggregate models like FOCUS and Focus-Ontario we must assume that the burden

of the current RST on investment goods or exports is, in effect, spread evenly across all such types of goods. Then, if the RST is removed, more of the "average" investment goods will be bought and added to the capital stock, with "average" effects on productivity. And the price of the average export good will decline, leading to an increase in exports at the average rate. But, the impact of the RST varies widely across investment goods and exports; indeed, this is one of its faults. Thus, it is possible that the RST burden will fall primarily on particular investment goods the demand for which responds little to price changes, or which have very little impact on measured productivity.[7] Similarly, for exports it is possible that the RST burden will fall most heavily on exports whose demand is very insensitive to price. The net result of this unevenness of RST burden, which the model cannot address, is that we may be overestimating the impact of removing the RST on productivity and competitiveness. Of course, it is also possible for the caution to go the other way; that is, because the burden of the RST is unevenly distributed we may also be underestimating the impact of the RST removal on productivity and export competitiveness. And the more uneven the RST burden on exports and investment goods, the greater the potential for one-time productivity gains from increasing efficiency by eliminating tax distortions across goods, which, again, the aggregate macro model does not take into account.[8]

2. The second caution has to do with the current state of the provincial RST system and its relationship to the so-called "underground" economy. There is some recent evidence (Spiro 1993) that the introduction of the GST has pushed some economic activity underground or into an unreported state. This may have affected RST revenues, and perhaps even PIT revenues, as well. It is possible that further increasing the sales tax burden on services or other items previously not taxed before the GST might push additional economic activity underground. The aggregate macro models cannot estimate the extent of additional underground activity that might result from harmonization. Obviously, any increase in underground activity would affect our estimates for economic impacts and our calculation of "revenue-neutral" or "deficit-neutral" tax rates, whether for the harmonized RST or for any necessary changes in PIT rates. It should be noted, however, that serious enforcement and auditing for the GST has only just begun, and that RST–GST harmonization would further simplify compliance, auditing, and enforcement, possibly stem-

ming any further movements underground or even forcing some underground activity back into the light of day.

3. The third caution concerns interprovincial impacts. We have simplified the analysis by measuring the impact of harmonization as if all provinces moved to harmonization simultaneously. In this case, there is likely to be little net interprovincial effect. In reality, Quebec has already partially harmonized, and other provinces may not do so even if Ontario does. In this case, harmonization by Ontario may reduce capital costs in Ontario relative to Quebec (where they have already been reduced by partial harmonization) and relative to provinces that do not harmonize, and might thereby cause new investments to come to Ontario that would otherwise have gone to other provinces. Similarly, harmonization by Ontario alone, by removing the tax burden from intermediate inputs, might make Ontario's goods relatively cheaper in other provinces and increase production in Ontario (slightly) at the expense of other provinces. Again, there are no long-term benefits on this score for Ontario if it harmonizes and if all other provinces harmonize as well. Of course, it should also be kept in mind that these effects work negatively on Ontario if it fails to harmonize when most of the other provinces do so; in this case, it becomes relatively less competitive in producing for the domestic market and somewhat less attractive for new investments.

4. The change in relative prices caused by harmonization may also set off structural changes because some industries will benefit and others will lose. The existing stock of physical and human capital must be shifted to the now relatively more profitable sectors. In the long run, this will mean efficiency gains, but the change-over can be time-consuming, and, in the interim, some workers and capital may be unemployed and output can be lost. Unfortunately, the models do not permit us to measure these effects, but it is important to recall that some structural change is always in progress and a modest additional amount need not be severely disruptive.

5. A final caution concerns our result that a lower harmonized rate, together with a PIT increase, would reduce the costs of transition to a harmonized system. This result depends upon an important asymmetry: namely, that labour will attempt to pass through into wages and salaries any increases in the cost of living due to indirect tax increases, but they will not attempt to bargain up their wages and salaries to offset income tax increases. Our two simulations are both increasing the tax burden on individuals (because

they are lowering the tax burden on investment goods and exports, and revenue neutrality is required), but simulation I does it through increasing consumer prices. This leads to a wage–price spiral choked off by anti-inflationary monetary policy and, in turn, to temporary output losses and added unemployment. Simulation II increases the tax burden on individuals through higher income taxes that are "accepted" by individuals with no direct impact on wage demands. That this asymmetry exists is strongly suggested by the equations of the models. But relying on asymmetries can be uncomfortable. It is possible that, especially with careful political "salesmanship" or even some resort to legislative means to limit pass-through, the extent of sales tax pass-through to wages might be les than what is found in simulation I, reducing the short-term negative impacts and making simulation II, with its PIT increase, appear less attractive.

Notes

1 There are, of course, many more microeconomic impacts that are of concern for a proper assessment of harmonization. These would include, for example, the amount of administrative savings expected for both governments and business; the impacts on different sectors or types of businesses across the economy; additional incentives or disincentives harmonization would add to tax evasion; and the impacts on cross-border shopping and tourism. There are also potential impacts on income distribution that are of concern. Some of these micro impacts might obviously have macroeconometric implications, but they cannot be directly estimated by macroeconometric models.

2 For detailed model descriptions see Dungan and Jump (1992) and Dungan (1992).

3 The base was developed for the Fair Tax Commission and is decribed in Dungan (1993).

4 Technically, the base case we use was developed before the Ontario budget of May 1993 and does not include the changes in items subject to RST (primarily insurance) announced in the budget. These new items would be virtually free of tax under a harmonized system. Therefore, our simulation of harmonization required that the additional revenues estimated in the budget be removed when we simulated the harmonized regime.

5 But the May 1993 budget also increased high-income surtaxes significantly.

6 For further discussion of the merits of higher indirect taxes on con-

sumption versus higher income taxes, see Wilson and Dungan (1993). Among other issues, putting greater reliance on income taxes increases the urgency of reforming the income tax system to increase shelters for savings and steer the system more in the direction of taxing consumption and not income.

7 For example, the burden of the RST on investment goods might fall much more heavily on company automobiles than on computer-controlled machine tools. If the RST burden were lifted, it might be asked how many new company cars would be bought, and if so, how more company cars would add to productivity in comparison with adding new machine tools.

8 The argument here is that if some types of investment goods are taxed and others are not, then producers will be buying relatively too much of the untaxed goods and too little of the other. If the tax distortion were to be removed, which it would be if all taxes are zero, then firms would gradually restructure their production to use somewhat more of the formerly taxed good and relatively less of the untaxed good, obtaining more output or productivity for a given investment dollar. The potential productivity gains from removing tax distortions across different kinds of investment goods cannot be estimated in an aggregate model, but would add to the productivity estimates obtained in our model work.

Bibliography

Dungan, D. Peter. 1992. "The Focus-Ontario Model – Version 92A" (Reference Manual), Institute for Policy Analysis, University of Toronto
– 1993. "The Economic Environment for Tax Reform in Ontario." In *The Economic and Social Environment for Tax Reform*, ed. Allan M. Maslove. Fair Tax Commission, Research Studies. Toronto: University of Toronto Press.
Dungan, D. Peter, and Gregory Jump. 1992. "The FOCUS Model of the Canadian Economy – Version 92A" (Reference Manual), Institute for Policy Analysis, University of Toronto
Dungan, D. Peter, Jack M. Mintz, and Thomas Wilson. 1990. "Alternatives to the Goods and Services Tax." *Canadian Tax Journal* 38: 644–65
Dungan, D. Peter, and Thomas A. Wilson. 1989a. "The Proposed Federal Goods and Services Tax: Its Economic Effect under Alternative Labour Market and Monetary Policy Conditions." *Canadian Tax Journal* 37: 341–67
– 1989b. "The Macroeconomic Effects of the Proposed Federal Goods and Services Tax." PEAP Policy Study 89-9, Institute for Policy Analysis, University of Toronto

Ontario. Fair Tax Commission. 1992. "Retail Sales Tax/Goods and Services Tax." Working Group Report. Mimeo. Toronto

Ontario. Ministry of Finance. 1993. *1993 Ontario Budget*, 19 May, Toronto

Spiro, Peter S. 1993. "Evidence of a Post-GST Increase in the Underground Economy." *Canadian Tax Journal* 41: 247–58

Wilson, Thomas A., and D. Peter Dungan. 1993. "Sales Tax Reform." In *Fiscal Policy in Canada: An Appraisal*. Canadian Tax Paper No. 94. Toronto: Canadian Tax Foundation

6 Wealth Tax Proposals
Distributional Impacts and Revenue Potential

JAMES B. DAVIES and DAVID G. DUFF

Introduction

The purpose of this paper is to discuss the possible impacts of two alternative wealth tax proposals on the distribution of income and wealth and on government revenue in Ontario. The two wealth tax variants analysed are an annual net wealth tax and a wealth transfer tax.

The key ingredients in any study of this type are information on the distributions of income and wealth and on patterns of wealth holding, and a model of tax impacts. As we will explore, while all of these ingredients are available in some form, the latter is typically far from ideal. This imposes inevitable limitations on the kind of study provided here, and it is important to keep them in mind.

Data on wealth holding are less reliable than those on income in all countries and are relatively less developed in Canada than elsewhere. Modelling the full impacts of these taxes would require specifying the transitional and long-run response of households, capital markets, and the economy in general to the tax innovations. This analysis ought to be rooted in a carefully parametrized model with a firm empirical and theoretical basis. Unfortunately, comprehensive models of this sort are not readily available and it would require sizeable resources to construct such a model from scratch. Despite the necessary limitations of this study, we can nevertheless say quite a bit about possible effects of new wealth taxes, on the basis of existing knowledge and data.

Two quite different forms of wealth tax are analysed here. The first is an annual net wealth tax. Each year individuals, or perhaps families, would pay a tax on their year-end net worth. The tax could have flat or graduated rates and would, no doubt, be introduced with fairly sizeable thresholds. In practice, special exemptions or reduced rates for particular assets (homes, farms, small businesses, and so on) are likely. There are considerable problems in administration, valuation, and so on, that have dogged annual wealth taxes in the countries where they are in force. There is no Canadian experience with comprehensive annual wealth taxes, although taxes on real property and corporate paid-up capital are often identified as forms of wealth taxation on particular categories of assets. From time to time tax reformers call for the introduction of a comprehensive annual net wealth tax, and it is that kind of initiative that is examined here.

The second kind of wealth tax that we study is a wealth transfer tax that is levied on gifts and/or bequests. This tax, like the annual net wealth tax, could also have flat or graduated rates with sizeable thresholds. There are many possible forms of wealth transfer tax. Here we have limited our attention to an estate tax. While a good case can be made that something like a lifetime accessions tax is superior on equity grounds, the data requirements for modelling such a tax are beyond our resources. In addition, the estate tax is similar to existing taxes in other jurisdictions and to wealth transfer taxes formerly levied in Canada. It may therefore have greater relevance in terms of the kind of tax that might emerge if this form of taxation were revived in Canada.

The final sections of this paper present some calculations of simulated distributional and revenue impacts. These calculations have important limitations that must be borne in mind. First, they are based on adjusted 1984 survey data updated to 1989. Changes in real wealth holding, asset values and incomes (other than pure inflation), and demographic changes since 1989 are therefore not taken into account. In addition, the calculations are only as good as the underlying survey data. The latter have been adjusted to represent more accurately the upper tail of the distribution of wealth, but as is always true with this kind of data, reliability in the upper regions of wealth holding is not very high.

A second important limitation of the calculations presented in this paper is that they assume each wealth tax applies to all assets without exception and that individual behaviour and economic conditions remain unaltered when the tax is introduced. Enforcement is never perfect in the real world and individual behaviour and economic phenomena are not unaffected by tax measures. Any of the wealth tax options simulated in this paper would experience leakage through avoidance and evasion and would also likely result in reduced asset values as the expected burden of the tax is capitalized in the market price of assets subject to tax.

A further limitation of the calculations is that they reflect only first-round or impact effects. The distributional effects of wealth taxes may well grow over time as the taxes and redistribution in successive years accumulate. Associated with this may be a decline in annual revenue if extremes in the distribution of wealth (and income) are narrowed over time. None of these effects is taken into account here.

This paper is organized as follows. Section two discusses what would be involved in an ideal investigation of the distributional and revenue impacts of wealth tax initiatives. Section three looks at actual experience with wealth taxes in other countries and in Canada in the past. In the fourth section we examine the available evidence on patterns of wealth holding in Canada and in Ontario. Calculations of the short-run impact of a comprehensive annual wealth tax are presented in the fifth section; the sixth section examines wealth transfer tax impacts; and we draw our conclusions in section seven.

Theoretical Analysis

Intuition suggests that if one levies a progressive wealth tax, and spends the proceeds on public goods and services or transfer payments, wealth and income inequality will tend to decline. Intuition also suggests that wealth taxes should increase government revenue. To what extent can we expect this intuition to be correct? In order to answer this question, we need to analyse the general equilibrium effects of wealth taxes, taking into account the phenomena of capital flight, impacts on saving and investment, and asset price effects.

Capital Flight

The possibility of capital flight tends to reinforce intuition in the case of the distributional effect, but to run against it in terms of revenue impacts. Part of the avoidance response to wealth taxes is for investors to relocate assets in other jurisdictions, and if that doesn't work to leave the country themselves. In the short run neither of these effects is likely very strong, but it seems naïve to believe they would be weak in the long run, given the increasing international mobility of capital and of wealthy investors.

Capital flight, whether accompanied by emigration of wealthy investors or not, has an immediate equalizing effect on the distribution of wealth. But this is a very special kind of equalization. What is lost from the upper tail is not transferred to people lower down in the distribution. The country becomes more equal, but it also becomes poorer in aggregate. There is an associated loss of tax revenue. Not only are wealth tax revenues eroded, but the income taxes that would be generated by the relocated capital are also affected. It is entirely possible that the net impact of levying a wealth tax on government revenues may be negative simply because of capital flight.

Effects on Saving and Investment

What is the likely impact of wealth taxation on people who remain in the country and cannot move assets across borders? The answer is that we really do not know, but that we can make guesses based on plausible assumptions about their motivations for saving and wealth holding. The effects of an annual wealth tax and of wealth transfer taxes should be considered in turn.

If all assets and all forms of asset income were taxable, and if the pre-tax rate of return, r, on all assets were the same, an annual net wealth tax levied at rate t would be fully equivalent to a capital income tax at rate t/r. Actual taxation of capital income is far from being at a flat rate on a comprehensive base, and the same would no doubt be true of actual wealth taxes. In addition, riskier assets earn higher average rates of return. Nevertheless, it is instructive to consider what we know, or think we know, about the effects of capital income taxes as a starting point for the discussion of the distributional and revenue impacts of an annual wealth tax.

It is a theoretical possibility that a capital income tax could increase saving (Feldstein 1978). However, both empirical evidence and tax policy simulations based on various versions of the life-cycle model of saving strongly suggest that the saving effect takes the more intuitive negative sign (see Boskin 1978; Summers 1981;

Auerbach, Kotlikoff, and Skinner 1983; and Auerbach and Kotlikoff 1987). On this basis, one might expect an annual net wealth tax to reduce household saving as well. It is hard to imagine that the possible narrowness of a real-world annual net wealth tax base, or the fact that it would fall more heavily on riskier, higher return assets, relative to a capital income tax, would reverse the direction of this effect.

It is sometimes claimed that the saving disincentive effects of a wealth transfer tax would be much weaker than those of an annual wealth or capital income tax. This argument is made by those who believe that bequests are largely "accidental." Bequests are accidental if individuals really only save to provide for their own future consumption, or to enjoy the power and privileges of wealth, and leave bequests simply because death is inescapable (and they like their heirs a bit more than other possible beneficiaries). In this situation, the taxation of bequests would have little or no disincentive effect on saving. On the other hand, some people think that there is very active altruism behind bequests, or at least concern that power and privileges be passed down in the family.

Even if there is strong bequest motivation for saving, it is not clear that taxing bequests will reduce saving very much in the short or long run. Suppose that an unanticipated permanent change to a flat 50 per cent tax on all capital transfers were instituted. This might reduce saving among all those currently saving to make a bequest. However, it would also cut in half any gifts or bequests currently being received. The sizeable decrease in lifetime income of inheritors would reduce their consumption, that is, increase their saving. The effects might be approximately offsetting.

What would be the long-run consequences of a decline in household saving due to the introduction of an annual net wealth tax, or possibly as a result of a wealth transfer tax? Thinking simply in partial equilibrium terms, the wealth-eroding, first-round impact of the tax would clearly be reinforced. Suppose that in the absence of the tax, the real wealth of the top 0.5 per cent of wealth holders would rise at a rate of 3 per cent per year. A comprehensive 1 per cent annual net wealth tax would cut this growth rate to about 2 per cent per year in the absence of any change in saving and portfolio choice. With a reduction in saving, and a possible substitution away from the now less-favoured, higher-yielding riskier assets, the growth rate would decline further. Suppose the growth rate in the real wealth of the top 0.5 per cent of wealth holders fell to 1 per cent per year. If the economy in general was growing at a 3 per cent real per capita rate, so that both incomes and assets of the bottom 99.5 per cent of wealth holders were growing at a 3 per cent rate, the ratio of the assets of the rich to those of the rest of us would be declining at an annual rate of 2 per cent.

What happens if we try to take a general equilibrium view, that is, if we take into account possible induced changes in the economy's factor endowments (labour, human capital, physical capital) and their rewards? The answer depends on taking an open-economy view. In a closed economy the decline in saving would lead to slower growth of the physical capital stock, and there would be a tendency to increase investment in human capital since its relative rate of return would rise compared with physical capital (subject to the annual net wealth tax). However, with free international capital mobility the result would be quite different. Assuming the tax would be a residence-based tax, like the personal income tax, it would not deter foreign investors. Opportunities for profitable investment in Canada would be little affected by the tax or the associated decline in Canadians' saving. In fact, if Canadians responded by investing more in human capital, opportunities for expanding – for example, high-tech industries – in Canada might even become more profitable. The investment would be by foreigners, rather than by Canadians, reinforcing the already high level of foreign ownership of Canadian industry.

In a closed economy, the reduction in capital formation caused by a decline in domestic saving would lead to lower growth of real wages and an increase in the before-tax rate of return to physical capital. These effects would offset the first-round equalizing impact of the tax. In the Canadian situation, however, such consequences do not appear very likely. The distribution of wealth among Canadians would likely become more equal, but Canadians in aggregate would become poorer, and a larger chunk of their economy would be foreign owned. Associated with these trends would be slow growth of the wealth tax base, so that with constant tax rates the revenue generated by the wealth tax would tend to fall over time as a proportion of total government revenue or gross domestic product.

Asset Price Effects

Consider the impact on asset prices of an unanticipated one per cent tax being imposed on six-cylinder cars. Given a fixed stock of such cars in the short run, the fact that a new stream of tax liabilities, T, was now attached to the ownership of such a car would reduce the demand price for six-cylinder cars by the amount T. Current owners of such cars would suffer a windfall capital loss. The decline in market price would result in a reduced rate of output and sales of such cars, tending to restore their price to its starting point over a period of years. In the long run the true incidence of the tax would fall on users of these vehicles, but there would be an important initial transition period before the stock of six-cylinder cars had been fully adjusted relative to that of other cars. During this period, it would primarily be the owners of the cars at the time the tax was imposed, rather than current owners, who would suffer from the tax. And they would suffer immediately, in the form of their capital loss, rather than on a year-by-year basis.

If an annual net wealth tax were to affect all asset prices in the same way that a tax on six-cylinder cars would affect their price, there would be profound implications for a discussion of the distributional effects of annual wealth taxes. Distributional effects in the form of capital losses would be very sizeable and would occur at the instant the tax was announced. There is, however, a difference between imposing a wealth tax on a single asset type and imposing one on all assets. A completely comprehensive tax would reduce the after-tax rate of return on all assets. If all assets had the same before-tax rate of return this would mean that both income streams and discount rates would decline by the same fraction, so that there would be no change in the present values of the income stream in any asset. The result would be no change in asset prices.

A real-world annual net wealth tax would differ from an across-the-board proportional wealth tax in that, for example, with a threshold of, say, $1 million, the great majority of asset holders would escape the tax entirely. For assets not held primarily by the wealthy, one would therefore expect very little asset price effect. What would be the anticipated impact on assets outside this category – for instance, expensive homes, shares in Canadian corporations, corporate bonds, and so on? The impact depends on what happens to the relevant discount rate for wealthy Canadians, and on the importance of foreign investors (and whether the tax also applies to foreign owners of Canadian assets). At least some wealthy Canadians would be operating sufficiently in foreign capital markets that their relevant after-tax interest rates on interest-bearing deposits or debt would be little affected by a Canadian annual net

wealth tax. (This would tend to be the case even if wealthy Canadians were theoretically taxable on world-wide wealth including
offshore deposits.) This would lead to a decreased demand price
on their part for fully taxed Canadian real estate, bonds, debt, and
the like. Prices would be depressed, except in those cases where
foreign investors are active. Thus, expensive Toronto homes and
shares in Canadian corporations might decline in value, but it is
unlikely that the value of Canadian corporate or government bonds
would decline.

Conclusion

The purpose of this section was to ask how general equilibrium
considerations would affect intuitive expectations that progressive
wealth taxes should reduce inequality and raise revenues significantly. Capital flight, effects on saving and investment, and asset
price impacts have all been predicted to reinforce the equalizing impact of wealth taxes, but at the cost of reduced aggregate wealth
and rising foreign ownership. In contrast, each of these effects weak-
ens the positive revenue impact suggested by intuitive expectations.
In combination, the factors considered could produce a negative net
effect of wealth taxes on overall government revenue.

The illustrative calculations of distributional and revenue impacts
of alternative wealth taxes presented later in this paper ignore all
the factors discussed in this section. This is an important limitation.
It implies, for example, that revenue impacts will tend to be overstated. It is possible to get a handle on this error by comparing
our hypothetical calculations for Canada with actual experience
where wealth taxes are currently imposed, and with former Canadian experience of estate taxes and succession duties.

Not considered in this section are avoidance and evasion. These
factors reinforce the doubts raised here about revenues, but act in
the opposite direction with regard to the impact on inequality. It
is often asserted that the opportunities for avoidance are greatest
for the wealthiest individuals and families. If this is the case, taking
avoidance into account would weaken the prediction that wealth
taxes will reduce inequality, as discussed below.

Wealth Taxes

Wealth taxes of one kind or another exist in most OECD countries, and were levied at the federal level in Canada from 1941 to 1971 and in Ontario from 1892 to 1979. This is not the place to examine these taxes in detail, nor to review the history of their existence and abolition in Canada.[1] Nonetheless, for our purposes, it is helpful to summarize the basic structure of these taxes and the main design elements that are likely to influence the amount of revenue that each tax might raise as well as the distributional impact of these taxes. Further, in order to assess the plausibility of our own estimates, it is useful to consider comparative data based on actual experience with wealth taxes.

Annual Net Wealth Taxes

Although annual net wealth taxes have never existed in Canada, they are common among OECD member countries, particularly Scandinavian and continental European countries where these taxes often predate taxes on income. Key design features that are likely to influence the revenue potential and distributional impact of these taxes include the breadth of assets included in the base, the rates of tax applicable to taxable wealth, the size of any tax-exempt threshold and whether this threshold applies to individuals or families.

Typically, annual net wealth taxes apply to a relatively broad base, calculated by subtracting the aggregate value of residents' world-wide liabilities from the total value of their world-wide assets, while non-residents are taxed on the net value of property located within the taxing jurisdiction. Pensions, household and personal effects, life insurance, modest personal savings, works of art and collections are often exempt. No OECD member country exempts owner-occupied homes from annual net wealth tax, although Ireland did so under its short-lived tax in the mid-1970s, and other countries provide special relief to owner-occupied housing through favourable methods of valuation. Special valuation rules are also often available to reduce the tax burden on agricultural property and private businesses.

Tax rates in OECD member countries with annual net wealth taxes generally range from 0.5 per cent to 3.0 per cent of taxable net wealth, with some countries levying tax at a single flat rate and others employing a graduated rate structure whereby higher rates apply to larger amounts of wealth. Several countries impose eilings on the amount of wealth tax payable, usually by limiting the combined amount of wealth and income tax payable to a specific percentage of taxable income. Thresholds below which no tax is payable range from as little as $10,000 in Luxembourg to over $500,000 in France. For the most part, tax is levied on a family basis so that these thresholds apply to the total amount of net wealth held by spouses and dependent children rather than individuals.

Comparative figures on revenues raised from annual net wealth taxes can be expressed as a share of total tax revenues or as a share of gross domestic product. The latter set of figures likely provide a better measure of the revenue potential of annual net wealth taxes in different countries with different-sized public sectors and different mixes of taxes. In order to assess the accuracy of our own estimates, however, we present both sets of figures.

Table 1 presents figures on the share of total tax revenues raised by OECD member countries (all levels of government) from annual net wealth taxes at ten-year intervals from 1970 to 1990. In 1990, these percentages ranged from 0.08 per cent in Finland to 2.32 per cent in Switzerland and averaged 0.66 per cent (unweighted average) in OECD countries with annual net wealth taxes.

Table 2 presents figures on revenues raised from annual net wealth taxes as a percentage of the gross domestic product of OECD member countries at ten-year intervals from 1970 to 1990. Calculated on this basis for 1990, annual net wealth taxes raised as little as 0.03 per cent of gross domestic product in Finland and as much as 0.73 per cent of gross domestic product in Switzerland, and averaged about 0.26 per cent of GDP across all OECD member countries with annual net wealth taxes (unweighted average). Compared with the first set of figures, these ratios are less variable among countries and more stable over time.

Based on these statistics, it is possible to make rough estimates of the revenue potential of a provincial annual net wealth tax, against which our own theoretical estimates can be compared. Relying strictly on annual net wealth tax revenues as a percentage of total tax revenues, estimates that Ontario raised roughly $30 billion in tax revenues in 1992–3 (Ontario Budget 1993, 91) suggest that Ontario might be able to obtain anywhere from about $25 million (0.08 per cent of total tax revenue as in Finland) to $700 million (2.32 per cent of total tax revenue as in Switzerland) from a provincial annual net wealth tax, though a more cautious estimate would be in the range of $200 million (0.66 per cent of total tax revenue, the OECD average).

TABLE 1
Annual Net Wealth Tax Revenue as a Percentage of Total Tax Revenues
OECD Member Countries

Country	1970	1980	1990
Australia	–	–	–
Austria	0.68	0.47	0.43
Belgium	–	–	–
Canada	–	–	–
Denmark	0.56	0.56	0.24
Finland	0.49	0.21	0.08
France	–	–	0.22
Germany	1.06	0.34	0.31
Greece	–	–	–
Iceland	0.80	0.61	1.29
Ireland	–	0.03	–
Italy	–	–	–
Japan	–	–	–
Luxembourg	0.43	0.18	0.33
Netherlands	0.84	0.74	0.53
New Zealand	–	–	–
Norway	0.83	0.68	1.17
Portugal	–	–	–
Spain	–	0.49	0.62
Sweden	0.70	0.27	0.41
Switzerland	3.31	2.64	2.32
Turkey	–	–	–
United Kingdom	–	–	–
United States	–	–	–
Average % of countries with tax (unweighted)	0.99	0.65	0.66

Source: OECD, *Revenue Statistics of OECD Members Countries, 1965–1991*

Using revenues as a percentage of gross domestic product as the standard for comparison, projections that Canada's gross domestic product will reach $724.6 billion in 1993 (Conference Board of Canada 1993) and estimates that Ontario households hold roughly 45 per cent of Canadian household net wealth (Ernst & Young 1990, 4) suggest that an annual net wealth tax might raise anywhere from $100 million (45 per cent of 0.03 per cent of GDP as in Finland) to $2.4 billion (45 per cent of 0.73 per cent of GDP as in Switzerland) in Ontario, but would most likely raise about $850 million (45 per cent of 0.26 per cent of GDP, the OECD average). These

TABLE 2
Annual Net Wealth Tax Revenue as a Percentage of Gross Domestic Product
OECD Member Countries

Country	1970	1980	1990
Australia	–	–	–
Austria	0.23	0.20	0.18
Belgium	–	–	–
Canada	–	–	–
Denmark	0.23	0.25	0.12
Finland	0.15	0.07	0.03
France	–	–	0.09
Germany	0.35	0.13	0.12
Greece	–	–	–
Iceland	0.25	0.19	0.42
Ireland	–	0.01	–
Italy	–	–	–
Japan	–	–	–
Luxembourg	0.13	0.08	0.17
Netherlands	0.32	0.34	0.24
New Zealand	–	–	–
Norway	0.32	0.32	0.54
Portugal	–	–	–
Spain	–	0.12	0.21
Sweden	0.28	0.13	0.23
Switzerland	0.79	0.81	0.73
Turkey	–	–	–
United Kingdom	–	–	–
United States	–	–	–
Average % of countries with tax (unweighted)	0.31	0.22	0.26

Source: OECD, *Revenue Statistics of OECD Members Countries, 1965–1991*

estimates represent the revenues that might be collected from Ontario residents from a national wealth tax, and do not account for
revenue losses that would likely result from additional opportunities
to avoid or evade a tax levied only at the provincial level. Nonetheless, they are probably more reliable than revenue estimates
based on comparative shares of total tax revenues raised through
annual net wealth taxes, since they ignore national differences in
the sizes of public sectors and in the mix of taxes levied.

The distributional impact of an annual net wealth tax depends
partly on its design, particularly its rate structure and the threshold
above which the tax applies. In France, for example, where annual

net wealth tax is imposed on household wealth above $500,000, less than 0.5 per cent of households were subject to tax in 1986 (Kessler and Pestieau 1991, 319). In other European countries, lower thresholds ensure that the tax is much more broadly based. In each of these countries, however, annual net wealth taxes are imposed at low rates and are intended to be paid out of income, not capital. As a result, it is generally agreed that their impact on the overall distribution of wealth or income is no greater than the impact of progressive income taxes. Perhaps not surprisingly, therefore, there is no indication they have had a significant effect on the distribution of wealth in the countries where they exist.

Wealth Transfer Taxes

Although wealth transfer taxes are currently not levied anywhere in Canada, this kind of tax existed at the federal level from 1941 to 1971 and in Ontario from 1892 to 1979. In addition, of 24 OECD member countries, all but Australia, Canada, and New Zealand levy some kind of wealth transfer tax.

Like annual net wealth taxes, the revenue potential and distributional impact of wealth transfer taxes can be influenced by the kinds of assets that are included in the tax base, the size of any tax-exempt threshold, the rates of tax applicable to wealth transfers, and the unit (individual or family) that is subject to tax. In addition, the overall impact of a wealth transfer tax may depend on the form of the tax – does it apply to gifts as well as transfers at death; is it calculated by reference to amounts given away by donors, or to amounts received by beneficiaries; and what is the period of time over which gifts and transfers at death are aggregated for purposes of assessing tax?

In general, wealth transfer taxes take one of two basic forms: An estate-type tax is based on the net value of all property owned by a person at death, whereas an inheritance-type tax is charged to recipients according to the net value of the transfers that they receive either from each individual donor or from all donors over a given period of time (accessions tax). Typically, these taxes are supplemented by a gift tax, which is often integrated with the tax at death by adding the value of lifetime gifts to the value of the property transferred at death and providing credit for gift taxes already paid. Among OECD member countries, most levy inheritance-type taxes, though estate-type taxes are more prevalent among common-law countries such as the United Kingdom and the United States. In Canada, the federal wealth transfer tax that was abolished in 1972 took the form of an integrated gift and estate tax, while Ontario combined estate- and inheritance-type features in its succession duty, added gifts made within five years of the donor's death to the base of the tax at death, and levied a separate gift tax on transfers made more than five years before death.

Jurisdictionally, wealth transfer taxes usually apply to transfers of property situated within the taxing jurisdiction (usually real property and unincorporated businesses) and to transfers made by resident donors (living and deceased) regardless of where the property is situated. Some countries, most notably Germany and Japan, also tax resident beneficiaries on property that is situated outside the country and received from non-resident donors. Ontarios succession duty applied to property located in Ontario (situs) and to transfers from resident donors to resident beneficiaries (transmissions), whereas most other provinces levied tax on transfers of property situated within the province and on transfers received by resident beneficiaries, regardless of the residence of the donor or the location of the property.

Notwithstanding the specific form or jurisdictional scope that these wealth transfer taxes may take, they generally apply to most kinds of assets, though favourable treatment is often provided for household and personal effects, works of art and national treasures (provided they are made accessible to public viewing), pension rights, life insurance proceeds, agricultural property, and family businesses. Ontario's succession duty allowed, for example, a $75,000 deduction in determining the taxable value of farms and small businesses and fully exempted transfers of farm assets and shares of a small business corporation to family members who continued to operate the farm or business for a period of ten years after the transfer. In addition, all wealth transfer taxes exempt transfers below certain threshold amounts, which range from a few hundred dollars in some countries with inheritance-type taxes to $600,000 under the U.S. Gift and Estate Tax (which also contains a separate gift tax threshold of $10,000 per donor, per year). Ontario's succession duty included a basic threshold of $250,000 per estate from 1975 to 1977 and $300,000 thereafter, while Ontario's Gift Tax allowed donors to transfer up to $50,000 per year ($10,000 per recipient) without incurring any tax.

Above these thresholds, wealth transfer taxes are generally imposed at graduated rates, with top marginal rates typically higher than the highest rates for income tax. In the United States, for example, rates range from 18 per cent on the first $10,000 of taxable value to 50 per cent on taxable amounts exceeding $2.5 million, whereas income taxes are levied at rates ranging from 15 per cent to 36 per cent. Rates under Ontario's succession duty depended on the relationship between the donor and the beneficiary, and ranged from 18 per cent to 58 per cent for "preferred" beneficiaries (children, children-in-law, grandchildren, and parents), 33 per cent to 60 per cent for "collateral" beneficiaries (siblings, nieces, nephews, and great-grandchildren), and 35 to 70 per cent for other recipients.

With respect to the unit of taxation, wealth transfer taxes are usually calculated on an individual basis, though Denmark and The Netherlands regard spouses as a single tax unit for purposes of gift and inheritance taxes. However, all countries with wealth transfer taxes provide special relief for transfers to spouses or dependent children. In countries with estate-type taxes, like the United Kingdom and the United States, this relief takes the form of an exemption or deduction for the total value of all transfers to spouses, provided they are domiciled in the United Kingdom or are citizens of the United States, and non-taxation of transfers for the purpose of maintenance, medical care, and education. In countries with inheritance-type taxes, maintenance costs are also excluded, and further relief is generally provided through exemptions or higher thresholds, and/or through different rate schedules, with lower rates on transfers from spouses, parents, or other "blood relatives." In Germany, for example, rates range from 3 to 35 per cent on transfers from parents or spouses; from 6 to 50 per cent on transfers from grandparents; from 11 to 65 per cent on transfers from aunts, uncles, and siblings; and from 20 to 70 per cent on transfers from other persons. Similarly, thresholds are DM 250,000 for transfers from spouses; DM 90,000 for transfers from parents; DM 50,000 for transfers from grandparents; DM 10,000 for transfers from aunts, uncles, and siblings; and DM 3,000 for transfers from other persons.

As with annual net wealth taxes, comparative figures on revenues raised from wealth transfer taxes can be expressed as a share of total tax revenues or as a share of gross domestic product. Table 3 summarizes information on the percentage of total tax revenues raised by OECD member countries (all levels of government) from wealth transfer taxes at ten-year intervals from 1970 to 1990. In 1990, these percentages ranged from 0.12 per cent in Turkey to

TABLE 3
Wealth Transfer Tax Revenues as a Percentage of Total Tax Revenues
OECD Member Countries

Country	1970	1980	1990
Australia	2.67	0.44	–
Austria	0.22	0.17	0.14
Belgium	1.01	0.81	0.69
Canada	1.00	0.07	–
Denmark	0.35	0.43	0.56
Finland	0.26	0.25	0.44
France	0.72	0.57	0.95
Germany	0.24	0.18	0.33
Greece	1.28	1.20	1.26
Iceland	–	0.13	0.21
Ireland	1.25	0.35	0.40
Italy	0.64	0.21	0.14
Japan	0.94	0.71	1.41
Luxembourg	0.39	0.34	0.31
Netherlands	0.58	0.48	0.50
New Zealand	1.88	0.51	0.29
Norway	0.24	0.09	0.15
Portugal	1.44	0.24	0.50
Spain	0.85	0.41	0.43
Sweden	0.36	0.21	0.19
Switzerland	1.03	0.75	0.89
Turkey	0.23	0.22	0.12
United Kingdom	1.98	0.55	0.65
United States	1.61	1.09	0.96
Average % of countries with tax (unweighted)	0.92	0.43	0.52

Source: OECD, *Revenue Statistics of OECD Members Countries, 1965–1991*

1.41 per cent in Japan and averaged 0.52 per cent in OECD countries with wealth transfer taxes. In the United Kingdom and the United States, the share of total tax revenues raised by wealth transfer taxes were 0.65 per cent and 0.96 per cent, respectively.

Table 4 presents figures on revenues raised from wealth transfer taxes as a percentage of the gross domestic products of OECD member countries at ten-year intervals from 1970 to 1990. Calculated on this basis for 1990, wealth transfer taxes raised between 0.03 per cent of gross domestic product (Turkey) and 0.46 per cent of gross domestic product (Greece) and averaged 0.20 per cent of GDP in OECD member countries that levied wealth transfer taxes

TABLE 4
Wealth Transfer Tax Revenues as a Percentage of Gross Domestic Product
OECD Member Countries

Country	1970	1980	1990
Australia	0.65	0.12	–
Austria	0.08	0.07	0.06
Belgium	0.36	0.36	0.31
Canada	0.31	0.02	–
Denmark	0.14	0.20	0.27
Finland	0.08	0.08	0.17
France	0.25	0.24	0.42
Germany	0.08	0.07	0.13
Greece	0.32	0.35	0.46
Iceland	–	0.04	0.07
Ireland	0.39	0.12	0.15
Italy	0.17	0.06	0.06
Japan	0.18	0.18	0.44
Luxembourg	0.12	0.16	0.15
Netherlands	0.22	0.22	0.23
New Zealand	0.52	0.17	0.11
Norway	0.09	0.04	0.07
Portugal	0.33	0.07	0.17
Spain	0.14	0.10	0.15
Sweden	0.14	0.10	0.11
Switzerland	0.24	0.23	0.28
Turkey	0.04	0.05	0.03
United Kingdom	0.73	0.19	0.24
United States	0.47	0.32	0.29
Average % of countries with tax (unweighted)	0.26	0.15	0.20

Source: OECD, *Revenue Statistics of OECD Members Countries, 1965–1991*

in 1990. In the United Kingdom and the United States, wealth transfer tax revenues amounted to 0.24 per cent and 0.29 per cent of gross domestic product.

Given these statistics, rough estimates of the revenue potential of an Ontario wealth transfer tax can be calculated in the same way as the annual net wealth tax estimates presented earlier. Looking at wealth transfer tax revenues as a percentage of total tax revenues, estimates that Ontario raised roughly $30 billion in tax revenues in 1992–93 (Ontario Budget 1993, 91) suggest that Ontario could raise between about $35 million (0.12 per cent of total tax revenue as in Turkey) and $425 million (1.41 per cent of total tax revenue as in Japan), but would most likely obtain something in the range of $150 million (roughly 0.52 per cent of total tax revenue, the average in OECD countries with wealth transfer taxes) to $300 million (approximately 0.96 per cent of total tax revenue as in the United States).

Turning to revenues as a percentage of gross domestic product as the standard for comparison, projections for Canada's gross domestic product in 1993 and estimates of the share of Canadian net wealth held by Ontario households suggest that a wealth transfer tax could raise as little as $100 million (45 per cent of 0.03 per cent of GDP as in Turkey) or as much as $1.5 billion (45 per cent of 0.46 per cent of GDP as in Greece), though a more cautious estimate would be in the range of $650 million (45 per cent of 0.20 per cent of GNP, the OECD average) to $950 million (45 per cent of 0.29 per cent of GDP as in the United States). As with the annual net wealth tax estimates, these figures represent the revenues that might be collected from Ontario residents from a national wealth tax, and do not account for revenue losses that would likely result from additional opportunities to avoid or evade a tax levied only at the provincial level. Nonetheless, as before, because comparative statistics on the share of gross domestic product raised through wealth transfer taxes ignore national differences in the sizes of public sectors and in the mix of taxes levied, they may be more reliable than revenue estimates based on the percentage of total tax revenues raised by wealth transfer taxes.

Although one might expect that the distributional impact of a wealth transfer tax could be shaped effectively by its design (particularly rates, thresholds, exemptions, and the form of the tax), a frequent criticism levelled against wealth transfer taxes is that they are easily avoided by the wealthiest taxpayers and therefore fall most heavily on those with medium-sized estates, irrespective of the particular design. Although it is impossible to measure the extent of avoidance or evasion among different wealth groups, Canadian and U.S. taxation statistics indicate a progressive pattern of wealth transfer tax payments in both countries, at least when measured against assessed net values of estates. According to figures reported 25 years ago by the Ontario Committee on Taxation (1967), average effective tax rates under Ontarios succession duty increased steadily from 6.7 per cent on estates with net values of less than $25,000 to 7.0 per cent for estates with net values of

$25,000–$100,000; 9.2 per cent for estates with net values of $100,000–$200,000; 12 per cent for estates with net values of $200,000–$500,000; 15 per cent for estates with net values of $500,000–$1,000,000; and 18.1 per cent on estates valued at more than $1 million.[2] In the United States, federal gift and estate tax returns filed by 1986 decedents indicate a steady increase in average effective tax rates from 0.6 per cent for estates with net worth of $500,000–$600,000, to 6.6 per cent for estates with net values of $600,000–$1,000,000; 17.2 per cent for estates with net values of $1,000,000–$2,500,000; 28.7 per cent for estates with net values of $2,500,000–$5,000,000; 35.8 per cent for estates with net values of $5,000,000–$10,000,000; and 38.5 per cent on estates with net values of more than $10 million.[3]

Whether wealth transfer taxes have had any noticeable long-term impact on the distribution of wealth is much less certain. Evidence from the United Kingdom, Sweden, and the United States indicates long-term reductions in the concentration of wealth, especially in the United Kingdom and Sweden (Wolff 1987, table 3.8; Aaron and Munnell 1992, fig. 3), trends that are certainly consistent with the conclusion that wealth transfer taxes may reduce the concentration of wealth over time. On the other hand, although one study indicates a statistical relationship between the British estate tax and long-term reductions in the share of wealth held by the top one per cent of British wealth holders (Atkinson and Harrison 1978),[4] empirical verification of any connection between wealth transfer taxes and the distribution of wealth is almost non-existent.

The Composition and Distribution of Wealth in Canada and Ontario

Information on the composition and distribution of wealth in Canada and Ontario is available from a number of sources, though none of these contains data approaching the comprehensive scope or reliability of statistics on personal and household income.

In its annual national balance sheet accounts, Statistics Canada provides a detailed account of the aggregate value of Canadian assets and liabilities at the end of each calendar year (Statistics Canada 1990a). The values of these assets are based on historical cost but are adjusted for changes in price levels. Similar information is collected by statistical agencies in other developed countries.

Many countries also conduct periodic surveys to estimate the composition and distribution of wealth among different types of house-holds. In Canada, the most recent survey was conducted by Statistics Canada in 1984 (Statistics Canada 1986). Prior to this survey, Statistics Canada had conducted five large-scale surveys in 1955, 1959, 1964, 1970, and 1977. Although recent history suggests a pattern of surveys every seven years, Statistics Canada did not conduct a wealth survey in 1991 and has no plans to do so in the near future. Fortunately, however, the accounting firm of Ernst & Young has filled this gap somewhat by using survey data and National Balance Sheet figures to estimate the composition and distribution of wealth in Canada and in each province at the end of 1989 (Ernst & Young 1990).

Finally, where countries levy an annual net wealth tax or a tax on the transfer of wealth, taxation statistics can be used to estimate the composition and distribution of wealth – either directly, by examining the wealth and the households that are subject to annual net wealth tax, or indirectly, by projecting an overall pattern of wealth holding on the basis of information contained in estate or inheritance tax returns.

Before summarizing the data from these sources, it is important to note some of the limitations of the data and to consider the implications of different methods of estimation for making comparisons with other jurisdictions and for tracking trends.

The first limitation applies to each of these sources and has to do with the definition of wealth itself. While economists define wealth as the market value of assets minus liabilities at a given point in time, views differ as to precisely which assets should be listed as components of wealth. According to the broadest definitions, measures of personal wealth should include the value of "human capital" – the expected stream of future earnings measured in present-value terms – and "social security wealth" – the present value of expected future benefits minus contributions under public pension plans. More narrow definitions exclude these items and emphasize only transferable assets.

Although alternative definitions of wealth can have enormous influence on estimates of wealth distribution,[5] it would be mistaken to characterize either of these basic definitional approaches as conceptually wrong. Instead, like most economic concepts, it is reasonable to expect that definitions of wealth will vary according to the purpose they are intended to serve. While broad definitions of wealth (including human capital and social security wealth) likely provide a good measure of one's ability to consume goods and services during one's lifetime, some believe that more narrow definitions provide a better measure of economic independence and economic power, including the power to transfer wealth via gifts or bequests.

The implications of these definitional approaches, particularly for estimates of wealth distribution, should be kept in mind when considering the data presented in this section. Each of the sources outlined employs a relatively narrow definition of wealth, excluding human capital and social security wealth. In addition, for administrative more than conceptual reasons, Statistics Canada's wealth surveys exclude equity in life insurance and employer-sponsored pension plans, the value of consumer durables other than vehicles, and interests in trusts. Likewise, for practical rather than conceptual reasons, Ernst & Young's study includes life insurance, employer-sponsored pension plans, and consumer durables, but excludes trusts, tax shelters, professional practices, real property located outside Canada, and registered retirement savings plan savings held with insurance companies. The net effect of these exclusions on estimates of the distribution of wealth is unclear.

A second limitation has to do with methods of estimating the composition and distribution of wealth. Whereas measures of personal income are readily available in most countries from annual income tax returns, jurisdictions that do not levy a broad-based annual net wealth tax lack a similar statistical basis to produce comprehensive annual measures of net wealth. In fact, thresholds, exemptions, and special valuation techniques can make accurate measurements of net wealth difficult even in countries with annual net wealth taxes.

As a result, researchers typically employ one of two methods to estimate the type of assets and the amount of wealth held by households or individuals. The survey method estimates the composition and distribution of wealth among various household types on the basis of survey information collected from a small but statistically significant sample of the total population. The estate-multiplier method estimates the distribution of wealth for a given year on the basis of the number of people in different age and sex categories who die and pay estate tax in that year. Since Canadian jurisdictions no longer levy estate taxes or succession duties, the survey method is the only method currently possible in Canada.

Neither approach is free of imperfections. Since the survey method depends on voluntary responses to study questionnaires, it may reflect incomplete or inaccurate reporting of particular assets or liabilities. For example, Statistics Canada's 1984 wealth survey concluded that stocks account for only 2.2 per cent of household wealth whereas the National Balance Sheet Account for the end of 1983 (the date closest to the time of the survey) estimated that stock holdings represented 11.2 per cent of the value of total assets for persons and unincorporated businesses at that time. Further, since the number of very wealthy households surveyed in a random sample is likely to be small, surveys provide an unreliable source of information on the composition of wealth among these households and are apt to underestimate their share of total wealth.

Alternatively, while estate-multiplier estimates are based on a non-random sample of top wealth holders subject to estate tax, they are extremely sensitive to minor variations in mortality rates (which are used to transform estate tax data into estimates of wealth held by the living). Moreover, since estate tax returns involve mainly elderly and single decedents,[6] estate tax data are often unreliable sources of information on wealth holdings among younger or married persons.

An important implication of these two methods is that they involve different wealth-holding units. While estate tax data are based on wealth had by individual decedents and therefore measure wealth holdings among individuals, survey results are based on household interviews and measure the composition and distribution of wealth among "households" (a concept that may itself vary from one study to another[7]). Since household estimates indicate a much greater concentration of wealth than individual measures, one must attempt to use consistent measures in making comparisons with other jurisdictions and in examining trends over time.

National Balance Sheet Accounts

The national balance sheet accounts provide information on the composition and total amount of household wealth in Canada, but contain no data on the distribution of wealth, or any statistics on the composition or share of wealth by province.

As figure 1 indicates, at the end of 1989 the assets of persons and unincorporated businesses were divided almost equally between financial assets (cash and deposits, bonds, shares, life insurance, pensions, and other financial assets) and non-financial assets (residential and non-residential structures, land, consumer durables, ma-

FIGURE 1
Estimated Composition of Assets – Canada, Persons and Unincorporated Businesses
(National Balance Sheets – 1989

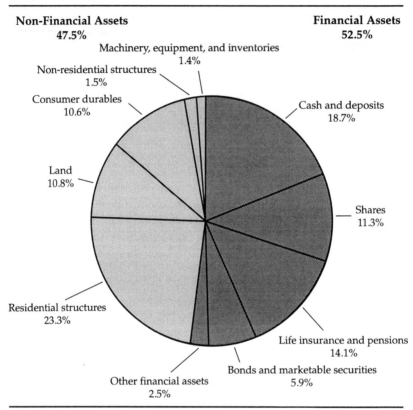

Non-Financial Assets
47.5%

Financial Assets
52.5%

Machinery, equipment, and inventories
1.4%

Non-residential structures
1.5%

Consumer durables
10.6%

Cash and deposits
18.7%

Land
10.8%

Shares
11.3%

Residential structures
23.3%

Life insurance and pensions
14.1%

Other financial assets
2.5%

Bonds and marketable securities
5.9%

Source: Statistics Canada (1990a): Table P3-1

chinery, equipment and inventories), with the former accounting
for 52.5 per cent of the value of all assets and the latter representing
47.5 per cent of total value. In order, the most important assets
held by persons and unincorporated businesses were residential
structures (23.3 per cent), cash and deposits (18.7 per cent), life
insurance and pensions (14.1 per cent), shares (11.3 per cent), land
(10.8 per cent), consumer durables (10.6 per cent), and bonds and
marketable securities (5.9 per cent). Liabilities totalled 18.5 per cent
of the value of all assets, two-thirds of which represented
mortgages.

Total net worth of persons and unincorporated businesses at the end of 1989 was estimated at $1,714 billion, with another $544 billion held by non-financial private corporations. Since there were an estimated 10,288,000 families and unattached individuals in Canada in 1989 (Statistics Canada 1990b, table 33), these data suggest that mean net wealth at the end of 1989 was about $220,000 per household. This figure represents an increase of almost 50 per cent over average household wealth of about $150,000 at the end of 1983 (the time of Statistics Canada's last wealth survey), and a 300 per cent increase over average household wealth of $46,500 in 1971 when Canada abolished its federal gift and estate tax.[8]

Statistics Canada's 1984 Wealth Survey

Statistics Canada's 1984 wealth survey contains estimates of the percentage composition of household wealth both nationally and regionally; national and regional figures on average wealth and the distribution of households by wealth group; and Canada-wide data on the distribution and percentage composition of wealth by age group.

As figure 2 indicates, survey estimates suggest that in 1984 Canadian households held a much smaller percentage (22 per cent) of wealth in the form of financial assets (cash and deposits, registered savings plans, bonds, stocks, and other financial assets) than in the form of non-financial assets (principal residences, other real estate, business equity, and vehicles, which were estimated to account for 78 per cent of the value of household assets), and that most household wealth was held in the form of principal residences (42.9 per cent) and private businesses (21.3 per cent). These figures are noticeably different from those based on the National Balance Sheet Accounts, both in 1989 (figure 1) and at the end of 1983,[9] and likely reflect both the exclusion of life insurance and employer-sponsored pension plans from the wealth survey as well as the survey's tendency to underestimate the proportion of wealth held in the form of shares. On average, according to the survey, liabilities totalled about 12.5 per cent of the value of household assets, with mortgages comprising roughly two-thirds of these debts.

These national proportions were only marginally different in Ontario, where survey statistics indicate that 23.2 per cent of wealth was held in the form of financial assets, 76.8 per cent was held in the form of non-financial assets – primarily principal residences

FIGURE 2
Estimated Composition of Assets – Canada (Statistics Canada Wealth Survey – 1984)

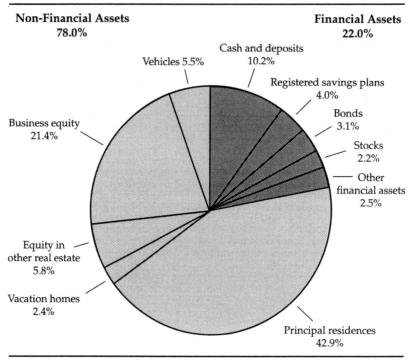

Non-Financial Assets
78.0%

Financial Assets
22.0%

Cash and deposits
10.2%

Vehicles 5.5%

Registered savings plans
4.0%

Bonds
3.1%

Business equity
21.4%

Stocks
2.2%

Other
financial assets
2.5%

Equity in
other real estate
5.8%

Vacation homes
2.4%

Principal residences
42.9%

Source: Statistics Canada (1986): Table 28

(47.2 per cent) and private businesses (16.8 per cent) – and that debts accounted for 12.4 per cent of the value of household assets. Compared with the rest of Canada, residents of Ontario were reported to hold a larger share of wealth in the form of stocks (2.7 versus 2.2 per cent), bonds (3.2 versus 2.6 per cent), and principal residences (47.2 versus 42.9 per cent), and a lower share in the form of business equity (16.8 versus 21.3 per cent) (Statistics Canada 1986, table 28).

With respect to average household wealth, the survey reports a slightly higher average in Ontario ($91,770) as compared with the country as a whole ($85,344) (Statistics Canada 1986, table 8). Nevertheless, both figures are substantially below the $150,000 figure for the end of 1983 calculated on the basis of the national balance sheet accounts. This difference likely reflects the exclusion of some assets from the wealth survey, under-reporting of other assets, and inadequate representation of the upper tail of the wealth distribution.

Figure 3 summarizes evidence on the distribution of households by wealth group both nationally and for the province of Ontario. According to the survey, 7.6 per cent of Ontario households had negative net wealth in 1984, while 5.4 per cent had net wealth of $300,000 or more. Compared with Canada as a whole, a smaller percentage of Ontario households had net wealth of less than $75,000 (62.4 versus 67.3 per cent), while a larger percentage of Ontario households reported net wealth in each wealth group above this amount.

Limitations in the survey approach suggest that estimates of the share of total wealth held by the wealthiest households should be viewed as lower bounds on the true shares of these groups. With this caveat in mind, the results of Statistics Canada's 1984 wealth survey suggest that the wealthiest 1 per cent of Canadian households owned 16.8 per cent of net wealth, that the top 5 per cent owned 37.5 per cent, and that the top 20 per cent held 68.8 per cent (Davies 1993, table 1). These ratios are considerably more unequal than those for the distribution of income, which indicate that the top 20 per cent of Canadian households received 43 per cent of pre-tax income in 1984 (Statistics Canada 1990b, table 55).

Figure 4 presents evidence on mean and median wealth by age group and on the distribution of wealth within each age group. While the shape of these curves indicates a noticeable "life-cycle pattern" according to which net wealth tends to increase up to the age of retirement and to decrease thereafter, data on the distribution of wealth within each age group also show a considerable degree of wealth disparity even among persons of the same age. However, since employer-sponsored pension plans are not included, the survey data probably underestimate the degree of life-cycle saving and exaggerate the degree of wealth disparity within each age group.

Finally, figure 5 reports evidence on the composition of wealth by age group. Most notably, these data indicate a consistently declining debt/asset ratio from 36.9 per cent for the lowest age group (24 and under) to 1.5 per cent for the highest age group (65 and over), and a marked tendency for households with older members (55 and over) to hold a much larger share of their wealth in the form of financial assets (especially cash and deposits, stocks, and

FIGURE 3
Estimated Distribution of Families by Wealth Group – 1984

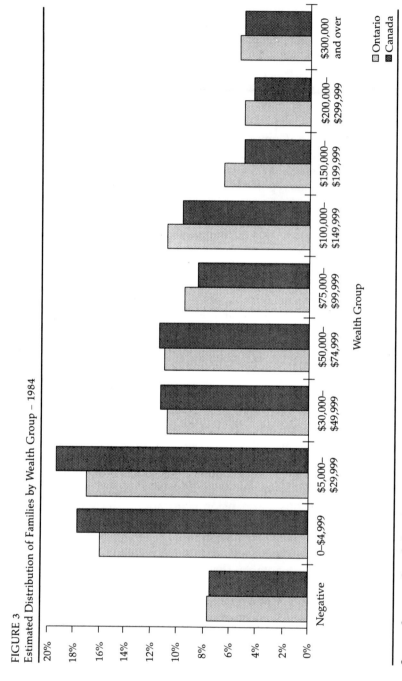

Source: Statistics Canada (1986): Table 8

FIGURE 4
Average and Median Wealth by Age – All Families (Canada, 1984)

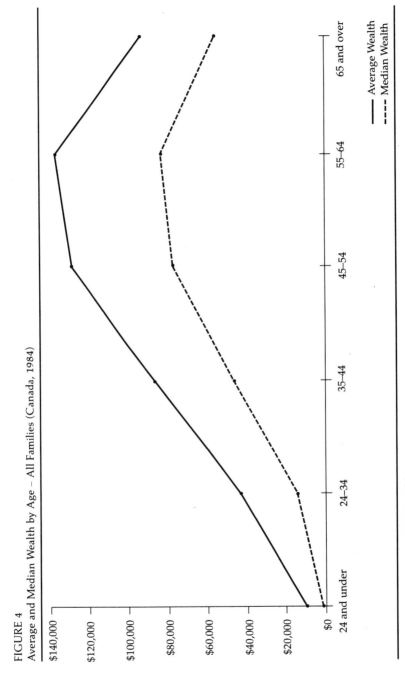

Source: Statistics Canada (1986): Table 5

bonds). These figures are consistent with U.S. estate tax data indicating a high percentage of liquid assets (stocks, bonds, cash,
notes, and mortgages) among estates subject to tax, and suggest
that the base of a wealth transfer tax is likely to include a larger
proportion of financial assets than the base of an annual net wealth
tax.

Ernst & Young's Wealth Report

Ernst & Young's *The Wealth Report* contains estimates on the composition and distribution of wealth in Canada and in Ontario at
the end of 1989; estimates on the distribution of net wealth and
particular assets by income group; and projections on the amount,
distribution, and composition of household wealth up to the year
2000. Although its methodology may make it a more accurate source
of information on the upper "tail" of the wealth distribution than
Statistics Canada's 1984 wealth survey,[10] it does not contain information on the composition and distribution of wealth by age.

Figure 6 summarizes Ernst & Young's estimates of the composition of household wealth in Ontario at the end of 1989. Following
Statistics Canada's categorization of assets as financial or non-
financial,[11] Ernst & Young's figures imply that 34.7 per cent of
household wealth was held in the form of financial assets, and 65.3
per cent in the form of non-financial assets. As with the National
Balance Sheet Accounts and Statistics Canada's 1984 wealth survey,
the most important assets were residential real estate (40 per cent);
cash and deposits (12.1 per cent); private businesses including farms
(10.8 per cent); pensions and life insurance (9.7 per cent); consumer
durables including vehicles (8.7 per cent); stocks (7.4 per cent); and
bonds and marketable securities including mutual funds (5.5 per
cent). The total value of liabilities was estimated at 11.4 per cent
of the value of all assets, two-thirds of which represented
mortgages.

Aside from the low debt/asset ratio reported in the Ernst & Young
report, the most striking difference between these estimates and
those of the National Balance Sheet Accounts is the high value of
residential real estate, both in absolute dollar amounts and as a percentage of total wealth. Compared with National Balance Sheet estimates of $489 billion in residential structures and $227 billion
in land at the end of 1989, the Ernst & Young study estimates that

FIGURE 5
Estimated Composition of Wealth within Age Groups – All Families (Canada, 1984)

24 and under

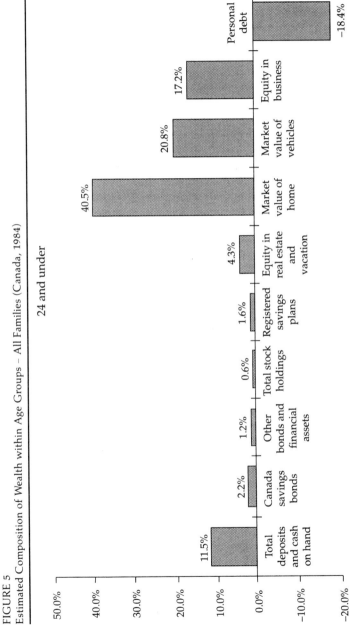

FIGURE 5 *(continued)*

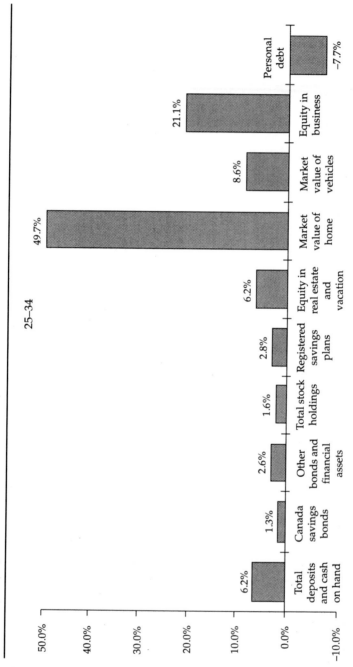

FIGURE 5 (continued)

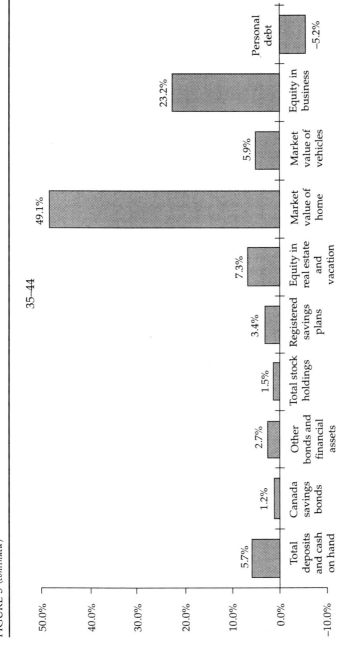

35–44

FIGURE 5 (continued)

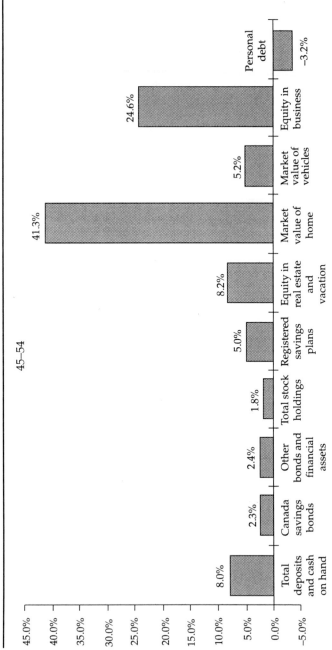

45–54

N

FIGURE 5 *(continued)*

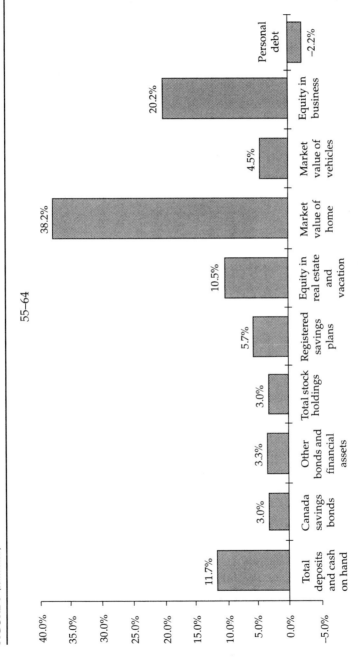

55–64

FIGURE 5 (*continued*)

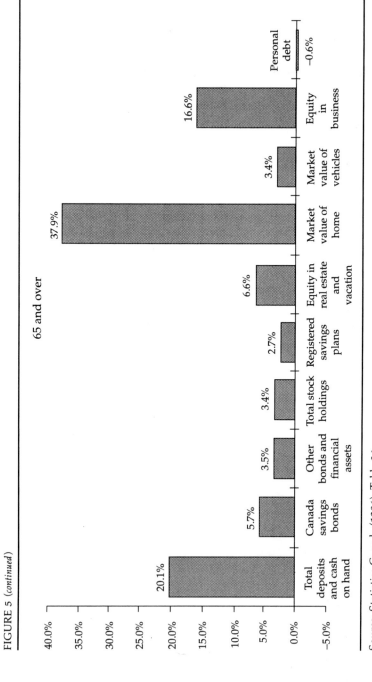

65 and over

Source: Statistics Canada (1986): Table 26

FIGURE 6
Estimated Composition of Household Wealth in Ontario (Wealth Report – 1989)

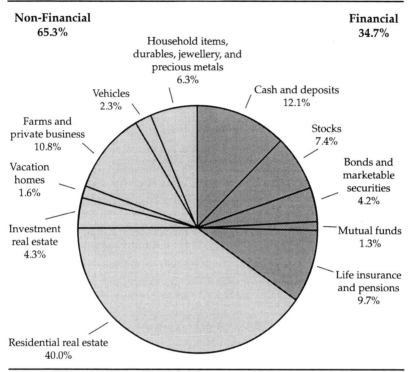

Non-Financial
65.3%

Financial
34.7%

Household items,
durables, jewellery, and
precious metals
6.3%

Vehicles
2.3%

Cash and deposits
12.1%

Farms and
private business
10.8%

Stocks
7.4%

Vacation
homes
1.6%

Bonds and
marketable
securities
4.2%

Investment
real estate
4.3%

Mutual funds
1.3%

Life insurance
and pensions
9.7%

Residential real estate
40.0%

Source: Ernst & Young (1990): Tables 1.3.1 and 1.3.2

the total value of residential real estate in Canada at that time was nearly $1 trillion. In addition, while the National Balance Sheet Accounts estimate that the value of residential structures and land (both residential and non-residential) accounted for 34.1 per cent of the total wealth of Canadian persons and unincorporated businesses, *The Wealth Report* estimates that 40 per cent of the total wealth of Ontario households was held in the form of residential real estate. This contrast likely reflects different valuation techniques (adjusted historic cost versus estimated market value) and a relatively larger role for residential real estate in the total wealth of Ontario households than in Canada as a whole.

Other comparisons between Ontario and national data indicate that Ontario households were generally wealthier than Canadian households and that Ontario had a disproportionate share of wealthy households. With 36 per cent of the population in 1989, Ontario households were estimated to hold 45.3 per cent of the net wealth of Canadian households, 52.9 per cent of the total value of residential real estate, and 50.8 per cent of the total value of stocks. Ernst & Young also estimates that the average wealth of Ontario households was about $330,000 versus $260,000 for Canadian households, and that Ontario was home to 50.3 per cent of Canada's 427,000 millionaire households (Ernst & Young 1990, table 8.2.1).

Ernst & Young estimates on the distribution of Ontario and Canadian households by wealth group are presented in table 5. These figures indicate that Ontario had a larger share of millionaire households in 1989 than Canada as a whole (6.3 per cent of Ontario households versus 4.5 per cent of Canadian households), and that these households owned a substantial share of total wealth (50.1 per cent in Ontario, and 44 per cent nationally). These statistics suggest that the wealthiest 1 per cent of Ontario households owned roughly 23 per cent of the net wealth of all Ontario households in 1989, that the top 5 per cent held approximately 46 per cent of household wealth, and that the top 20 per cent owned about 74 per cent of household wealth.[12] As with the 1984 statistics summarized earlier, these ratios are considerably more unequal than those for the distribution of income, which indicate that the top 1 per cent of Ontario households received about 4 per cent of total income earned by Ontario households in 1989, that the top 5 per cent received 14 per cent, and that the top 20 per cent received roughly 42 per cent.

Finally, table 6 represents data on the estimated joint distribution of household wealth and income in Ontario at the end of 1989. While these figures suggest a strong correlation between household wealth and income, they also indicate that some high-income households have accumulated little wealth (an estimated 17,400 households are estimated to have annual incomes of more than $100,000 but wealth of less than $100,000) while some wealthy households have low annual incomes (10,500 millionaire households are estimated to have annual incomes of less than $25,000).

The implications for an annual net wealth tax are twofold. First, to the extent that the tax is intended to substitute for increases in marginal rates of personal income tax, an annual net wealth tax is an imperfect approach that can impose a relatively light burden on some high-income earners (with little wealth) and a potentially

TABLE 5
Estimated Distribution of Ontario Households by Aggregate Wealth Group
As of 31 December 1989

| | Households by Aggregate Wealth Group | | | | | | | |
	Under $10,000	$10,000 –$100,000	$100,000 –$250,000	$250,000 –$500,000	$500,000 –$1,000,000	$1,000,000 –$2,000,000	Over $2,000,000	All Households
# households	631,900	864,400	880,000	520,300	296,500	130,000	84,900	3,408,000
# households above lower bound	3,408,000	2,776,100	1,911,700	1,031,700	511,400	214,900	84,900	
% households above lower bound	100.0%	81.5%	56.1%	30.3%	15.0%	6.3%	2.5%	
Average wealth	$0	$46,600	$171,660	$325,000	$675,000	$1,300,000	$4,640,377	$329,487
Total wealth ($ billions)	$0	$40,280	$151,068	$169,095	$200,152	$168,976	$393,321	$1,122,892
Total wealth above lower bound	$1,122,892	$1,122,892	$1,082,612	$931,544	$762,449	$562,297	$393,321	
% Wealth above lower bound	100.0%	100.0%	96.4%	83.0%	67.9%	50.1%	35.0%	

Source: Ernst & Young (1990): Vol. 1, Tables 1.5.1 and 8.4.1; Vol. 2, Appendix N.
Note: Averages and totals may not compute due to rounding.

TABLE 6
Estimated Distribution of Ontario Households by Income and Aggregate Wealth Group as of 31 December 1989

Households by income group	Number of Households by Aggregate Wealth Group							
	Under $10,000	$10,000 –$100,000	$100,000 –$250,000	$250,000 –$500,000	$500,000 –$1,000,000	$1,000,000 –$2,000,000	Over $2,000,000	All Households
Under $10,000	125,800	38,700	20,800	8,900	3,300		200	198,500
$10,000–$25,000	262,600	206,200	155,100	68,000	28,700	6,800	2,900	730,600
$25,000–$50,000	191,400	391,900	321,200	166,000	89,700	31,700	16,900	1,209,100
$50,000–$100,000	51,000	210,800	342,900	244,300	141,600	59,600	34,500	1,084,800
$100,000–$250,000	1,000	16,400	37,900	31,000	29,400	27,400	23,600	166,400
Over $250,000	0	0	2,100	2,100	3,800	3,800	6,800	18,500
All households	631,900	864,400	880,000	520,300	296,500	130,000	84,900	3,408,000
	Percentage of Households by Wealth Group							
Under $10,000	3.7	1.1	0.6	0.3	0.1		0.0	5.8
$10,000–$25,000	7.7	6.1	4.6	2.0	0.8	0.2	0.1	21.4
$25,000–$50,000	5.6	11.5	9.4	4.9	2.6	0.9	0.5	35.5
$50,000–$100,000	1.5	6.2	10.1	7.2	4.2	1.7	1.0	31.8
$100,000–$250,000	0.0	0.5	1.1	0.9	0.9	0.8	0.7	4.9
Over $250,000	0.0	0.0	0.1	0.1	0.1	0.1	0.2	0.5
All households	18.5	25.4	25.8	15.3	8.7	3.8	2.5	100.0

Source: Ernst & Young (1990): Vol. 2, Appendix N
Note: Figures may not sum due to rounding.

large burden on the other low-income earners (with substantial net wealth). Second, where an annual net wealth tax does not contain a ceiling based upon each taxpayer's income, it is entirely possible that some taxpayers will be unable to cover their taxes out of income and may actually have to sell assets in order to pay the tax.

Annual Net Wealth Tax Estimates

The annual net wealth tax simulations, whose results are reported here, are based on data from Ernst & Young's *The Wealth Report*, on the distribution of Ontario households by income and aggregate wealth group, and on average wealth held within each wealth group. Table 7 reproduces the most relevant of these data, showing the income distribution and average (mean) wealth of all households and of households with aggregate wealth of more than $500,000.

Given these data, the alternative annual net wealth tax options that can be modelled are limited in two key ways. First, since the Ernst & Young data are presented on a household basis, it is impossible to model an annual net wealth tax imposed on individuals without obtaining further information or making assumptions about the distribution of aggregate household wealth among individual members. While *The Wealth Report* contains some information on the number of households by household size, there is no information on the average household size for each wealth group, nor on the distribution of wealth within households. Further, although it would be possible to devise rough estimates for the distribution of wealth among individuals, it is doubtful whether this exercise would provide reliable figures on the performance of an individually based annual net wealth tax – particularly since the distribution of wealth within households is almost certain to be influenced by the imposition of the tax. As a result, each of the annual net wealth tax options simulated in this section assumes the same household unit employed in Ernst & Young's *The Wealth Report*: that is, individuals whether or not they are related, who share a common dwelling. Although it is unlikely that this grouping would be selected as the unit of taxation for an annual net wealth tax, it is plausible that such a tax might be imposed on a family basis. In practice, the differences between such a family unit and Ernst & Young's household unit are not substantial. Whereas Statistics Canada estimates the number of families and unattached individuals resident in Ontario in 1989 at 3,710,000, Ernst & Young reports that there were 3,408,000 Ontario households in 1989.

TABLE 7
Estimated Distribution of Households by Income and Aggregate Wealth Group – Ontario, 1989

Households by income group	Households by Aggregate Wealth Group				
	$500,000 –$1,000,000	$1,000,000 –$2,000,000	Over $2,000,000	All households over $500,000	All households
Under $25,000	32,000	7,400	3,100	42,500	929,100
$25,000–$50,000	89,700	31,700	16,900	138,300	1,209,200
$50,000–$100,000	141,600	59,700	34,500	235,800	1,084,800
$100,000–$150,000	21,000	20,100	15,700	56,800	125,900
$150,000–$200,000	6,200	5,600	5,000	16,800	30,000
$200,000–$250,000	2,200	1,700	2,900	6,800	10,500
Over $250,000	3,800	3,800	6,800	14,400	18,500
All households	296,500	130,000	84,900	511,400	3,408,000
Average wealth	$675,000	$1,300,000	$4,640,377	$1,492,000	$329,487

Source: Ernst & Young (1990): Vol. 2, Appendix N

A second limitation has to do with the base of the simulated annual net wealth tax under different options. Since information on the composition of wealth by income and aggregate wealth groups is unreliable or incomplete (Statistics Canada's wealth survey is extremely unreliable at the upper tail, while the Ernst & Young study contains only limited data on the composition of assets within each wealth group), it is difficult to model the combined impact of a dollar threshold and/or graduated rates on the one hand and exemptions for specific assets (for example, principle residences, family farms, small businesses, or pensions) on the other. Where the tax includes a dollar threshold and/or graduated rates, the distributional and revenue effects of exempting a specific asset will depend on its incidence of ownership and its share in total asset composition among different wealth groups. Similarly, where the tax exempts a specific asset, the distributional and revenue impact of a variation in rate structure (including a threshold or "zero rate band") will depend on the distribution of the exempt asset by income or wealth group. In the absence of information on the incidence of asset ownership and composition of assets by income or wealth group, it is impossible to model the combined effects of a threshold and/ or graduated rate structure and exemptions for specific classes of assets.

This leaves two alternatives: to show the effects of different rate structures assuming a fully comprehensive base, or to show the effects of various exemptions assuming a flat rate tax with no threshold. There are two reasons why we have chosen the former approach. First, since these taxes typically include at least some threshold and generally aspire to a relatively broad base, examples with different thresholds and rates but a fully comprehensive base seem more realistic and more relevant. Second, although the revenue impact of alternative exemptions might be calculated under the latter approach (assuming a flat rate annual net wealth tax without a dollar threshold), it is impossible to calculate the distributional impact of any exemption without adequate information on the percentage composition of assets by income or wealth group, both of which are lacking. As a result, each of the annual net wealth tax options simulated in the appendix assumes a fully comprehensive base without any exemption for specific assets.[13]

Recognizing these limitations (as well as those outlined in the introduction), it is nonetheless possible to simulate the distributional impact and revenue potential of various thresholds and rate structures for a comprehensive annual net wealth tax applied on a household basis. For each income group, the total amount of revenue raised is calculated as the product of average household wealth within each wealth group less the threshold amount, the applicable tax rate, and the number of households within each wealth group. Once this estimate is determined, it is easy to calculate the average amounts of tax paid (by taxpaying households and by all households) within each income group and overall, and average tax payments as a percentage of the average wealth (both for taxpaying households and for all households). Calculations of average taxes as a percentage of income assume that average incomes within each income group are at the midpoint of the income range that defines the group (except for the under $10,000 category for which average income is assumed to be $50,000, and for the over $250,000 category for which – on the basis of procedures [described in the appendix] used to model the upper tail of income and wealth distributions – average income is assumed to be three times the lower bound, namely, $750,000).

The results of six such simulations are presented in tables 8–13 and in figures 7–10. In each case, the tables indicate for each income group the estimated number and percentage of households subject to the tax, the average amount of tax paid by taxpaying households and by all households within the income group, the average rate of tax (as a percentage of income and wealth) paid by taxpaying households and all households within the income group, and the estimated amount of revenue raised.

Tables 8–10 simulate the distributional and revenue impacts of a 1 per cent flat rate annual net wealth tax with three different thresholds. With a $500,000 threshold, it is estimated that 511,000 households (15 per cent of Ontario households) would have been subject to the tax at the end of 1989; that the average annual net wealth tax payment by these households would have been $9930; and that the tax could have raised about $5 billion (table 8).

With a $1 million threshold, the estimated number of households subject to tax drops to 214,500 (6.3 per cent of Ontario households), the average tax payment increases to roughly $16,000, and potential revenues decline to $3.5 billion (table 9).

Increasing the threshold to $2 million causes the estimated number of households subject to tax to fall below 85,000 (2.5 per cent of Ontario households), increases the average annual net wealth tax payment by these households to approximately $26,000, and reduces the amount of revenue raised to $2.2 billion (table 10).

TABLE 8
Comprehensive Flat-Rate Annual Net Wealth Tax
Estimated Distributional Impact and Revenue Potential,
Upper Bound, 1989

Simulation 1: Threshold: $500,000
Rate: 1.0% above $500,000

Households by income group	Taxpaying households		Average tax paid by		Average tax paid by		Average tax paid by		Revenue raised ($ millions)
	#	%	Taxpaying households ($)	All households ($)	Taxpaying households (% income)	All households (% income)	Taxpaying households (% wealth)	All households (% wealth)	
Under $25,000	42,500	4.6	4,677	214	37.4	1.7	0.48	0.19	198.8
$25,000–$50,000	138,300	11.4	6,440	737	17.2	2.0	0.56	0.31	890.6
$50,000–$100,000	235,800	21.7	7,384	1,605	9.8	2.1	0.60	0.39	1,741.2
$100,000–$150,000	56,800	45.1	14,816	6,684	11.9	5.3	0.75	0.67	841.5
$150,000–$200,000	16,800	56.0	20,828	11,664	11.9	6.7	0.81	0.75	349.9
$200,000–$250,000	6,800	64.8	46,536	30,138	20.7	13.4	0.90	0.88	316.4
Over $250,000	14,400	77.8	51,084	39,763	6.8	5.3	0.91	0.90	735.6
All households	511,400	15.0	9,922	1,489			0.66	0.45	5,074.1

TABLE 9
Comprehensive Flat-Rate Annual Net Wealth Tax
Estimated Distributional Impact and Revenue Potential,
Upper Bound, 1989

Simulation 2: Threshold: $1,000,000
Rate: 1.0% above $1,000,000

Households by income group	Taxpaying households		Average tax paid by		Average tax paid by		Average tax paid by		Revenue raised ($ millions)
	#	%	Taxpaying households ($)	All households ($)	Taxpaying households (% income)	All households (% income)	Taxpaying households (% wealth)	All households (% wealth)	
Under $25,000	10,500	1.1	8,596	97	68.8	0.8	0.46	0.09	90.3
$25,000–$50,000	48,600	4.0	10,096	406	26.9	1.1	0.50	0.17	490.6
$50,000–$100,000	94,200	8.7	10,853	942	14.5	1.3	0.52	0.23	1,022.4
$100,000–$150,000	35,800	28.4	17,480	4,971	14.0	4.0	0.64	0.49	625.8
$150,000–$200,000	10,600	35.3	26,986	9,535	15.4	5.4	0.73	0.62	286.1
$200,000–$250,000	4,600	43.8	62,956	27,581	28.0	12.3	0.86	0.81	289.6
Over $250,000	10,600	57.3	63,770	36,538	8.5	4.9	0.86	0.83	676.0
All households	214,900	6.3	16,197	1,021		4.9	0.62	0.31	3,480.7

TABLE 10
Comprehensive Flat-Rate Annual Net Wealth Tax
Estimated Distributional Impact and Revenue Potential,
Upper Bound, 1989

Simulation 3: Threshold: $2,000,000
Rate: 1.0% above $2,000,000

Households by income group	Taxpaying households		Average tax paid by		Average tax paid by		Average tax paid by		Revenue raised ($ millions)
	#	%	Taxpaying households ($)	All households ($)	Taxpaying households (% income)	All households (% income)	Taxpaying households (% wealth)	All households (% wealth)	
Under $25,000	3,100	0.3	11,953	40	95.6	0.3	0.37	0.03	37.1
$25,000–$50,000	16,900	1.4	13,405	187	35.7	0.5	0.40	0.08	226.5
$50,000–$100,000	34,500	3.2	14,443	459	19.3	0.6	0.42	0.11	498.3
$100,000–$150,000	15,700	12.5	26,019	3,245	20.8	2.6	0.57	0.32	408.5
$150,000–$200,000	5,000	16.7	43,851	7,309	25.1	4.2	0.69	0.47	219.3
$200,000–$250,000	2,900	27.6	88,102	24,333	39.2	10.8	0.81	0.71	255.5
Over $250,000	6,800	36.8	87,729	32,246	11.7	4.3	0.81	0.73	596.6
All households	84,900	2.5	26,404	658			0.57	0.20	2,241.7

Despite these differences in projected revenues, average tax payments, and numbers of households subject to tax, the distributional impacts of these three simulations are broadly similar. Reflecting a strong (though imperfect) correlation between household income and wealth, for each simulation the share of taxpaying households within each income class steadily increases from a small fraction of low-income households to a substantial percentage of high-income households. Further, as figure 7 indicates, when average tax payments are measured as a percentage of average income, each simulation is regressive for taxpaying households and relatively proportional for all households up to household incomes of $80,000–$90,000, and (both for taxpaying households and for all households) progressive at income levels above these amounts, except for the very top income group with household incomes of more than $250,000.

Finally, as figure 8 shows, when average tax payments are expressed as a percentage of average wealth within each income group, each simulation is proportional or mildly progressive up to about $80,000 in household income and noticeably progressive above that level.

These patterns remain largely unchanged when a single flat rate is replaced by a graduated rate structure, as simulated in tables 11–13. In order to isolate the impact of the graduated rate structure, these simulations repeat the thresholds of tables 8–10, and are designed to raise similar amounts of revenue as the flat-rate simulations.

As figures 9 and 10 demonstrate, the distributional effects of each graduated-rate annual net wealth tax simulation are strikingly similar to the distributional impacts of the flat-rate simulations.

Wealth Transfer Tax Estimates

The Distribution of Estates in Ontario

Wealth transfer tax simulations are based on estimates for the distribution of Ontario estates in 1989, which are themselves derived from Statistics Canada's 1984 survey estimates for the distribution of wealth by age and family type, from Ernst & Young and Statistics Canada estimates of average (mean) household wealth in Ontario in 1989 and 1984, from Statistics Canada estimates of population by age and family type, and from mortality figures compiled by Statistics Canada. Most of these underlying data are summarized in tables 14–16.

FIGURE 7
Comprehensive Flat-Rate Annual Net Wealth Tax
Average Tax as a Percentage of Income,
Upper Bound, 1989

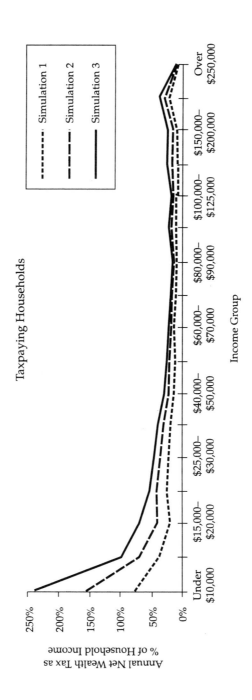

FIGURE 7 (continued)

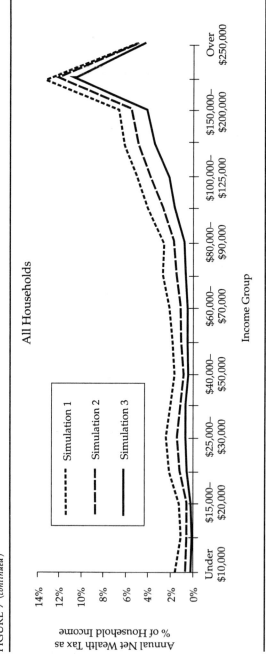

All Households

Simulation 1
Simulation 2
Simulation 3

Income Group

Annual Net Wealth Tax as
% of Household Income

14%
12%
10%
8%
6%
4%
2%
0%

Under
$10,000

$15,000–
$20,000

$25,000–
$30,000

$40,000–
$50,000

$60,000–
$70,000

$80,000–
$90,000

$100,000–
$125,000

$150,000–
$200,000

Over
$250,000

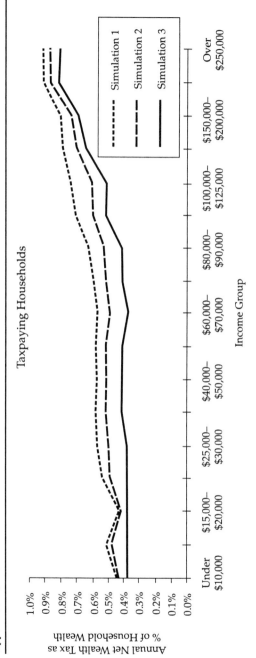

FIGURE 8
Comprehensive Flat-Rate Annual Net Wealth Tax
Average Tax as a Percentage of Wealth,
Upper Bound, 1989

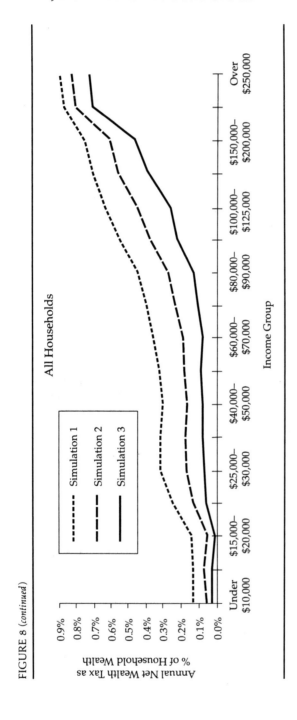

FIGURE 8 (continued)

TABLE 11
Comprehensive Graduated-Rate Annual Net Wealth Tax
Estimated Distributional Impact and Revenue Potential,
Upper Bound, 1989

Simulation 4: Threshold: $500,000
Rate: 0.5% up to $1,000,000 from $1,000,000 to $2,500,000; 1.5% above $2,500,000

Households by income group	Taxpaying households		Average tax paid by		Average tax paid by		Average tax paid by		Revenue raised ($ millions)
	#	%	Taxpaying households ($)	All households ($)	Taxpaying households (% income)	All households (% income)	Taxpaying households (% wealth)	All households (% wealth)	
Under $25,000	42,500	4.6	3,654	167	29.2	1.3	0.38	0.15	155.3
$25,000–$50,000	138,300	11.4	5,507	630	14.7	1.7	0.48	0.27	761.7
$50,000–$100,000	235,800	21.7	6,551	1,424	8.7	1.9	0.53	0.35	1,544.7
$100,000–$150,000	56,800	45.1	15,822	7,138	12.7	5.7	0.80	0.71	898.7
$150,000–$200,000	16,800	56.0	24,709	13,837	14.1	7.9	0.96	0.89	415.1
$200,000–$250,000	6,800	64.8	62,282	40,335	27.7	17.9	1.21	1.18	423.5
Over $250,000	14,400	77.8	68,546	53,355	9.1	7.1	1.22	1.21	987.1
All households	511,400	15.0	10,141	1,522			0.68	0.46	5,186.0

TABLE 12
Comprehensive Graduated-Rate Annual Net Wealth Tax
Estimated Distributional Impact and Revenue Potential,
Upper Bound, 1989

Simulation 5: Threshold: $1,000,000
Rate: 0.5% up to $2,000,000; 1% from $2,000,000 to $5,000,000; 1.5% above $5,000,000

Households by income group	Taxpaying households		Average tax paid by		Average tax paid by		Average tax paid by		Revenue raised ($ millions)
	#	%	Taxpaying households ($)	All households ($)	Taxpaying households (% income)	All households (% income)	Taxpaying households (% wealth)	All households (% wealth)	
Under $25,000	10,500	1.1	6,062	69	48.5	0.5	0.33	0.06	63.7
$25,000–$50,000	48,600	4.0	7,594	305	20.3	0.8	0.38	0.13	369.1
$50,000–$100,000	94,200	8.7	8,460	735	11.3	1.0	0.41	0.18	796.9
$100,000–$150,000	35,800	28.4	17,076	4,856	13.7	3.9	0.62	0.48	611.3
$150,000–$200,000	10,600	35.3	30,252	10,689	17.3	6.1	0.82	0.69	320.7
$200,000–$250,000	4,600	43.8	79,722	34,926	35.4	15.5	1.09	1.02	366.7
Over $250,000	10,600	57.3	80,754	46,270	10.8	6.2	1.09	1.05	856.0
All households	214,900	6.3	15,749	993		6.2	0.60	0.30	3,384.4

TABLE 13
Comprehensive Graduated-Rate Annual Net Wealth Tax
Estimated Distributional Impact and Revenue Potential,
Upper Bound, 1989

Simulation 6: Threshold: $2,000,000
Rate: 0.5% up to $5,000,000; 1.5% above $5,000,000

Households by income group	Taxpaying households		Average tax paid by		Average tax paid by		Average tax paid by		Revenue raised ($ millions)
	#	%	Taxpaying households ($)	All households ($)	Taxpaying households (% income)	All households (% income)	Taxpaying households (% wealth)	All households (% wealth)	
Under $25,000	3,100	0.3	5,977	20	47.8	0.2	0.19	0.02	18.5
$25,000–$50,000	16,900	1.4	7,941	111	21.2	0.3	0.24	0.05	134.2
$50,000–$100,000	34,500	3.2	9,344	297	12.5	0.4	0.27	0.07	322.4
$100,000–$150,000	15,700	12.5	25,006	3,118	20.0	2.5	0.54	0.31	392.6
$150,000–$200,000	5,000	16.7	49,131	8,189	28.1	4.7	0.77	0.53	245.7
$200,000–$250,000	2,900	27.6	108,999	30,104	48.4	13.4	1.01	0.88	316.1
Over $250,000	6,800	36.8	108,494	39,879	14.5	5.3	1.01	0.90	737.8
All households	84,900	2.5	25,527	636	14.5	5.3	0.55	0.19	2,167.2

FIGURE 9
Comprehensive Graduated-Rate Annual Net Wealth Tax
Average Tax as a Percentage of Income,
Upper Bound, 1989

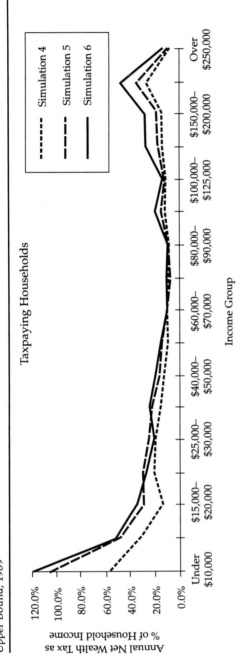

FIGURE 9 (continued)

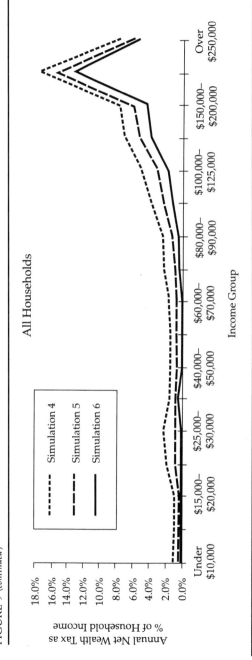

All Households

Annual Net Wealth Tax as % of Household Income

Income Group

Simulation 4
Simulation 5
Simulation 6

FIGURE 10
Comprehensive Graduated-Rate Annual Net Wealth Tax
Average Tax as a Percentage of Wealth,
Upper Bound, 1989

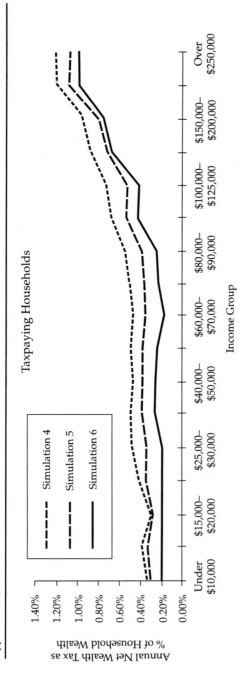

FIGURE 10 (continued)

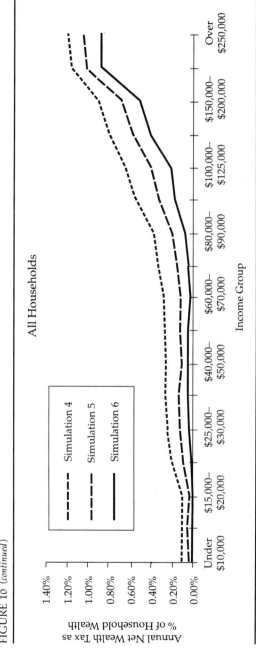

All Households

Simulation 4
Simulation 5
Simulation 6

Annual Net Wealth Tax as
% of Household Wealth

1.40%
1.20%
1.00%
0.80%
0.60%
0.40%
0.20%
0.00%

Under
$10,000

$15,000–
$20,000

$25,000–
$30,000

$40,000–
$50,000

$60,000–
$70,000

$80,000–
$90,000

$100,000–
$125,000

$150,000–
$200,000

Over
$250,000

Income Group

TABLE 14
Estimated Distribution of Household Wealth by Age and Family Type – Canada, 1984

	Families (by Age of "Head")				
Wealth group	45–54 All	55–64 All	65+ Husband-wife	65+ Not husband-wife	65+ Average
Negative	2.7%	1.8%	1.0%	3.4%	1.3%
$0–999	3.3%	1.8%	2.3%	1.9%	2.3%
$1,000–$4,999	3.3%	3.0%	4.4%	6.4%	4.7%
$5,000–$14,999	5.5%	3.5%	3.7%	4.4%	3.9%
$15,000–$29,999	6.1%	5.9%	5.5%	8.3%	5.8%
$30,000–$49,999	10.2%	9.3%	12.0%	18.1%	12.6%
$50,000–$74,999	12.8%	13.0%	16.3%	13.6%	15.7%
$75,000–$99,999	13.2%	12.9%	13.8%	10.2%	13.3%
$100,000–$149,999	16.5%	17.1%	15.9%	14.7%	16.0%
$150,000–$199,999	8.4%	9.2%	8.5%	8.2%	8.4%
$199,000–$299,999	8.9%	9.4%	7.7%	6.3%	7.5%
$300,000 and over	9.0%	13.2%	9.1%	4.5%	8.4%
Total	100.0%	100.0%	100.0%	100.0%	100.0%
Mean wealth	$141,484	$159,920	$131,931	$118,431	$131,005
Median wealth	$86,476	$97,867	$83,942	$63,789	$81,733

	Unattached Individuals (by Age)				
Wealth group	45–54 All	55–64 All	65+ Male	65+ Female	65+ Average
Negative	10.1%	8.1%	1.5%	1.1%	1.2%
$0–$999	23.2%	13.7%	12.2%	16.2%	15.2%
$1,000–$4,999	12.7%	6.6%	14.4%	13.3%	13.6%
$5,000–$14,999	11.1%	10.0%	10.3%	10.8%	10.7%
$15,000–$29,999	8.6%	9.7%	11.5%	10.1%	10.4%
$30,000–$49,999	8.4%	11.9%	12.2%	13.3%	13.0%
$50,000–$74,999	6.6%	12.0%	11.7%	15.0%	14.2%
$75,000–$99,999	3.5%	7.6%	8.4%	8.0%	8.1%
$100,000–$149,999	6.0%	9.4%	8.0%	6.8%	7.1%
$150,000 and over	9.8%	11.0%	9.8%	5.4%	6.4%
Total	100.0%	100.0%	100.0%	100.0%	100.0%
Mean wealth	$56,611	$65,446	$65,357	$47,999	$52,185
Median wealth	$8,531	$33,132	$30,053	$27,734	$28,351

Source: Statistics Canada (1986): Tables 5 and 6

TABLE 15
Population by Age and Family Type – Canada and Ontario, 1989

	Families							
	Canada						Ontario	
	All families		Male "head"		Female "head"		All families	
Age of "head"	#	% of total	#	% of group	#	% of group	#	% of total
24 or less	247,000	3	197,000	80	50,000	20	77,000	3
25–34	1,591,000	22	1,408,000	88	183,000	12	557,000	21
35–44	1,852,000	26	1,661,000	90	191,000	10	674,000	26
45–54	1,326,000	19	1,194,000	90	132,000	10	504,000	19
55–59	543,000	8	499,000	92	44,000	8	205,000	8
60–64	509,000	7	460,000	90	49,000	10	205,000	8
65–69	421,000	6	383,000	91	38,000	9	158,000	6
69 +	601,000	8	525,000	87	76,000	13	216,000	8
Total	7,090,000	100	6,327,000	89	763,000	11	2,596,000	100

continued

TABLE 15 (continued)
Population by Age and Family Type – Canada and Ontario, 1989

	Unattached Individuals							
	Canada						Ontario	
	All individuals		Male		Female		All individuals	
Age	#	% of total	#	% of group	#	% of group	#	% of total
24 or less	425,000	13	216,000	51	209,000	49	145,000	13
25–34	760,000	24	458,000	60	302,000	40	290,000	26
35–44	449,000	14	261,000	58	188,000	42	147,000	13
45–54	290,000	9	141,000	49	149,000	51	90,000	8
55–59	162,000	5	75,000	46	87,000	54	59,000	5
60–64	196,000	6	73,000	37	123,000	63	59,000	5
65–69	220,000	7	66,000	30	154,000	70	72,000	6
69 +	698,000	22	163,000	23	535,000	77	252,000	23
Total	3,200,000	100	1,453,000	45	747,000	56	1,114,000	100

Source: Statistics Canada (1990b): Tables 5, 6, 7, 17, and 37
Note: Of 6,327,000 families with a male "head," 6,104,000 were husband-wife families and 223,000 were not.

TABLE 16
Mortality Rates – Ontario, 1989

	45–54	55–64	65+
Deaths by Marital Status, Age, and Sex			
Married			
Male	1,643	4,226	16,438
Female	950	2,217	6,046
Total	2,593	6,443	22,484
Unattached			
Male	609	1,563	9,013
Female	470	1,097	20,644
Total	1,079	2,660	29,657
Population by Marital Status, Age, and Sex			
Married			
Male	444,800	379,400	358,200
Female	421,000	343,300	276,000
Total	865,800	722,700	634,200
Unattached			
Male	63,900	57,200	97,500
Female	89,700	114,200	368,800
Total	153,600	171,400	466,300
Mortality Rates by Marital Status, Age, and Sex			
Married			
Male	0.37%	1.11%	4.59%
Female	0.23%	0.65%	2.19%
Total	0.30%	0.89%	3.55%
Unattached			
Male	0.95%	2.73%	9.24%
Female	0.52%	0.96%	5.60%
Total	0.70%	1.55%	6.36%

Sources: Statistics Canada (1990c): Table 3; Statistics Canada (1991): Table 5
Note: Statistics Canada (1991) lists deaths by marital status, age, and sex only for an aggregated 45–64 age group. These figures have been disaggregated by distributing these deaths among the 45–54 and 55–64 age groups according to the proportion of all male and female deaths (regardless of marital status) within each of these two age groups.

Given these data, estimates for the distribution of Ontario estates in 1989 are produced in four steps. First, to compensate for in-adequate sampling of the upper tail in Statistics Canada's 1984 wealth survey and to account for changes in mean household wealth between 1984 and 1989, the wealth groups listed in table 14 are augmented by a Pareto tail and adjusted by a multiple (roughly 3.5) calculated by dividing Ernst & Young's 1989 estimate for mean household wealth in Ontario ($329,487) by Statistics Canada's 1984 estimate for mean household wealth in Ontario ($91,770).

The resulting estimates, presented in table 17, assume that the distribution of household wealth in Ontario at the end of 1989 was the same as the distribution of household wealth nationally in 1984. Since Statistics Canada's 1984 wealth survey indicates that a larger share of Ontario households belong to upper-wealth groups, this assumption understates the percentage of Ontario households in the top wealth groups.

Second, from the information presented in table 15, the Ontario population aged 45 or over in 1989 was classified according to the same age and family type categories used in Statistics Canada's estimates of the distribution of wealth. The under-45 age group is ignored in estimating the distribution of Ontario estates because few members of this age group are likely to leave substantial estates and because statistical information on the upper tail of the wealth distribution is extremely unreliable for younger wealth holders (since their numbers are few). Further, since published information on Ontario is incomplete, these estimates assume that the proportion of males and females within each age and family type is the same in Ontario as in Canada, and that Ontario has the same percentage of "not-husband-wife" families (as a share of all families) as Canada. This assumption does not seem to be unreasonable, since table 14 indicates that the distribution of Ontario's population by age and family type corresponds quite closely to that of Canada as a whole. The resulting profile appears in table 18.

Third, assuming (in the absence of specific data) that spouses are the same ages so that for "husband-wife" families the numbers of men and women within each age group are the same, applying the mortality rates from table 15 to the Ontario population aged 45 and over in table 18 generates estimated deaths by sex and family type. These estimates are presented in table 19.

Finally, assuming that the distribution of wealth owned by Ontario decedents is the same as the distribution of wealth among

TABLE 17
Estimated Distribution of Household Wealth by Age and Family Type – Ontario, 1989

	Families (by Age of "Head")				
Wealth group	45–54 All	55–64 All	65+ Husband-wife	65+ Not husband-wife	65+ All
Negative	2.7%	1.8%	1.0%	3.4%	1.3%
$0–$3,500	3.3%	1.8%	2.3%	1.9%	2.3%
$3,500–$17,500	3.3%	3.0%	4.4%	6.4%	4.7%
$17,500–$52,500	5.5%	3.5%	3.7%	4.4%	3.9%
$52,500–$105,000	6.1%	5.9%	5.5%	8.3%	5.8%
$105,000–$175,000	10.2%	9.3%	12.0%	18.1%	12.6%
$175,000–$262,500	12.8%	13.0%	16.3%	13.6%	15.7%
$262,500–$350,000	13.2%	12.9%	13.8%	10.2%	13.3%
$350,000–$525,000	16.5%	17.1%	15.9%	14.7%	16.0%
$525,000–$700,000	8.4%	9.2%	8.5%	8.2%	8.4%
$700,000–$1,050,000	8.9%	9.4%	7.7%	6.3%	7.5%
$1,050,000–$2,500,000	6.6%	9.6%	6.6%	3.3%	6.1%
$2,500,000–$5,000,000	1.6%	2.3%	1.6%	0.8%	1.5%
Over $5,000,000	0.8%	1.3%	0.9%	0.4%	0.8%
Total	100.0%	100.0%	100.0%	100.0%	100.0%
Mean wealth	$495,194	$559,720	$461,759	$414,509	$458,518
Median wealth	$302,666	$342,535	$293,797	$223,262	$286,066

	Unattached Individuals (by Age)				
Wealth group	45–54 All	55–64 All	65+ Male	65+ Female	65+ All
Negative	10.1%	8.1%	1.5%	1.1%	1.2%
$0–$3,500	23.2%	13.7%	12.2%	16.2%	15.2%
$3,500–$17,500	12.7%	6.6%	14.4%	13.3%	13.6%
$17,500–$52,500	11.1%	10.0%	10.3%	10.8%	10.7%
$52,500–$105,000	8.6%	9.7%	11.5%	10.1%	10.4%
$105,000–$175,000	8.4%	11.9%	12.2%	13.3%	13.0%
$175,000–$262,500	6.6%	12.0%	11.7%	15.0%	14.2%
$262,500–$350,000	3.5%	7.6%	8.4%	8.0%	8.1%
$350,000–$525,000	6.0%	9.4%	8.0%	6.8%	7.1%
$525,000–$700,000	3.4%	3.9%	3.4%	1.9%	2.2%
$700,000–$1,050,000	2.9%	3.2%	2.9%	1.6%	1.9%
$1,050,000–$2,500,000	2.5%	2.8%	2.5%	1.4%	1.7%
$2,500,000–$5,000,000	0.6%	0.7%	0.6%	0.3%	0.4%
Over $5,000,000	0.4%	0.4%	0.4%	0.2%	0.2%
Total	100.0%	100.0%	100.0%	100.0%	100.0%
Mean wealth	$198,139	$229,061	$228,750	$167,997	$182,648
Median wealth	$29,859	$115,962	$105,186	$97,069	$99,229

TABLE 18
Estimated Population Aged 45 and Over by Age and Family Type – Ontario, 1989

Family type	Age of Head					
	45–54	55–59	60–64	65–69	69+	All 45+
Families						
Husband-wife Male "head"	437,830	182,180	178,080	138,840	181,170	1,118,100
Not husband-wife Male "head"	15,770	6,420	6,420	4,940	6,750	40,300
Not husband-wife Female "head"	50,400	16,400	20,500	14,220	28,080	129,600
All families	504,000	205,000	205,000	158,000	216,000	1,288,000
Unattached individuals						
Male	44,100	27,140	21,830	21,600	57,960	172,630
Female	45,900	31,860	37,170	50,400	194,040	359,370
All individuals	90,000	59,000	59,000	72,000	252,000	532,000

TABLE 19
Estimated Mortality among Population Aged 45 and Over – Ontario, 1989

Age of "head"	Estimated Population		Mortality Rates		Estimated Deaths		
	Male	Female	Male	Female	Male	Female	Total
Husband-Wife Families with Male "Head" Aged 45 or Over							
45–54	437,830	437,830	0.37%	0.23%	1,620	1,007	2,627
55–64	360,260	360,260	1.11%	0.65%	3,999	2,342	6,341
65+	320,010	320,010	4.59%	2.19%	14,688	7,008	21,697
Total	1,118,100	1,118,100			20,307	10,357	30,664
Not Husband-Wife Families with "Head" Aged 45 or Over							
45–54	15,770	50,400	0.95%	0.52%	150	262	412
55–64	12,840	36,900	2.73%	0.96%	351	354	705
65+	11,690	42,300	9.24%	5.60%	1,080	2,369	3,449
Total	40,300	129,600			1,581	2,985	4,566
Unattached Individuals Aged 45 or Over							
45–54	44,100	45,900	0.95%	0.52%	419	239	658
55–64	48,970	69,030	2.73%	0.96%	1,337	663	2,000
65+	79,560	244,440	9.24%	5.60%	7,351	13,689	21,040
Total	172,630	359,370			9,107	14,591	23,698

the living, the wealth distribution of table 18 can be used to estimate a distribution of estates for the population of Ontario decedents aged 45 and over that was derived in table 19.[14] The results appear in table 20 and require some further explanation.

First, in order to estimate the value of individual estates and in the absence of data on the distribution of wealth within families, we assume that net wealth is equally divided between spouses in husband-wife families and wholly owned by the family head in not-husband-wife families. The former assumption about equal property ownership by spouses may not be true for older couples, but is likely increasingly the case for younger spouses. Further, this assumption produces a lower-bound estimate on the potential revenue yield of a wealth transfer tax since it maximizes the impact of an individual threshold and lessens the effect of graduated rates. The latter assumption that all wealth is held by the family head in not-husband-wife families probably exaggerates the number of wealthy households, since at least some wealth is likely to be owned by other family members, but seems more reasonable than any other assumption.

Second, in order to allow calculations based on Ernst & Young estimates of average (mean) wealth within different wealth groups, we have adjusted the estate sizes in table 20 from the dollar ranges that appear in table 17 to dollar ranges that correspond to those appearing in the Ernst & Young study. This adjustment assumes that estate sizes are distributed proportionally within each estate size group (for example, that 50 per cent of decedents with estates of between $1,000,000 and $2,000,000 have estates of $1,500,000 or more). The results of these calculations appear in table 20.

Revenue and Distributional Impact

As with the annual net wealth tax simulations, these estimates for the distribution of Ontario estates impose two significant constraints on our ability to effectively model alternative wealth transfer tax options. First, without reliable information on the composition of estates by different estate sizes, it is impossible to accurately model the combined impact of a dollar threshold (and/or graduated rates) and exemptions for specific assets (for example, principal residences, family farms, or small businesses). Although rough estimates for the composition of Ontario estates by estate size might be based on old Ontario succession duty statistics or on more recent

TABLE 20
Estimated Distribution of Estates – Ontario, 1989

Estate size	Type of Decedent					
	Decedents with surviving spouses		Single decedents		All decedents	
	#	%	#	%	#	%
Negative	402	1.3	704	2.5	1,106	1.9
$0–$10,000	1,703	5.6	5,384	19.0	7,087	12.0
$10,000–$100,000	7,940	25.9	7,202	25.5	15,142	25.7
$100,000–$250,000	11,710	38.2	7,265	25.7	18,975	32.2
$250,000–$500,000	5,503	17.9	4,858	17.2	10,361	17.6
$500,000–$1,000,000	1,811	5.9	1,927	6.8	3,738	6.3
$1,000,000–$2,000,000	800	2.6	497	1.8	1,297	2.2
$2,000,000–$5,000,000	689	2.2	342	1.2	1,031	1.7
Over $5,000,000	106	0.3	85	0.3	191	0.3
Total	30,664	100.0	28,264	100.0	58,928	100.0

information on the composition of U.S. estates by estate size, it is uncertain whether these figures accurately describe the current composition of Ontario estates. Consequently, as with the annual net wealth tax simulations, each of the wealth transfer tax options simulated in the appendix assumes a fully comprehensive base without any exemption for specific assets.[15]

A second major limitation of the estimates in table 20 concerns the form of the wealth transfer tax options that can be effectively modelled. Without some information (or assumptions) on how estates are distributed among beneficiaries, on the volume of lifetime giving, on the extent of inheritances from non-resident decedents, or on the value of Ontario property owned by non-resident decedents, it is impossible to model any wealth transfer tax except an estate-type tax applied only to the estates of Ontario decedents. To model an inheritance-type tax, one would need information on the average number of beneficiaries for different estates sizes and on the distribution of these estates among these beneficiaries. To model a gift tax, one would need information on the total value of lifetime gifts either transferred by Ontario donors or obtained by Ontario recipients (or both). To model an accessions-type tax, one would need information on the total value of gifts and inheritances received by Ontario residents over a given period of time. Finally, information on the number of non-resident decedents owning Ontario property and the value of Ontario property owned by non-residents would be necessary to simulate a tax on foreign estates. Since reliable data are unavailable in any of these areas, each of the wealth transfer tax options simulated in this section applies only to the estates of deceased residents of Ontario.

Despite these limitations, the information in table 20 can be used to simulate the distributional impact and revenue potential of various thresholds and rate structures as well as the distributional and revenue effects of exempting transfers to surviving spouses. For each estate size, the total amount of revenue raised is calculated as the product of Ernst & Young's estimate for average wealth within each wealth group less the threshold amount, the applicable tax rate, and the number of households within each estate size group. Once this estimate is determined, it is easy to calculate average amounts and rates of tax paid (by taxpaying estates and by all estates) within each estate size group and overall.

Further, although there is no readily available source of information from which estimates of lifetime gifts and foreign estates might be simulated, U.S. estate tax data and old Ontario succession duty statistics provide some indication of the impact of separate levies on lifetime gifts and foreign estates. According to a study of U.S. estate tax returns filed by 1986 decedents, lifetime gifts accounted for 14.2 per cent of the aggregate value of all estates and 15.8 per cent of the total value of taxable estates. These percentages were lower for estates of less than $2.5 million and higher for larger estates, especially estates worth $10 million or more (calculated from Johnson 1990, table 3). In Canada, statistics from 1970–1 indicate that foreign estates accounted for roughly 20 per cent of estates subject to tax and between 3.5 per cent and 9.5 per cent of total revenues raised under both the Federal Estate Tax and the Ontario succession duty (Department of National Revenue 1971, tables 2 and 7). Given these figures, the addition of these levies to a tax on the estates of deceased residents would be expected to increase total revenues by about 20 per cent.

The results of our simulations are presented in tables 21–23 and in figure 11. In each case, the tables indicate both overall and, for each estate size, the estimated number and percentage of estates subject to the tax, the average amount of tax paid by taxpaying estates and by all estates, the average rate of tax (as a percentage of the average value of estates) paid by taxpaying estates and all estates, and the estimated amount of revenue raised.

Table 21 simulates the distributional and revenue impacts of three different thresholds for a 30 per cent flat-rate estate tax with no exemption for transfers to surviving spouses. With a $500,000 threshold, it is estimated that roughly 6260 estates (10.6 per cent of the estates of Ontario decedents) would have been subject to the tax at the end of 1989, that the average tax paid by these taxable estates would have been approximately $350,000, and that the tax could have raised almost $2.2 billion (simulation 1). With a $1 million threshold, the estimated number of taxable estates drops to 2519 (6.3 per cent of Ontario estates), the average tax paid by these estates increases to almost $645,000, and potential revenues decline to about $1.6 billion (simulation 2). Doubling the threshold to $2 million causes the number of taxable estates to fall by slightly more than 50 per cent to 1222 (2.1 per cent of Ontario estates), increases the average amount of tax paid by these estates to almost $934,000, and reduces total revenues by 30 per cent to $1.1 billion (simulation 3).

Table 22 simulates the impact of a full exemption for transfers to surviving spouses by assuming that decedents with surviving spouses leave the entirety of their estates to their surviving spouses. Although this assumption seems to be justified by experience in the United States, where most decedents leave the bulk of their estates to their spouses (Johnson 1990, 28), to the extent that decedents with surviving spouses transfer some part of their wealth to other beneficiaries, it may underestimate the number of estates subject to tax and, consequently, the amount of revenue raised.

With the same 30 per cent flat rate and thresholds as simulations 1–3, simulations 4–6 indicate a substantial reduction in the number of taxable estates and in the estimated amount of revenue raised. With a $500,000 threshold, a full spousal exemption reduces the number of taxable estates by 54 per cent to 2851 (4.8 per cent of Ontario estates) and decreases total revenues by 60 per cent to $880 million (simulation 4). With a $1,000,000 threshold, a full spousal exemption causes a 63 per cent drop in the number of taxable estates to 924 (1.6 per cent of Ontario estates) and a 61 per cent decline in total revenues to $640 million (simulation 5). With a threshold set at $2,000,000, a full spousal exemption reduces the number of taxable estates by 65 per cent to 427 (0.7 per cent of Ontario estates) and decreases total revenues by 59 per cent to $466 million (simulation 6).

TABLE 21
Comprehensive Flat-Rate Estate Tax with No Exemption for Transfers to Surviving Spouses
Estimated Distributional Impact and Revenue Potential, Upper Bound, 1989

Estate size	Taxable estates		Average tax paid by				Revenue raised ($ millions)
			Taxpaying estates		All estates		
	#	%	$	%	$	%	
			Simulation 1: Threshold: $500,000		Rate: 30% above $500,000		
$500,000–$1,000,000	3,738	100.0	52,500	7.8	52,500	7.8	196.2
$1,000,000–$2,000,000	1,297	100.0	240,000	18.5	240,000	18.5	311.3
$2,000,000–$5,000,000	1,031	100.0	808,599	25.3	808,599	25.3	833.7
Over $5,000,000	191	100.0	4,489,137	29.0	4,489,137	29.0	857.4
All estates	6,257	10.6	351,385	21.0	37,310	12.4	2,198.6
			Simulation 2: Threshold: $1,000,000		Rate: 30% above $1,000,000		
$1,000,000–$2,000,000	1,297	100.0	90,000	6.9	90,000	6.9	116.7
$2,000,000–$5,000,000	1,031	100.0	658,599	20.6	658,599	20.6	679.0
Over $5,000,000	191	100.0	4,339,137	28.1	4,339,137	28.1	828.8
All estates	2,519	4.3	644,907	20.5	27,568	9.1	1,624.5
			Simulation 3: Threshold: $2,000,000		Rate: 30% above $2,000,000		
$2,000,000–$5,000,000	1,031	100.0	358,599	11.2	358,599	11.2	369.7
Over $5,000,000	191	100.0	4,039,137	26.1	4,039,137	26.1	771.5
All estates	1,222	2.1	933,871	18.3	19,366	6.4	1,141.2

TABLE 22
Comprehensive Flat-Rate Estate Tax with Full Exemption for Transfers to Surviving Spouses
Estimated Distributional Impact and Revenue Potential, Upper Bound, 1989

Estate size	Taxable estates		Average tax paid by				Revenue raised ($ millions)
			Taxpaying estates		All estates		
	#	%	$	%	$	%	
Simulation 4: Threshold: $500,000 Rate: 30% above $500,000							
$500,000–$1,000,000	1,927	51.6	52,500	7.8	27,065	4.0	101.2
$1,000,000–$2,000,000	497	38.3	240,000	18.5	91,966	7.1	119.3
$2,000,000–$5,000,000	342	33.2	808,599	25.3	268,226	8.4	276.5
Over $5,000,000	85	44.5	4,489,137	29.0	1,997,783	12.9	381.6
All estates	2,851	4.8	308,160	20.2	14,909	4.9	878.6
Simulation 5: Threshold: $1,000,000 Rate: 30% above $1,000,000							
$1,000,000–$2,000,000	497	38.3	90,000	6.9	34,487	2.7	44.7
$2,000,000–$5,000,000	342	33.2	658,599	20.6	218,468	6.8	225.2
Over $5,000,000	85	44.5	4,339,137	28.1	1,931,029	12.5	368.8
All estates	924	1.6	691,339	20.9	10,840	3.6	638.8

continued

TABLE 22 (continued)

| Estate size | Taxable estates | | Average tax paid by | | | | | Revenue raised ($ millions) |
| | # | % | Taxpaying estates | | All estates | | |
			$	%	$	%	
			Simulation 6: Threshold: $2,000,000 Rate: 30% above $2,000,000				
$2,000,000–$5,000,000	342	33.2	358,599	11.2	118,953	3.7	122.6
Over $5,000,000	85	44.5	4,039,137	26.1	1,797,522	11.6	343.3
All estates	427	0.7	1,091,258	19.4	7,907	2.6	466.0

Finally, table 23 simulates the distributional impact of replacing the 30 per cent flat-rate estate taxes in simulations 4–6 with a graduated rate structure designed to raise a similar amount of revenue. In order to isolate the impact of the graduated rate structure, simulations 7–9 retain a full spousal exemption and the same thresholds as simulations 4–6.

As simulations 7–9 indicate, while average amounts and rates of tax remain the same for all estates in aggregate, a graduated rate structure reduces the burden on smaller estates (in each case, average taxes decrease for estates valued at less than $5 million) and increases the burden on very large estates (over $5 million). This impact is further demonstrated in figure 11, which shows that both rate structures are progressive overall. For the flat-rate taxes, this effect is produced by the existence of a threshold or "zero-rate band" that exempts the first $500,000, $1,000,000, or $2,000,000 from estate tax. However, as figure 11 demonstrates, the flat-rate estate tax simulations are more steeply progressive among smaller estates while the graduated-rate estate tax simulations produce a more even distribution of average tax rate increases throughout all estate sizes.

Conclusions

This paper has discussed the possible impacts of two alternative wealth tax proposals: an annual net wealth tax and a wealth transfer tax. Impacts on the distribution of income and wealth, and on government revenues in Ontario have been analysed. The qualitative analysis has emphasized the importance of such factors as capital flight, effects on saving and investment, asset price impacts, and avoidance and evasion. However, in the quantitative analysis it has been possible only to study these aspects partially and indirectly – for example by looking at revenues in other countries where these taxes are currently levied and by referring to the evidence from the earlier period when estate taxes and succession duties were levied in Canada. Our tax simulations ignore all of these special aspects, and are therefore only intended to be exploratory and illustrative. We nonetheless believe that the data and calculations presented here are worthwhile since they bring out some important points about the distributional and revenue impacts as well as design issues.

One very interesting point that emerges from our annual net wealth tax simulations, and that would, with the appropriate data,

TABLE 23
Comprehensive Graduated-Rate Estate Tax with Full Exemption for Transfers to Surviving Spouses
Estimated Distributional Impact and Revenue Potential, Upper Bound, 1989

| | Taxable estates | | Average tax paid by | | | | Revenue raised ($ millions) |
| | | | Taxpaying estates | | All estates | | |
Estate size	#	%	$	%	$	%	
Simulation 7: Threshold: $500,000							
Rate: 10% from $500,000 to $1,000,000; increasing by 5% for each $500,000 above $1,000,000 up to 55% above $5,000,000							
$500,000-$1,000,000	1,927	51.6	17,500	2.6	9,022	1.3	33.7
$1,000,000-$2,000,000	497	38.3	95,000	7.3	36,403	2.8	47.2
$2,000,000-$5,000,000	342	33.2	573,365	17.9	190,195	6.0	196.1
Over $5,000,000	85	44.5	7,105,084	45.9	3,161,948	20.4	603.9
All estates	2,851	4.8	309,001	20.2	14,950	5.0	881.0
Simulation 8: Threshold: $1,000,000							
Rate: 12% from $1,000,000 to $1,500,000; increasing by 4% for each $500,000 above $1,500,000 up to 44% above $5,000,000							
$1,000,000-$2,000,000	497	38.3	36,000	2.8	13,795	1.1	17.9
$2,000,000-$5,000,000	342	33.2	414,692	13.0	137,560	4.3	141.8
Over $5,000,000	85	44.5	5,644,067	36.5	2,511,758	16.2	479.7
All estates	924	1.6	692,059	20.9	10,852	3.6	639.5

continued

Simulation 9: Threshold: $2,000,000

Rate: 18% from $2,000,000 to $2,500,000; increasing by 3% for each $500,000 above $2,500,000 up to 36% above $5,000,000

$2,000,000–$5,000,000	342	33.2	241,879	7.6	80,235	2.5	82.7
Over $5,000,000	85	44.5	4,531,964	29.3	2,016,843	13.0	385.2
All estates	427	0.7	1,095,877	19.4	7,941	2.6	467.9

FIGURE 11
Flat-Rate versus Graduated-Rate Estate Tax
Estimated Distributional Impacts

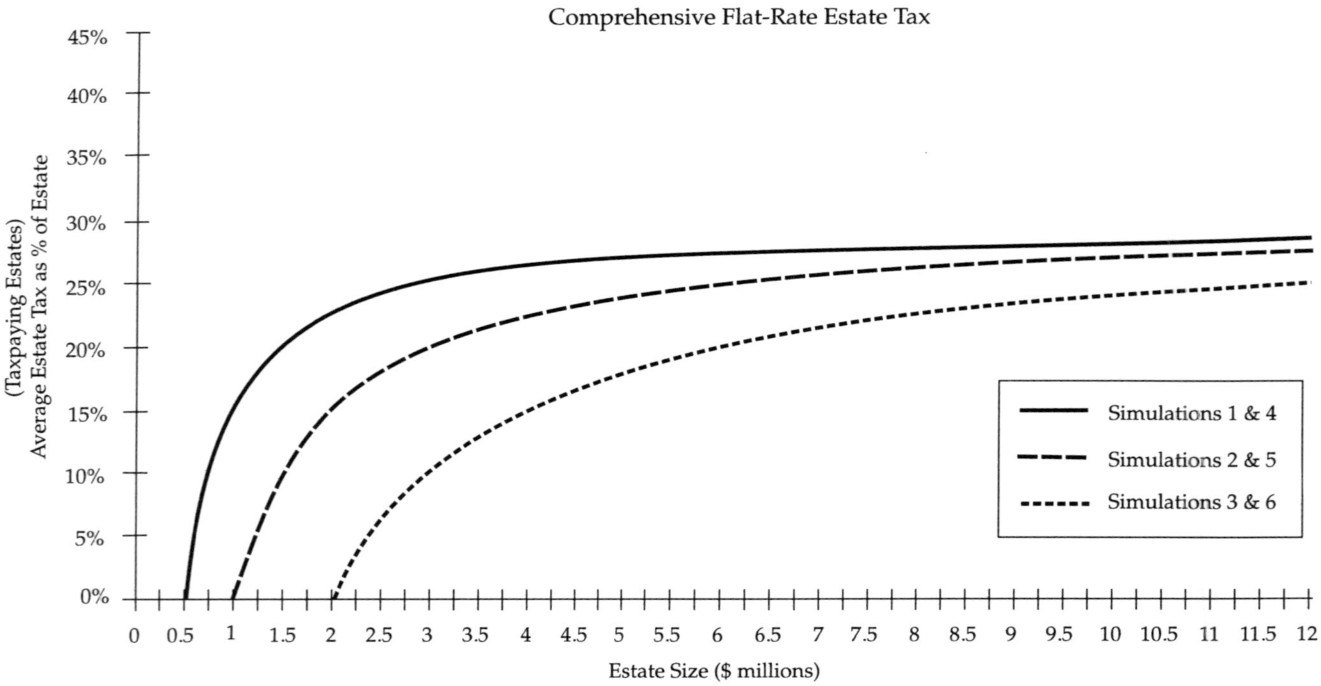

Comprehensive Flat-Rate Estate Tax

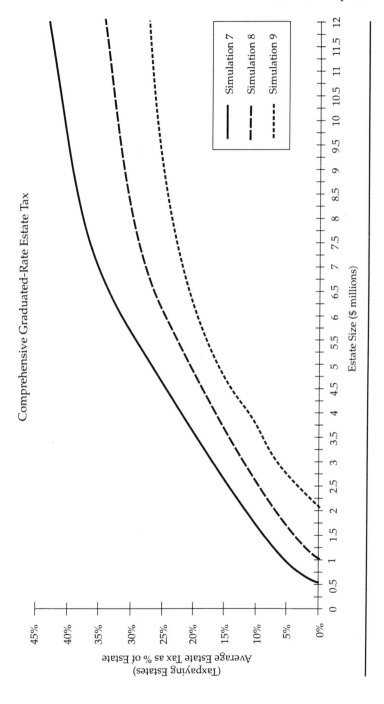

Comprehensive Graduated-Rate Estate Tax

Average Estate Tax as % of Estate
(Taxpaying Estates)

Estate Size ($ millions)

Simulation 7
Simulation 8
Simulation 9

show up under a wealth transfer tax as well, is that even if incidence is progressive in relation to wealth it can be highly regressive in relation to income. This is because there is a highly imperfect correlation between wealth and annual income. Traditionally, the redistributive effects of Canadian taxes have been studied in relation to income. For those who believe such an evaluative framework makes sense, the regressive incidence of wealth taxes over lower income ranges will appear very significant.

Another interesting point to emerge from both the annual net wealth tax and wealth transfer tax simulations is that with judicious selection of thresholds and tax rates, almost as much redistributive "bang" can be wrung out of either tax using a single marginal tax rate as can be achieved using graduated rates. Uniform marginal tax rates have considerable advantages from an administrative and compliance standpoint, and also help to assuage fears and perhaps dampen avoidance and evasion at extreme wealth levels. Our calculations indicate that these benefits can be reaped at little cost in terms of reduced redistributive impact (assuming, of course, that one decides to adopt such taxes).

The significance of the precise distributional effects of the annual net wealth tax and wealth transfer tax options according to the simulations reported here are less important than these lessons about distributional side-effects and design issues. Capital flight, and effects on saving, investment, and asset prices, all suggest that the simulations would understate the equalizing effects of the taxes (and overstate the revenue impact). Similarly, our calculations only look at the impact in a single initial year, whereas the taxes should theoretically have a cumulative downward impact on inequality over time. Acting in the other direction, avoidance and evasion are important forces eroding the equalizing effects of these taxes. Avoidance is generally considered most likely to be important for the wealthiest individuals and families. This helps to explain the widespread scepticism about the efficacy of these taxes in altering the distributions of income and wealth.

On the revenue side we are fortunate in being able to make comparisons with real-world experience. Clearly, the annual net wealth tax simulations exaggerate revenue potential considerably. Our calculations suggest revenue of between $2.2 billion and $5 billion per annum with higher thresholds than used in other countries (but similar rates), whose experience suggests a revenue figure of $850 million might be more plausible. Even the latter figure must be assessed keeping in mind the possible negative effect on revenues from other taxes (for example, personal and corporate income taxes) due to capital flight, reduced domestic saving and investment, and lower asset prices.

Surprisingly, the wealth transfer tax estimates with a full spousal exemption ($466 million to $880 million) are not far off the comparative estimates based on wealth transfer tax revenues as a percentage of GDP in OECD countries on average in the United States ($650 million to $950 million). Since the former also assumes a fully comprehensive base and allows for no avoidance or evasion, this is a puzzle that must be explained. Two factors may be at work. First, the generally conservative method of generating simulated estates and simulating the impact of various taxes may have underestimated the number of transfers that would be actually subject to tax under the simple estate tax described. Second, to the extent that our simulated tax – unlike most actual estate taxes – does not apply to gifts or to transfers to or between non-residents, it underestimates the potential base of any real-world wealth transfer tax. In fact, the impact of this latter limitation may be substantial: U.S. estate tax data indicate that gifts made during decedents' lifetimes accounted for 15 per cent of the tax base of the U.S. Gift and Estate Tax for 1986 decedents (Johnson 1990, table 3), and Canadian statistics reveal that in 1970–1 levies on non-residents accounted for 3.5 per cent of revenues collected under the federal estate tax and 9.5 per cent of revenues raised by the Ontario succession duty. As a result, the similarity between our estimates and those reached by comparative analysis seem to be the result of offsetting influences. Overall, we conclude that revenues of $500 million to $1 billion might be expected from either kind of tax in Ontario.

Appendix: Methods of Extrapolation

At various points in the calculations performed in this paper it was necessary to extrapolate frequency distributions of wealth or estates into the upper tail. This is because the data are typically provided in the form of frequency tables with open-ended upper groups (see, for example, table 5).[16] Thus, for example, when we were computing the impact of an annual net wealth tax, we knew that 84,900 Ontario households had wealth exceeding $2 million, according to the Ernst & Young estimates for 1989. However, we did not know how they were distributed above that point, or the value of their average net worth.

Without an estimate of the latter it is impossible to compute annual net wealth tax revenues from this group. Similarly, in table 20 we have an estimate of 191 decedents in the open-ended group leaving estates worth $5 million or more. It is, of course, impossible to guess estate tax revenues from this group if we do not make some assumption about the average estate in this group.

Pareto (1897) observed that the upper tails of income distribution data from many countries followed a simple mathematical law quite closely. The frequency distribution implied by this law is known as the Pareto distribution. Over the last 100 years it has been found to approximate fairly well the upper tail of the distribution of wealth wherever the shape of that tail has been subjected to close scrutiny (see, for example, Cowell 1977, 88, 100-1). We have therefore used as a working hypothesis the assumption that the distributions of wealth and estates left on death in Ontario could be reasonably well approximated by a Pareto distribution.

The Pareto distribution has a very simple form. Let W represent a wealth level, and let N be the number of families (or individuals, or whatever) with wealth above this level. Then, if the distribution of wealth is "Pareto" above some cut-off, W, a plot of the logarithm of N against that of W (log N vs. log W) will follow a straight line above log W. We plot log W on the horizontal axis and log N on the vertical, as in figure A.1. The line slopes downwards to the right (that is, has a negative slope) because as W rises there are fewer people who have a higher level of wealth.[17] The less steep this line, the longer is the upper tail of the distribution of wealth, and the greater is the degree of inequality. The slope is conventionally known as "α," and has been found to take on values in the range of 1.0 to 2.0 in the large number of statistical studies that have been performed in various countries at various times. The value $\alpha = 1.5$ was originally found by Pareto in income data, but has also cropped up repeatedly as a reasonable approximation to the upper tail of the distribution of wealth (see, for example, Cowell 1977, 101; Atkinson and Harrison 1978, 25).

An extremely convenient feature of the Pareto distribution is that the average wealth above any W is always the same multiple of W. The multiplier is $\alpha/(\alpha - 1)$. Thus, if we know, for example, that a particular dataset suggests $\alpha = 1.5$, then the average wealth of those with wealth above $1 million will be $3 million; the average

FIGURE A.1
General Form of the Pareto Distribution

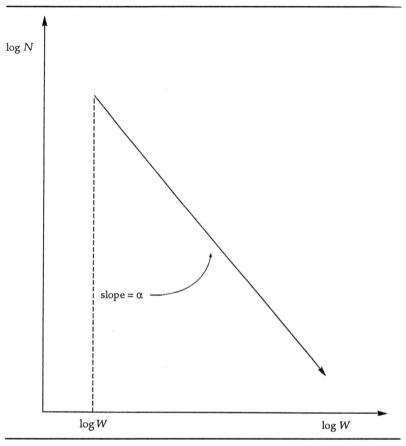

wealth of those with wealth over $2 million will be $6 million, and so on.

In order to make use of the Pareto distribution we need to have only an appropriate method of computing the parameter α for particular datasets. There are a variety of ways in which this can be done, and economists and statisticians have devoted considerable attention to the optimal method of estimation (see Aigner and Goldberger 1970; and Harrison 1981). We have opted for one of the simplest methods, since it is sufficiently robust for our purposes.

TABLE A.1
Estimates of Pareto's α, Canadian Data

I. 1984 Survey of Consumer Finance

Group	W ($,000)	N (%)	log W	log N	$\hat{\alpha}$	R^2
1	300	5.1	5.704	1.629	–	–
2	200	9.5	5.298	2.251	1.534	1.000
3	150	14.5	5.011	2.674	1.509	1.000
4	100	24.2	4.605	3.186	1.421	.998
5	75	32.7	4.318	3.487	1.345	.995
6	50	44.1	3.912	3.787	1.219	.984

II. 1989 Ontario Simulated Distribution of Estates

Group	W ($ million)	N	log W	log N	$\hat{\alpha}$	R^2
1	10	25	2.303	3.219	–	–
2	5	75	1.609	4.318	1.585	1.000
3	2.5	137	.916	4.920	1.227	.972
4	1.5	456	.406	6.123	1.444	.971
5	.75	1365	−.288	7.219	1.528	.984
6	.625	1807	−.470	7.500	1.551	.989
7	.45	2827	−.799	7.947	1.551	.992
8	.375	3491	−.981	8.158	1.542	.993

Source: Authors' calculations. See text for explanation.

Table A.1, panel I, reports the W, N, log W, and log N values for Statistics Canada's 1984 Survey of Consumer Finance (SCF) wealth data. Panel II of the same table shows the corresponding information for our estimate of the 1989 distribution of estates passing on death in Ontario. The last two columns of the table show the alternative estimates of α, which are obtained by performing an ordinary least squares (OLS) regression of log N on log W using the data points above each W level in turn, and the associated values of R^2.[18]

Panel I of table A.1 shows that our estimate of α tends to increase as the lower cutoff on the Pareto distribution, W, is increased. This reflects the fact that the relationship between log W and log N becomes steeper as W rises, as found in other studies (see, for example, Shorrocks 1975, 156). When we use the $50,000 cutoff, the estimated α is just 1.22, whereas when we get to a $150,000 cutoff the coefficient has risen to 1.51. The point of our exercise is to extrapolate beyond the highest cutoff, which is $300,000 in this case. Thus it is appropriate to put greatest emphasis on the values of α estimated with the higher W cutoffs, as long as the quality of the estimates is not declining due to the small number of data points as the cutoff is increased. The smooth increase in estimated α as W rises indicates that the latter is not a problem here.

The conclusion from panel I of table A.1 is that a Pareto distribution with $\alpha = 1.5$ provides a reasonable approximation to the upper tail of the 1984 SCF wealth distribution. We have assumed this distribution for all extrapolations of wealth distributions in this paper, since this SCF survey also provides the basis for the 1989 Ernst & Young data.[19]

Panel II of table A.1 reports W, N, log W, and log N for the 1989 distribution of estate left in Ontario simulated in the text. These data also turn out well approximated by the Pareto distribution. The estimate of α is less sensitive to the choice of W cutoff than is the case with the 1984 SCF data. A value of α equal to about 1.55 is fairly consistently obtained until the cutoff is raised beyond $1 million. Lower values are then obtained (except for the $5 million cutoff, which is not very persuasive since it is based on just two data points). As a compromise, we have assumed in the exercises reported in the text that, once again, the upper tail of the distribution is approximated by a Pareto distribution with $\alpha = 1.5$.

Notes

1 For a detailed summary of wealth taxes of OECD member countries as they existed in 1986, see OECD (1988). On the history of wealth taxes in Canada, see Carter (1973) and Bird (1978).

2 Calculated from statistics reported in Ontario Committee on Taxation 1967, vol. III, 140.

3 Calculated from statistics reported in Johnson 1990, table 3.

4 In order to measure the specific impact on top wealth holders, the researchers defined the explanatory estate tax variable as the cumulative amount (since 1923) of the difference between the percentage of estate duty paid by the top 1 per cent of wealth holders as a share of total wealth held by this group in any given year, and the percentage of total estate duty as a share of all household wealth in that year.

5 According to a recent U.S. study, the top one per cent of U.S. families

held 21 per cent of total wealth under a broad definition of wealth (including social security wealth but not human capital), versus 31.5 per cent of total wealth under a narrow definition of wealth (including only transferable assets, and with pensions valued according to their cash surrender value) (Aaron and Munnell 1992, 126–7).

6 Where married decedents transfer assets to their surviving spouses, their estates are often exempt from tax on account of spousal exemptions.

7 Statistics Canada divides households into families (defined as "a group of individuals sharing a common dwelling unit and related by blood, marriage or adoption") and unattached individuals (defined as "a person living by him/herself or rooming in a household where he/she is not related to any other household member"), and provides statistical information on the composition and distribution of wealth among both types of household. (Statistics Canada 1986, 11). In contrast, the Ernst & Young study employs a broader definition of the household unit, including all persons – even if unrelated – who share a common dwelling. Since the latter approach implies fewer households than the former (3,408,000 versus 3,710,000 in Ontario in 1989), it produces a larger estimate of mean wealth per household (roughly $330,000 versus $300,000 using Ernst & Young's estimate of total net wealth in Ontario in 1989).

8 These averages are calculated in the same manner as the calculation for mean net wealth in 1989, by dividing total net worth figures from the National Balance Sheet Accounts for 1983 ($1,045 billion + $348 billion) and 1971 ($234 billion + $84 billion) by the number of families and unattached individuals estimated for 1983 (9.2 million) and 1971 (6.8 million) (Statistics Canada 1990b, table 33; Statistics Canada 1975, table 35).

9 According to the national balance sheet accounts, at the end of 1983, persons and unincorporated businesses held 50.7 per cent of total wealth in the form of financial assets (18.0 per cent cash and deposits; 11.8 per cent life insurance and pensions; 11.2 per cent shares; 6.8 per cent bonds and marketable securities; and 2.9 per cent other financial assets) and 49.3 per cent in the form of non-financial assets (22.4 per cent residential structures; 12.0 per cent land; 10.3 per cent consumer durables; 2.5 per cent machinery, equipment, and inventories; and 2.1 per cent non-residential structures) (Statistics Canada 1990a, table P3-1).

10 The report first estimates the total value of various components of wealth and then allocates shares of this total wealth to households ac-

cording to the profiles of wealth by income group found in the 1984 Statistics Canada wealth survey. According to the authors, this approach is designed "to take into account inflation, as well as real growth in wealth and adjusts for excluded categories and under-reporting of assets in the 1984 survey" (Ernst & Young 1990, 107).

11 Although the Ernst & Young study categorizes assets as "liquid" or "non-liquid," these have been redesignated as "financial" or "non-financial" to maintain consistency with the Statistics Canada categories employed in the National Balance Sheet Accounts and the 1984 wealth survey.

12 These shares are estimated by fitting Pareto distributions based on the data presented in Ernst & Young 1990, vol. II, appendix N.

13 However, it is important to recall that the Ernst & Young data used for these simulations exclude interests in trusts, tax shelters, professional practice, real property located outside Canada, and registered retirement savings plan savings held with insurance companies. It should also be noted that *The Wealth Report* values farms as farmland, not on the basis of their value for residential or commercial development (Ernst & Young 1990, 61).

14 To the extent that the less affluent experience higher mortality rates, this assumption exaggerates the number of wealthy decedents.

15 Again, it is important to note that the data on which these simulations are based value farmland according to its agricultural use, and exclude interests in trusts, tax shelters, professional practice, real property located outside Canada, and registered retirement savings plan savings held with insurance companies.

16 There is also, of course, a problem of interpolation within the groups that have finite lower and upper bounds. That problem has been addressed here by assuming all those within such a group to have wealth at the midpoint range. This is a relatively crude technique, but it is unlikely to introduce much error compared with other possible sources of error in the exercises performed in this paper that have been discussed at length in the text. The size of the error arising from this source is limited by the fact that the data are fairly finely grouped.

17 For an example of actual log N vs. log W curves, see Shorrocks 1975, figure 1, 156. Shorrocks' curves, which are for separate age groups in the U.K. in 1961, show that the actual log N vs. log W curves tend to "droop" a little, rather than being perfectly linear; that is, they tend to become slowly steeper as wealth rises. A similar feature is found in the Canadian data used in the present study. The Pareto distribution is thus a reasonable, but not an ideal, approximation.

18 The OLS method is the simplest way to fit a straight line to a plot of
    data points. It is discussed in most introductory textbooks on statistics
    and in all elementary texts on econometrics (see, for example, Maddala
    1992). The R^2 statistic is the square of the correlation coefficient be-
    tween log W and log N. It measures the fraction of the variation in log
    N, which is explained by the variation in log W across the data points. A
    drawback of using the approach in the present context was discussed by
    Aigner and Goldberger (1970) – this is, that since N is a cumulative var-
    iable the residuals are not identically and independently distributed.
    Our assessment is that this disadvantage is not sufficiently serious to
    warrant the application here of the computationally much more de-
    manding alternative methods.

19 As discussed in the text, the Ernst & Young data are based on an updat-
    ing of the 1984 SCF data to 1989, the imputation of forms of wealth
    missing from the 1984 survey, and an extrapolation into the upper tail.
    The procedures used to perform the latter extrapolation are not speci-
    fied by Ernst & Young. It is evident from plotting the log W vs. log N
    relationship at high wealth levels in the Ernst & Young data, however,
    that a Pareto distribution was not used. (The relationship between
    these variables is far from being linear.) It is important to note that the
    shape of the true upper tail of the Canadian wealth distribution cannot
    be investigated by fitting functional forms to the upper tail of the Ernst
    & Young data, since that tail is the result of statistical extrapolation
    rather than observation.

Bibliography

Aaron, Henry J., and Alicia H. Munnell. 1992. "Reassessing the Role for
  Wealth Transfer Taxes." *National Tax Journal* 45(2): 11,943
Aigner, D.J., and A.S. Goldberger. 1970. "Estimation of Pareto's Law from
  Grouped Observations." *Journal of the American Statistical Association* 65:
  712–23
Atkinson, A.B., and A.J. Harrison. 1978. *Distribution of Personal Wealth in Brit-
  ain.* Cambridge: Cambridge University Press
Auerbach, Alan J., and Laurence J. Kotlikoff. 1987. *Dynamic Fiscal Policy.*
  Cambridge: Cambridge University Press
Auerbach, Alan J., Laurence J. Kotlikoff, and Jon Skinner. 1983. "The Effi-
  ciency Gains from Dynamic Tax Reform." *International Economic Review* 24:
  81–100

Beach, Charles M., Robin W. Boadway, and Neil Bruce. 1988. *Taxation and Savings in Canada*. Ottawa: Economic Council of Canada

Bird, Richard. 1978. "Canada's Vanishing Death Taxes." *Osgoode Hall Law Journal* 16: 133

Boskin, Michael J. 1978. "Taxation, Saving, and the Rate of Interest." *Journal of Political Economy* 86(2), Supplement (April): S3–28

Canada. Department of National Revenue. 1971. *Taxation Statistics, 1970–1971*. Ottawa: Department of National Revenue

Carter, George E. 1973. "Federal Abandonment of the Estate Tax: The Intergovernmental Fiscal Dimension." *Canadian Tax Journal* 21: 232–46

Conference Board of Canada. 1993. *Canadian Outlook: Economic Forecast* 8: 4

Cowell, F.A. 1977. *Measuring Inequality*. London: Philip Allan

Davies, James B. 1981. "Uncertain Lifetime, Consumption, and Dissaving in Retirement." *Journal of Political Economy* 89: 561–77

Davies, James B. 1993. "The Distribution of Wealth in Canada." In *Research in Economic Inequality*, ed. D.J. Slottje and E. Wolff, 159–80. Greenwich, CT: JAI Press

Davies, James B., and France St-Hilaire. 1987. *Reforming Capital Income Taxation in Canada*. Ottawa: Economic Council of Canada

Ernst & Young. 1990. *The Wealth Report*. Toronto: Ernst & Young

Feldstein, Martin S. 1978. "The Rate of Return, Taxation, and Personal Savings." *Economic Journal* 88: 482–7

Gauthier, Denis. 1986. "Taxation and Life-Cycle Savings Behaviour in a Small Open Economy." Discussion Paper No. 306. Ottawa: Economic Council of Canada

Harrison, Alan. 1981. "Earnings by Size: A Tale of Two Distributions." *Review of Economic Studies* 48: 621–31

Johnson, Barry W. 1990. "Estate Tax Returns, 1986–1988." *Statistics of Income Bulletin* 9: 27–78

Kessler, Denis, and Pierre Pestieau. 1991. "The Taxation of Wealth in the EEC: Facts and Trends." *Canadian Public Policy* 17: 309–21

Lord, William, and Peter Rangazas. 1991. "Saving and Wealth in Models with Altruistic Bequests." *American Economic Review* 81: 289–96

Maddala, G.S. 1991. *Introduction to Econometrics*, 2nd ed. New York: MacMillan

Ontario Budget. 1993. Toronto: Queen's Printer for Ontario

Ontario Committee on Taxation. 1967. *Report*, vol. 3. Toronto: Queen's Printer

Ontario. Department of Revenue. 1971. *Annual Report for Fiscal Year Ended March 31, 1971*. Toronto: Queen's Printer

Organization of Economic Cooperation and Development (OECD). 1988. *Taxation of Net Wealth, Capital Transfers and Capital Gains of Individuals.* Paris: OECD

- 1992. *Revenue Statistics of OECD Member Countries (1965–1991).* Paris: OECD
Pareto, Vilfredo. 1897. *Cours d'économie politique.* Lausanne: Rouge
Shorrocks, A.F. 1975. "The Age-Wealth Relationship: A Cross-Section and Cohort Analysis." *Review of Economics and Statistics* 57: 155–63
Statistics Canada. 1975. *Income Distributions by Size in Canada, 1973.* Publication No. 13-207. Ottawa: Minister of Industry, Trade and Commerce
- 1985. *National Balance Sheet Accounts, 1961–1984.* Publication no. 13-214. Calculated from table 02-24. Ottawa: Minister of Supply and Services
- 1986. *The Distribution of Wealth in Canada.* Publication no. 13-580. Ottawa: Minister of Supply and Services
- 1990a. *Financial Flow and National Balance Sheet Accounts.* Publication no. 13-214. Ottawa: Minister of Supply and Services
- 1990b. *Income Distributions by Size in Canada, 1989.* Publication no. 13-207. Ottawa: Minister of Industry, Science and Technology
- 1990c. *Postcensal Annual Estimates of Population by Marital Status, Age, Sex and Components of Growth for Canada, Provinces and Territories.* Publication no. 91-210. June 1, 1989, vol. 7. Seventh Issue. Ottawa: Minister of Supply and Services Canada
- 1991. *Health Reports.* Publication no. 82-003S15. Supplement no. 15, 1991, vol. 3, no. 1. Ottawa: Minister of Supply and Services Canada
Summers, Lawrence H. 1981. "Capital Taxation and Accumulation in a Life-Cycle Growth Model." *American Economic Review* 71: 533–44
Wolff, Edward N., ed. 1987. *International Comparisons of the Distribution of Household Wealth.* Oxford: Clarendon Press

Notes on Contributors

James Davies is professor of economics and chair of the Economics Department at the University of Western Ontario.

Kathleen M. Day is professor, Department of Economics, University of Ottawa.

David Duff was a research coordinator with the Ontario Fair Tax Commission. He is currently with the Tax Policy Branch, Ontario Ministry of Finance.

Peter Dungan is adjunct associate professor of economics and associate director of the Policy and Economic Analysis program at the University of Toronto.

Jonathan R. Kesselman is professor of economics and director of the Centre for Research on Economic and Social Policy at the University of British Columbia.

Maureen Maloney was dean of law, University of Victoria, British Columbia.

Stanley L. Winer is professor, School of Public Administration, Carleton University.

Commission Organization

Chair*
Monica Townson

Vice-Chairs
Neiol Brooks**
Robert Couzin**

Commissioners
Jayne Berman
William Blundell
Susan Giampietri
Brigitte Kitchen**
Gérard Lafrenière
Fiona Nelson
Satya Poddar**

Executive Director
Hugh Mackenzie

Director of Research
Allan M. Maslove

Assistant Director of Research
Sheila Block

Executive Assistant to Research Program
Moira Hutchinson

Editorial Assistant
Marguerite Martindale

*Chair of the Research Subcommittee
**Member of the Research Subcommittee